I0141289

Destiny Unfulfilled

Destiny Unfulfilled

A Critique of The Harry Potter Series

Revised Edition

Jim Adam

Gragthor Terrazin

Copyright © 2010 by Jim Adam

Cover Design by Cathi Stevenson
Background image © 2006 by Selahattin Bayram
Wizard's Study image © 2004 by Ethan Myerson
Both images from iStockPhoto.com

All rights reserved. Normal copyright restrictions apply. Quotes may be used as part of critiques, reviews, or educational material, so long as such quotes do not exceed the limits of reasonable fair use.

The Harry Potter series, including all characters, entities, and quotes, are copyrighted © by their author, J.K. Rowling.

Publisher's Cataloging-In-Publication Data

Adam, Jim.
    Destiny Unfulfilled / Jim Adam

        p. cm

Includes index.

ISBN-13: 978-0-9843525-1-7   (trade pbk. : alk. paper)
Library of Congress Control Number: 2010920558

1. Fiction, English—Criticism 2. Fiction—Authorship
3. Fiction—Technique 4. Rowling, J.K. I. Title.

Revised Edition

Regarding the Revised Edition

This revised edition includes a chapter focusing on the strengths of the Potter series, a new first chapter, and — because the revised edition will be available in hardcopy — a Table of Contents and an Index.

Our thanks to Jane Friedman, Publisher & Editorial Director of Writer's Digest, for posting a slightly altered version of "Strengths of the Potter Series" on her blog *There Are No Rules*: http://blog.writersdigest.com/norules.

Contents

Introduction

The Harry Potter series has justly become one of the bestselling works of fiction in history. J.K. Rowling's flowing narrative style and endlessly inventive imagination brought her creation to life as she blended elements of the boarding school and coming-of-age tales with fantasy, horror, mystery, and alternate reality.

Her decision to have the series end after seven books was ingenious and added to its unique quality, clearly separating the Potter saga from both the fantasy trilogy crowd as well as from episodic tales such as L. Frank Baum's Oz series, which can effectively go on forever because their protagonists never change in any meaningful way.

The often dark quality of Ms. Rowling's subject matter, along with her unflinching dedication to her own vision — her willingness to redefine "what is allowed" in young adult fiction — separated her opus from generic commercial pabulum and propelled the Potter series into that highest sphere of literature: the censored work.

As a result, Ms. Rowling seemed akin to a more-substantial Enid Blyton, challenging both her characters and her readers with deeper issues. The stakes were high. Not only the lives of the characters, but peace and freedom were in danger on a global scale.

Unfortunately, the very qualities that made the series so successful also led some readers to feel disappointed. Either our expectations were too high, or else we were misled by the apparent promise of a non-episodic tale that would grapple with difficult issues like trauma, abuse, and homicide. But whatever the answer, some nascent fans were driven off, while others gradually fell out of love with Harry Potter as the epic progressed. Given the success and popularity of the series, we have a lot of work to do, if we're to explain what led to these unhappy results. To begin with, we can at least summarize a few of the most potent issues.

First, Harry didn't remain the hero-protagonist of the series. Neither hero nor antihero, Harry too often resembled a video camera, observing key events without the power to affect them. In the final book of the series, *Deathly Hallows*, Harry sits in the woods even though a Hitler-esque Voldemort is wreaking havoc in the outside world. Harry's behavior is conscionable only because we know he isn't up to facing Voldemort in a fair fight — but this is one case where two wrongs don't make it right. Ultimately, Dumbledore became the true protagonist of the series, a role he mostly plays offstage.

Second, key characters in the series failed to evolve in any substantial way. Harry and Ron remain underachievers who never reach their full potential. Malfoy is locked into his role as a minor nuisance. Snape never moves past being the sniveling, petty tyrant. As for Dumbledore, his role in Book 7 was indistinguishable from his role in earlier volumes. He might be dead, but he continues as the wise mentor, showing up near the end of the story to help wrap things up.

Thus, though limited to seven books, the series still became episodic in nature. It discovered a formula and then worked that formula as if the series were a garden-variety TV sitcom or an endless series like *The Hardy Boys*. Each year, we start with Harry at the Dursley house. At the end of each year, we see him return there. In between, we see him spend far too much time playing wizard chess and trading chocolate frog cards with Ron in front of the Gryffindor fireplace, taking Hogwarts and his own abilities for granted.

In musical terms, the Potter series became not The Beatles — who evolved from toe-tapper hits to complex and surreal masterpieces — but The Beach Boys, recycling the same rhythms, the same harmonies, and the same melodic structures year after year, album after album ... book after book.

Third, while the series promotes positive values like the power of love, friendship, and teamwork, it also contains less congenial messages such as: it's better to be lucky than talented; it's a waste of time to work hard; and your best bet is to just sit around and wait for divine providence to solve your problems for you. Given the historical impact of this series, shouldn't it instead promote hard work, the intelligent use of one's talents, and having and pursuing meaningful goals?

While these claims will strike many fans of the series as ridiculous, for other fans it begins to seem that something went terribly wrong somewhere along the line.

Although *Destiny Unfulfilled* focuses primarily on what we perceive as weaknesses in the series, our goal isn't to deny the power and greatness of Ms. Rowling's masterwork. Rather, we hope to voice the complaints of a minority of readers, who expected more from the series and were ultimately disappointed.

This book is broken into two parts. Part 1 follows a topical organization, focuses primarily on high-level issues, and makes use of a few key examples to support its arguments. Part 2 goes sequentially book-by-book, delves down to lower-level issues, and offers a larger number of hypothetical alternatives — ideas not only as to what might be changed, but also what those changes might look like.

Creative writing students will likely benefit from reading this book, as the careful analysis someone else's writing often helps us analyze our own work.

Acknowledgments

Thanks to Kate Steele of The Editorial Department for annotating the manuscript of *Destiny Unfulfilled*. Having read the Potter series to children in after-school programs, Kate was able to catch me uttering a few falsehoods regarding the actual text of the books, as well as to give me several new ideas, and some much-needed validation. I'm not quite as alone as I at first feared.

Additional feedback came from various denizens of The Leaky Cauldron forums

http://www.leakylounge.com/forums.html

who responded with restraint and tact to my various assertions regarding the Potter series.

Thanks to Greg and Cindy for lots of free food and booze and for giving feedback on the manuscript. Actually, this book was Greg's idea, but I think he just hoped it would make me shut up about the Potter business.

Part 1:
Thematic Discussion

Chapter 1:
Something Rotten In Hogwarts

The Harry Potter series works fine for most readers, but for others it seems to be flawed. The best way to understand the complaints these readers have is to start with Book 6, *Half-Blood Prince*, where — more-so than in any other book from the series — Harry is robbed of his duties as protagonist. Relegated to the role of tag-along, his sometimes dejected manner suggests he may even be aware of his wretched condition.

To appreciate Harry's role in Book 6, consider the play *Rosencrantz and Guildenstern are Dead*, written by Tom Stoppard. For those shamefully deficient in their Shakespeare, Rosencrantz and Guildenstern are two minor characters from *Hamlet*, but in Stoppard's play they become the main characters, with Hamlet limited to a bit part.

In the Harry Potter series, Book 6 is J.K. Rowling's version of *Rosencrantz and Guildenstern are Dead*.

Has Anyone Seen the Protagonist?

In Book 6, the protagonist's goal, and thus the main plotline, is: "Prepare to defeat Voldemort." Perhaps "Finish preparing to defeat Voldemort" is an even better description, as Voldemort has been back for all of Book 5. At any rate, in Book 6 Voldemort is the villain: the primary obstacle between the protagonist and his goal of ensuring a peaceful world to live in.

What does Harry have to do with this hypothetical main plotline? Let's have a look.

To start with, recall the situation at the beginning of Book 6. Voldemort is not only back, but is now operating in the open. Giants, dementors, and death eaters are attacking both muggles and wizards. People are dying. In addition, Dumbledore has told Harry the Prophecy, which means Harry now knows he is the Chosen One — or at least, he was *supposed* to be the Chosen One: the one person with the power to destroy Voldemort permanently.

While Voldemort shifts into high gear, what does Harry do? He lounges in seclusion and safety at the home of his aunt and uncle. His first scene in Book 6 shows him in his room at the Dursley home, having fallen asleep waiting for Dumbledore to show up. Though Harry expects Dumbledore to take him out of the Dursley home for the remainder of the summer, Harry hasn't bothered to pack his things.

Consider that for a moment. Not only is our nominal hero sitting passively, waiting for permission to do something, he has become so tired of waiting that he has fallen asleep. Furthermore, the unpacked trunk implies that he has doubts that permission will *ever* be given.

Could this be a Freudian slip: the author's creative subconscious showing its resentment of a predefined plot outline, an outline constructed — and then set in concrete — by the rational, deterministic half of the author's brain? To put our question more dramatically, could it be that the fictional Harry fears he might not even have a role in Book 6? If so, his fears turn out to be unfounded, but understandable just the same. As we shall see, in terms of the main plotline, Harry is a candidate for the cutting room floor.

When Dumbledore finally shows up to escort Harry from the Dursley home, he lets Harry tag along for a chapter, using Harry to lure Horace Slughorn into accepting a professorship at Hogwarts. Harry knows that he's supposed to help in this task, but he has no idea *what* he's expected to do, and ultimately

Slughorn accepts the professorship because of Harry's fame. Which is to say, in this scene Harry is a kind of idiot device. He succeeds not through cunning, charisma, or intelligent effort, but by the lucky happenstance that he's famous. Famous, primarily, because of the sacrifice his mother made, which brought Voldemort's first reign of terror to an end.

Having accomplished this side goal, Dumbledore drops Harry off at the Weasley home and departs. One of the first questions that Ron asks Harry is, "So, what's been going on?" To which Harry replies, "Nothing much, I've been stuck at my aunt and uncle's, haven't I?" Ron objects that Harry has been out and about with Dumbledore, but Harry shrugs this off with, "It wasn't that exciting."

This apathetic, dispirited attitude again makes readers wonder, "What is Harry trying to tell us?"

Consider also the book's climactic scene atop the Astronomy Tower, where Dumbledore sacrifices himself for the cause. In that scene, Harry is forced to remain silent and immobile, hidden under his invisibility cloak. Not only is he invisible in the literal magical sense, he's invisible in the colloquial sense: overlooked, unimportant, impotent.

While these points are perhaps rather subtle, Book 6 contains more-obvious indications that Harry has ceased to be the protagonist of his namesake series.

Subplot vs. Plot

What is Harry obsessed with in Book 6? Getting hooked up with Ginny, captaining the Quidditch team, and finding out what Draco Malfoy is up to. In terms of the Big Three, Hermione has an additional goal of learning the identity of the half-blood Prince. What are all of these? They are subplots.

Harry's one meaningful task with regard to "prepare to defeat Voldemort," is to obtain a crucial memory from Professor Slughorn. Rather than coming up with this task himself, Harry is *assigned* the task by Dumbledore. Worse,

Dumbledore has to scold Harry before our hero takes the task seriously. Between one meeting with the headmaster and another, Harry effectively forgets that he's helping put an end to the genocidal Voldemort.

When Harry finally gets around to retrieving the memory from Slughorn, his success isn't based on ability, tenacity, or any other active characteristic. Rather, his success is a result of drinking a mouthful of a luck potion. Once again, Harry is an idiot device. Provided with a luck potion, *anyone* could retrieve the memory from Slughorn. As such, Harry brings nothing special to his role. (Or, at most, Harry brings his birthright; Slughorn knew Harry's mother and thinks highly of her, which provides Harry the final lever he needs for extracting the memory.)

In Book 6, Dumbledore is the one with the driving goal to destroy Voldemort, he's the one who develops a plan to achieve this goal, and ultimately he knowingly sacrifices his own life in order to bring the plan to fruition. While Dumbledore spends some time during Book 6 reviewing Voldemort's backstory with Harry, the headmaster keeps the most important bits of information to himself.

As for Harry, he has no part in developing the plan, nor is he even made a party to it. No doubt his role is an important one, but he will play his role just as he did when he helped recruit Slughorn: not fully understanding what he's doing, and not entirely sure why, in the end, he achieves success. He has no idea how to locate the Horcruxes, how to recognize them, or how to destroy them, all of which are tasks absolutely required before Voldemort can be destroyed. Moreover, in the final showdown, Harry's victory is made possible not by his own powers and abilities, but by the magical Deathly Hallows and an arcane ricochet effect outside Harry's control, just as Harry's fame (a force outside of his control) enabled him to recruit Slughorn.

What we see here, then, is that by Book 6, Dumbledore has usurped the role of protagonist, while Harry has become a dispirited character who goes where he's told to go, when he's told to go, without any real understanding of what he's doing.

As in the climactic buildup at the end of Book 1, *Philosopher's Stone,* Harry has become a bishop in someone else's game of chess. That the series is bookended with Harry-as-chess-piece makes one wonder if perhaps this is some sort of hint. Are we *meant* to see Harry as the hero or not? This is one of those alarming little nettles that — along with Harry's invisibility during most of the climactic battle in Book 7, *Deathly Hallows* — makes us wonder if, just possibly, Ms. Rowing might be having us on. But let's think positively and assume otherwise.

Which then leaves us with another question. To paraphrase *The Godfather*, "How did things ever get this messed up?"

Chapter 2:
Shaggy Dogs

Consider the following short story:

> Zaphod strode down the star cruiser's main passageway, his skin red with anger. At the end of the hall, Zaphod kicked open a blast door. In front of him, Black Bart stood holding a gun against Penelope's head. Zaphod raised a finger and pointed it threateningly. Only, nothing happened because Zaphod was actually a giant tomato and didn't have hands or fingers.

What's wrong with this picture? Probably more than one thing, but the fundamental flaw is that the writer has cheated us. Zaphod turning out to be a giant tomato doesn't constitute a surprise ending, it constitutes a gyp. A broken promise.

While the Zaphod story doesn't explicitly promise to play fair, that promise is there implicitly. In fact, almost all promises made by any piece of writing are implicit rather than explicit. Yet they are promises nonetheless, and faithful readers expect that such promises will be kept.

In the coming discussion, we divide the promises made by the Potter series into three categories: general-purpose promises common to all works of fiction, genre-specific promises, and promises unique to the Potter universe. We cover the first category here, and the other two in the next chapter.

Books on writing sometimes call the sum of these promises the writer's contract with the reader. Contract seems like a good word for it. Writers have a responsibility to fulfill both the letter and the spirit of the contracts they enter into. Doing so not only keeps readers happy, it helps the resulting work reach its full potential.

General-Purpose Promises

Before proceeding, we need to define several terms that loom large in the coming discussion. A "shaggy dog" is when a story cheats. The cheat can range from a total failure to resolve the attendant conflict (ex., "Zaphod was actually a tomato" or "It was all a dream") to resolution of the conflict by forces outside the protagonist's control. "Deus ex machina" is a kind of shaggy dog where some supernatural power resolves a dilemma. Examples of deus ex machina range from a god-like being literally showing up and snapping his fingers, to miracles, to plain old luck.

Shaggy Dog Examples

The Potter series contains a large number of shaggy dogs. Though some of the examples listed below may seem trivial, the cumulative effect of these cheats makes them devastating. Book 3, *Prisoner of Azkaban*, is the only book in the series that doesn't undercut the story's resolution with some sort of shaggy dog. (Even Book 3 diminishes Harry's achievement, using a time-travel effect to give Harry a second chance at saving the day, and forcing him to say, "I knew I could do it, because I'd already done it." Most unfortunate, that.) By resolving key challenges via one sort of cheat or another, every other book in the series robs Harry and/or the Big Three of the full responsibility and glory that should be theirs.

Cheating comes at a price, and for some readers the price is very high indeed, because we no longer sweat when the conflict escalates. Why should we? We know the story will turn out however it wants, whether or not the resolution makes sense or is consistent with the "rules" that have previously been established. Meanwhile, those of us not born lucky lose our ability to relate to Harry. In sum, the Potter series gradually ceases to involve us as it once did.

1. Harry's killing of Professor Quirrell is treated as if it never happened, Book 1, *Philosopher's Stone*.

At the end of Book 1, Harry faces Professor Quirrell in a chamber underneath Hogwarts where the Philosopher's Stone is being kept. Quirrell, with Voldemort riding about on the back of his head, is trying to locate the magical Stone because the elixir it produces can restore Voldemort's strength. When Voldemort realizes that Harry has the Stone in his pocket, he orders Quirrell to seize Harry, at which point Quirrell discovers that the very touch of Harry's skin burns him, due to the lingering protection of Lily Potter's sacrifice.

One potential problem with this solution is that it treats Harry like he's still a helpless infant. When he was one year old (or thereabouts) Harry was saved from Voldemort by his mother's sacrifice. Now that he's eleven going on twelve, he's again saved by this same mechanism. Still, this *is* Book 1. Harry isn't yet twelve, and it wouldn't make sense for him to either out-magic an adult, even if that adult is the unimpressive Quirrell. Having Harry figure a way to out-smart Quirrell and Voldemort would perhaps be the best answer, but it isn't apparent how he might do that under the circumstances.

On the plus side, Harry does at least cotton on to what is happening, and he makes maximum use of his unexpected ability to harm Quirrell/Voldemort. The pain of contact injures him nearly as much as it does Quirrell, but Harry continues to grab at Quirrell's head with his blistering hands until Quirrell is dead and Voldemort is forced to flee. As a result, Harry isn't an entirely passive entity, which clearly differentiates this encounter from the one ten years earlier.

Therefore, it isn't the power to harm Quirrell/Voldemort that we object to, but rather how Book 1 uses that ability to trivialize Harry's role. Specifically, because touching Quirrell hurts Harry, Harry passes out before the fight ends. Dumbledore arrives and carries the unconscious Harry from the chamber, so that responsibility for Quirrell's death is left unclear. Did Harry kill him? Was it Dumbledore? Was Quirrell doomed to begin with?

Interestingly, the first movie changes this scene, so that Harry isn't injured when he touches Quirrell, and thus is fully conscious when Quirrell disintegrates into a pile of dust. What the movie can't do, however, is have Harry face the implications of that event. Certainly, it can't carry the implications forward into the rest of the series.

Let us suppose that Harry does in fact kill Quirrell at the end of Book 1. By knocking Harry out before the fight is finished, the book tries to tap dance around the fallout from such an action. Dumbledore arrives, the waters get muddied, Quirrell's death is never dealt with, and as a result, Harry is robbed not only of the full credit due him but also of responsibility and guilt.

In a sense, this is a reverse shaggy dog. Harry did in fact save the day, but the book acts as if he didn't. Why? Because if our eleven-year-old protagonist killed someone with his bare hands, he couldn't possibly emerge unchanged.

And yet that is exactly what happens.

When Harry leaves the hospital at the end of Book 1, it's as if the fight with Quirrell and Voldemort never happened. If Harry is depressed at all, it's because he faces another summer with the Dursleys. The result is that he seems devoid of conscience and empathy.

Of course, Book 1 is ostensibly aimed at readers as young as Harry himself. Doesn't it make sense, then, that Ms. Rowling would obfuscate Harry's role in Quirrell's death out of consideration for that young audience? For several reasons, no.

(a) The movie shows Harry being clearly responsible. Surely Ms. Rowling could be as brave as Hollywood.

(b) Ultimately, Harry bears at least some responsibility. As such, we expect the series to deal honestly with the emotional repercussions. Hollywood heroes have no problem killing someone without losing a moment's sleep over it. But Harry isn't a Stallone or Schwarzenegger-type hero. Our hypothetical younger audience (along with some of us who are older as well) would be better served by an honest exploration of what it feels like to have killed another person, rather than having such realities swept under the rug, ignoring personal responsibility and treating homicide as something trivial and easily forgotten.

Note the similarity between the death of Quirrell and the death of the Wicked Witch in the first Oz book. An odd, unexpected effect (a splash of water in the *Wizard of Oz*) leads to the villain's death in both cases. In both cases, the hero emerges free of guilt – Dorothy because she didn't intend to splash the witch with water, and didn't realize the witch had a deathly allergy to the substance. The similarity is unfortunate because the Oz series is an episodic story where Dorothy remains unchanged throughout.

To reinforce a point made earlier, what is especially worrisome about the ending of Book 1 is that it establishes a precedent for the remainder of the series.

2. Harry and Ron are saved from giant spiders by the appearance of the Weasley's automobile, Book 2, *Chamber of Secrets*.

Late in Book 2, Harry and Ron follow a trail of spiders, which leads them to the giant spider Aragog's lair out in the Forbidden Forest. Aragog dispenses a few clues, then offers the two lads up as a late-night snack to his various descendants. In the nick of time, Mr. Weasley's magical car arrives and transports Ron and Harry to safety.

Because Harry and Ron fly Mr. Weasley's car to school at the start of Book 2, the appearance of the car at Aragog's lair is somewhat understandable. It doesn't just show up out of nowhere, after all. However, the car still represents a shaggy dog resolution to the spider problem.

That the car can maneuver through thick woods and knock down trees is a bit much, but as a magical car, that is a mere quibble. The real problems are that the car is still running and that it has any interest in helping Ron and Harry.

Keep in mind that the car crashed at the start of the year because it was running out of juice. Being cynical, we see the book playing a game of "the car is going dead" when a crash is wanted, then changing its mind to "actually the car was just tired" or some such later on.

More serious than motive power is the car's willingness to help. The last we saw of it, the car was mad at Ron and Harry for not only crashing it, but crashing it into the Whomping Willow. Given that the two heroes are now surrounded by spiders, some of which are even bigger than the car itself, the car should logically want nothing to do with the situation.

How else could the spider encounter be resolved? One option would be to have Ron and Harry talk their way out of the dilemma, use some form of magic, or otherwise effect an escape themselves. Such a radical change isn't required, however. The car will do, so long as we see Ron and/or Harry repairing it during the school year. That would have them *earn* their escape through a demonstration of industriousness and empathy toward the car, and would justify the car's friendliness and continued operation after so many months.

As a side benefit, having Ron perform this task would help to deepen his character by showing him taking after his father, and would give him a talent other than chess to draw upon.

The question of character depth and character abilities is a critical one for the Potter series. Shaggy dog resolutions such as the spider-and-car escape affect more than the immediate situation. They ultimately allow the series to keep its main characters weak and ineffectual, obscuring the fact that Harry and Ron aren't growing up, aren't developing into powerful wizards, and aren't becoming heroic forces in a world heading toward war.

3. Harry and Ron are saved from Professor Lockhart by the malfunctioning of Ron's wand, Book 2.

Ron and Harry force Professor Lockhart to accompany them down the drainpipe that leads to the Chamber of Secrets. Once there, Lockhart decides he's had enough, grabs Ron's wand, and tries to cast an Obliviate spell, designed to make the two lads forget what has happened. Unfortunately for Lockhart, Ron's wand is damaged and the spell rebounds upon the hapless professor, with the side-effect of collapsing part of the tunnel they're in.

As with the appearance of the car, we're quite prepared for Ron's wand to act up. He damaged his wand *in* the car crash, actually, and since then we've seen numerous examples of the wand misbehaving — Ron's vomiting slugs for the better part of a day being perhaps the most memorable. However, for Lockhart to use Ron's wand at this point is more than a happy coincidence, it makes sense only as a convenience for the story to get the results it wants.

Even worse, Ron and Harry are made to look stupid when they decide that, with Ginny's life on the line, Lockhart is just the man to help them take on a basilisk. However many times Book 2 shows us Ron's wand misbehaving, it shows us Lockhart's ineffectual, buffoonish nature twice as often. Readers expect Harry in particular to recognize that Lockhart represents an impediment rather than an aid.

Two simple changes would help make this particular sequence easier to swallow. First, have Lockhart — sensing that he has his next book in the making — force himself upon Ron and Harry, rather than vice-versa. Once he gets underground and spots a discarded basilisk skin, Lockhart naturally chickens out and decides he has enough information to be getting on with.

The second change would have Lockhart cast Obliviate with his own wand rather than Ron's. Instead of a wand backfire, let Harry block Lockhart's spell, but do so too energetically — not knowing his own strength yet and his adrenaline having kicked in.

The physical result of these changes is the same as in the original version. The roof caves in, Lockhart's memory is entirely erased, and Harry is forced to continue to the Chamber of Secrets alone. But this approach doesn't require Harry and Ron to act dumb by inviting Lockhart along, and it allows Harry to earn the escape from Lockhart.

This solution would even introduce a bit of irony, since Lockhart himself arranged for a dueling class earlier in the school year, and during that class introduced Harry to a spell (probably Protego) which can be used to block most other spells. What poetic justice for Lockhart to be zapped by that very spell. As side benefits, (a) Harry would begin to suspect that he can do this magic stuff after all, thus adding another crack to the eggshell of insecurity he's trapped in, and (b) he would have Lockhart's loss of memory on his conscience.

Unfortunately, this won't be the last time the Potter series uses some external solution (in this case, Ron's malfunctioning wand; in Book 7, *Deathly Hallows*, the three artifacts of the book's title) rather than allow Harry to solve a problem with either his natural or his magical abilities. Protego won't be the last spell to disappear from Harry's lexicon almost as soon as it appears, with the result that Harry ever remains the ineffectual, helpless orphan boy. He might be a wizard, but by no means is he a very good one. And in too many situations, he might as well not be one at all.

4. Harry is saved from Voldemort and the basilisk by the appearance of Dumbledore's phoenix Fawkes, the Sorting Hat, and Godric Gryffindor's sword, Book 2.

Following his arrival in the Chamber of Secrets at the very end of Book 2, Harry finds himself facing a ghostly Tom Riddle: a former Hogwarts student that Harry met earlier in the year via a seemingly blank diary. Riddle gets ahold of Harry's wand and patiently explains to a suddenly not-so-bright Harry that Riddle is the villain here. In fact, Riddle is the once and future Lord Voldemort — this version of him housed in a diary and now grown strong by feeding on Ginny's spirit during the school year.

Riddle then calls forth his pet basilisk to attack Harry. Although Harry is a Parselmouth and thus is able to communicate with creatures like the basilisk, he makes no attempt to counter Riddle's order — another example of an ability that has been set up and then forgotten in preference to miracles from above. In this case, the miracle takes the form of Dumbledore's phoenix Fawkes, who arrives carrying (of all things) the Sorting Hat.

Interestingly, Harry's wand contains one of Fawkes' tail feathers. Only one other wand in the world can make that claim, which might imply a connection between Harry and Fawkes. If so, the series fails to explore that connection. Dumbledore has become lifelong friends with a phoenix, but at no point does Dumbledore teach Harry how to accomplish such a feat.

More importantly for the situation here in the Chamber, Harry doesn't actively call for Fawkes and is surprised (and nonplussed) when Fawkes appears. What the heck is Harry going to do with a phoenix and the Sorting Hat? He hasn't a clue. This reinforces the cynical view that the appearance of Dumbledore's phoenix is a cheat by the author.

While Fawkes duels the basilisk, Harry closes his eyes and, eventually, jams the Sorting Hat onto his head as a blindfold, occasionally muttering, "Help. Someone help me," while cowering in the middle of the Chamber of Secrets deep below Hogwarts, with the unconscious Ginny the only friendly character in earshot.

By this time, the unsympathetic reader is cheering the basilisk on, hoping it will hurry up and finish this helpless loser off. But it is not to be, for something drops out of the Sorting Hat: not a rabbit, but Godric Gryffindor's sword.

Although Harry then uses Gryffindor's sword to kill the basilisk, his victory is robbed of any oomph by the preceding bone-headed maneuvers and deus ex machina moments.

True, earlier in Book 2 Dumbledore did promise that help would always be given if it was asked for, but that doesn't excuse this sort of "angels from on high" solution. Harry is supposed to be a powerful wizard, even if he doesn't quite realize it yet. More importantly, Harry is supposed to be clever, quick thinking, and calm under pressure. Here is an opportunity for him to demonstrate those traits, rather than be handed an unearned solution.

Yes, Harry does show loyalty by standing up for Dumbledore as he faces Tom Riddle. But in no way does that earn Harry the appearance of Fawkes and the Sorting Hat. In fact, this concept of "give all praise to Dumbledore and help will arrive" is an insidious cancer that will gut Harry and the series by the time we reach Book 7, casting Dumbledore as an ever-watchful protector who will surely step in if a situation starts to get out of hand.

What's surprising is how little needs to change in order for Harry to retain his place as the hero of the series while keeping Dumbledore in his role as the wise mentor, rather than turning him into some sort of demigod.

(a) Book 2 already has Harry visit Dumbledore's office during the middle of the school year. During that visit, Harry spots the Sorting Hat and is introduced to Fawkes. A simple addition would have Dumbledore mention that it's possible to pull objects out of the Sorting Hat. He might talk about his own attempts, all unsuccessful, to recover Gryffindor's missing sword via that very means. (If the sword isn't missing at this point, *let* it be missing.) "I think it has something to do with really needing an object," Dumbledore might say, "or perhaps having a strong connection to an object, rather than merely wanting it."

(b) Prior to venturing down to the Chamber of Secrets at the end of Book 2, Harry could again visit Dumbledore's office. Seeing that Dumbledore is gone, Harry grabs the Sorting Hat and either convinces Fawkes to accompany him down to the Chamber or else attempts to communicate the situation to Fawkes. (Hermione might have done research on phoenixes following Harry's first visit to the headmaster's office, thus giving Harry additional insight into the various powers of phoenixes and making Harry's interest in bringing Fawkes along more logical, while also allowing Hermione a larger role in Harry's final victory.)

Taking the Sorting Hat (and possibly Fawkes as well) to the Chamber shows Harry thinking ahead and being clever. Currently, he takes Professor Lockhart and Ron with him, and neither of them is the right answer. What exactly is Ron going to do when faced with a basilisk, other than be turned to stone?

The current resolution to Book 2 has Harry calling for help and talking to the walls about how wonderful Dumbledore is, making him appear both scatterbrained and very, very lucky. His subsequent victory over the basilisk demonstrates bravery and fortitude, but Harry's victory is diminished and the risk to his life robbed of intensity by the implication that Dumbledore is watching and surely won't let anything really bad happen.

5. Harry is assisted in the Tri-Wizard Tournament by Moaning Myrtle, Dobby, and the false Mad Eye Moody, Book 4, *Goblet of Fire.*

In Book 4, Moaning Myrtle helps Harry twice with the Tri-Wizard Tournament. The first time, she tells him how to unlock the secret of the golden dragon egg, which he needs for the second Tri-Wizard task. Myrtle then helps Harry during the second task itself while Harry is swimming in the lake, by telling him how to find the prisoners who need to be rescued.

The point isn't that Harry must do everything himself, but merely that readers expect Harry (and the other main characters) to earn any help they receive. While Harry does know Moaning Myrtle from Book 2, he has never been on terms with her. Worse, after she helps Harry figure out the clue inside the golden egg, Myrtle asks for a favor in return: that Harry come visit her. Harry's response to this? He says "sure" with his fingers crossed. He has no intention of so much as dropping by to say hello.

Far from helping Harry a second time, when Myrtle gives Harry directions in the Hogwarts lake during the second task, she should point him in the wrong direction! That would repay him for being an insensitive git, a liar, and an ingrate. That would be poetic justice and fair return.

In being put off by Myrtle's self-pitying personality, Harry behaves indistinguishably from Ron. Didn't Harry grow up as a muggle and spend his early years in an unloving home? Why would he turn up his nose not only at a friend, but at a friend who is a ghost? Sure she's whiny, but clearly Myrtle is also useful. She helped Harry figure out how to find the Chamber of Secrets in his second year, and now she's helping him again. Having a ghost on your side at Hogwarts certainly seems worth five minutes out of your day, once or twice a week.

Harry keeping his promise to visit Myrtle would not only earn her help during the second task, it would help to differentiate Harry as a character. Even if all teenage boys are insensitive gits, readers can tolerate Harry having certain unlikely characteristics — up to and including empathy for the feelings of others.

As for Myrtle's help with the golden egg, Harry could earn even that. One possibility is to have Harry begin visiting Myrtle regularly following his second year. Another possibility is that, rather than unilaterally telling Harry how to decipher the clue inside the golden egg, Myrtle could play hard to get. Harry has to make some sort of bargain with her. His promise to come visit her (i.e., the idea being his not hers) might be sufficient, but perhaps Myrtle is too cynical to trust such a promise. As a result, Myrtle counters with a bargain of her own. Given Myrtle's obvious curiosity in the matter, she might agree to help Harry in exchange for getting to look at him naked. While this is perhaps a bit racy for the series, this *is* Book 4, after all. But either way, at least let Harry earn the second bit of help from Myrtle, if not the first as well.

Dobby also helps Harry with the second Tri-Wizard task. Overhearing Mad Eye Moody say that gillyweed is the very thing Harry needs to complete the task, Dobby goes to Professor Snape's private stores, steals the gillyweed, and brings it to Harry just in the nick of time.

This bit of help is doubly disturbing. On the one hand, Harry has been insensitive, bordering on cruel, toward Dobby's friend Winky, cross-examining her while she's clearly distraught, and not even trying to help her overcome her depression and butterbeer addiction. Moreover, though Harry did help Dobby obtain his freedom at the end of Book 2, the connection between them is clearly tenuous. While Dobby tramped about the country looking for work (during the whole of Book 3), Harry failed to keep in touch with him and did nothing at all to help Dobby find employment. At a minimum, it should take more than an off-hand remark overheard in a third-party conversation for Dobby to steal gillyweed from Professor Snape — a master of the school that employs both Dobby and Winky.

The second disturbing part of Dobby's intercession is that Harry can find out about gillyweed merely by talking to Neville Longbottom. Neville's gift is herbology, and he's in possession of a book that specifically mentions gillyweed and its properties. Though the fake Moody suggests that honor and pride keep Harry from reaching out to Neville, readers know better. Harry eagerly accepts help from Hermione, takes the totally unearned gillyweed from Dobby, and callously follows Moaning Myrtle's directions in the lake. As a result, Harry's failure to get this information from Neville is clearly not a badge of honor, but rather a testament both to Harry's aloofness and his lack of empathy even when it involves a fellow orphan.

Finally, Mad Eye Moody helps Harry with each of the Tri-Wizard tasks. Though Moody has an ulterior motive, his help still serves as a shaggy dog, because it emphasizes that Harry isn't capable of handling these tasks on his own. We must keep in mind that, here in Book 4, the series is half over. For Harry to still be an ineffectual, helpless kid is a clear sign that something is broken. There isn't enough time left for him to evolve into the Chosen One, which makes us wonder if, just maybe, some other character's name should be on the cover of these books.

6. Harry overpowers Voldemort in the Riddle graveyard, Book 4.

At the end of Book 4, Voldemort is restored to his body by a magic ritual. After recalling his faithful death eaters, Voldemort hands Harry a wand and challenges him to a duel. This will allow Voldemort to prove who is the Dark Lord and who is road kill.

After Voldemort has toyed with Harry via the Cruciatus curse, Harry realizes that he's going to die. Although Harry has no illusions of being able to go toe-to-toe with Voldemort (more's the pity), he decides he isn't going to just lie down and let Voldemort kill him. He determines to go out swinging. As Voldemort casts the killing curse, Harry casts his own trademark spell, Expelliarmus, designed to knock the wand out of an opponent's hand.

At this point, Harry is saved by a happy coincidence. Harry's wand shares the same core as Voldemort's (one of Fawkes' tail feathers), and this unusual trait causes the wands to malfunction.

We've been told ahead of time that the cores match, and Harry quickly catches on to what is happening. Not only does he catch on, he magically overpowers Voldemort during the subsequent struggle to control the misbehaving wands. As a result, Harry demonstrates coolness under pressure, strength of will, and a most impressive amount of raw magical power. But the end result is still a shaggy dog.

If Harry is powerful enough to overpower Voldemort, why doesn't his power show up in other ways? How can he be stronger than Voldemort and yet struggle with the simple spells they teach in the classroom? If Harry can overmatch the most powerful dark wizard in a thousand years, why does Mad Eye Moody have to hold Harry's hand to get him through the Tri-Wizard Tournament?

The story wants Harry to remain an ineffectual wizard, a struggling student, and a generally-insecure kid, because it's easier to make him seem sympathetic that way than if he grows up into a full-blown hero. Moreover, writing about a character who undergoes radical evolution in both personality and ability has to be about as difficult as it gets in the world of fiction. Thus, it's much easier to leave Harry as we find him, the oppressed orphan who everyone feels sorry for.

On the other hand, the story needs Harry to escape the Riddle graveyard alive. Thus, for a few seconds Harry is granted great power. But as soon as it stops being expedient, that power is taken away and Harry goes back to being nothing special.

Such inconsistency is a problem because it undermines the reader's faith in the story. When a character gains and loses power inexplicably, and does so at critical moments, it makes us see that character not as a real person but as a widget, something that the author manipulates as the spirit moves her.

7. Harry is saved from the false Mad Eye Moody by Dumbledore, Book 4.

After his duel with Voldemort in the Riddle graveyard, Harry returns to Hogwarts and is taken into the castle by the false Mad Eye Moody. Moody questions Harry about what happened in the graveyard, reveals himself as one of Voldemort's faithful death eaters, and prepares to kill Harry, only to be stopped at the last moment by Dumbledore.

Within a few short pages, Harry has gone from being able to overpower Voldemort to being the helpless waif in need of rescue. What is especially worrisome about this particular scene is that it begins a pattern of Dumbledore actively intervening. In the past, Dumbledore has been more of a security blanket, reassuring us that nothing bad is really going to happen because help is just a prayer away. Here, Dumbledore is no longer an advisor or a distant benevolent figure. Instead, he rushes in to save the day, and it won't be the last time.

It isn't necessary for Harry to overpower the fake Mad Eye. However, readers expect him to at least be capable of seeing the shadows in Moody's foe-glass growing more solid, intuit that help is on the way, and endeavor to keep the imposter either talking or listening, thus allowing Harry an active part in his rescue. Does this lose the "surprise" of Dumbledore's entry? Yes, but that surprise would last another two paragraphs at most and is viable only on the first reading. A surprise that comes at such a high cost should be discarded.

8. Harry saved from Voldemort by Dumbledore, Book 5, *Order of the Phoenix.*

Late in Book 5, Harry goes to the Ministry of Magic, having seen in a vision that Sirius is being held there by Lord Voldemort. Reaching the Department of Mysteries, Harry learns that his vision was a false one. Death eaters arrive, followed by members of the Order of the Phoenix, and a fight ensues.

During the fight, Sirius is killed by his cousin Bellatrix. Harry chases after Bellatrix, who mocks and toys with Harry until Voldemort arrives. Luckily, before Voldemort can take any meaningful action, Dumbledore also puts in an appearance. Dumbledore pushes Harry aside to keep him from getting in the way and proceeds to duel Voldemort until the arrival of the Minister of Magic and various other people frightens Voldemort off.

This sequence is problematic for several reasons. (a) When we compare Harry's abilities with those that Dumbledore and Voldemort display in their duel, we see that Harry isn't in their same league. He's a mediocre fifteen-year-old basketball player being asked to go one-on-one with Magic Johnson. Moreover, given that we're at the very end of Book 5, we have to question whether Harry can ever *reach* the league he needs to be in. The delta here is so great, it forces us to either view Dumbledore and Voldemort as gods, or else to see Harry as a set of claws scuttling about on the tile floor.

(b) What was Harry thinking when he came to the Ministry in the first place? Let us ignore for now questions of why Snape did such a lousy job teaching Harry Occlumency (which theoretically would have shielded Harry from the intruding visions), why Harry would trust the vision, or why Harry would disregard the two-way mirror that Sirius gave him, which would allow Harry to determine that Sirius is in fact perfectly safe. Accepting the situation just as Harry does, still Harry's behavior doesn't add up.

Harry claims he wants to save Sirius from Voldemort, but this is a kid who struggles with school lessons. Just imagine if Harry's vision had been correct, and Voldemort really did have Sirius down in the Department of Mysteries. Harry would be tomato paste, along with the students who accompany him. Harry's behavior, far from showing bravery and loyalty, suggests that he is delusional.

(c) When Dumbledore arrives, he shoves Harry aside and pins him in a place where Harry will be safe. This turns Harry into a kind of video camera. This level of passivity in a protagonist is insidious and will ultimately suck the life out of the last two books of the Potter series. It shows us a Dumbledore who doesn't trust Harry to even stay out of the way on his own. It shows us a Dumbledore eager to relive his glorious defeat of Grindelwald. It shows us a Harry who might as well not be there.

9. Harry is saved from the undead by Dumbledore, Book 6, *Half-Blood Prince.*

Near the end of Book 6, Dumbledore locates a cave where he believes one of Voldemort's Horcruxes is hidden. He takes Harry with him to the cave, where they discover a lake filled with undead. Dumbledore informs Harry that the way to fight the undead is with fire.

They cross to the center of the lake and find what they believe is the locket Horcrux. However, the locket is protected by a potion that must be drunk in order to expose the Horcrux. Dumbledore takes this task upon himself and is ultimately rendered unconscious by the potion.

Harry wants to give Dumbledore a drink of water, hoping to revive him with it, and chooses to scoop water out of the surrounding lake. (Yuck.) This action causes the undead to rise up and advance threateningly. Once portrayed as cool under pressure, the Harry of Book 6 loses his head and fumbles the situation as if he were a first-year Neville Longbottom. He's forgotten what Dumbledore told him moments ago and uses a variety of spells to fight the undead, all to no effect.

In previous books, Harry's one strong subject was Defense Against the Dark Arts. As a sixth year student, he shouldn't need Dumbledore to explain to him how to handle the undead. That he does need such instruction again suggests that Harry hasn't really evolved as a wizard.

In just a few pages, Dumbledore will be dead. As the Chosen One, Harry should be ready to step in and fill Dumbledore's role in the fight against Voldemort. What the cave scene demonstrates beyond a doubt is that Harry is *not* ready.

It's a shameful moment for Harry and for the series as a whole. We can only guess, but it seems likely that the story wants to demonstrate Dumbledore's greatness one last time in preparation for his coming self-sacrifice. Unfortunately, Dumbledore is elevated at Harry's expense. Harry is rendered so ineffectual, so clueless, so motiveless, he becomes a kind of third-rate sidekick. The equivalent not of Batman's Robin, nor of Holmes' Dr. Watson, but of Dr. Frankenstein's Igor. A hapless dolt.

This sad state of affairs is made only worse when Dumbledore inexplicably recovers from his potion-induced coma and saves the day. If the story didn't feel free to change the rules of the game at will, if it had any interest in justifying the reader's trust, this scene would end with both Dumbledore and Harry dead, dragged into the water and drowned by the undead hoard. Such a result would at least acknowledge that, by the time we reach the end of Book 6, something in the Potter series is fatally broken.

10. Harry is saved from death eaters by Dumbledore and (indirectly) by Voldemort, Book 6.

Following their trip to the Horcrux cave, Harry and Dumbledore arrive back at Hogwarts only to find the castle under attack by death eaters. Harry and Dumbledore fly to the top of the Astronomy Tower. Just as they land, they hear someone climbing up to the roof. As at the end of Book 5, Dumbledore immobilizes Harry and pins him out of the way. Draco Malfoy then emerges onto the roof and knocks Dumbledore's wand out of his hand.

A long conversation ensues, where it becomes apparent that Draco is unable to kill Dumbledore for reasons of conscience. Eventually, Professor Snape arrives and kills Dumbledore himself, then Snape and the other death eaters flee the castle.

Harry chases after them and manages to catch up to Professor Snape near the castle gates. Snape toys with Harry and reminds Harry that shouting spells at the top of his lungs is pointless when dealing with a skilled opponent. A death eater arrives who wants to kill Harry, but Snape informs the death eater that Voldemort wants to kill Harry personally. At this point, Snape and the rest of the death eaters complete their escape.

In analyzing this scene, let us start by recognizing that Harry need not have been present. On the rooftop, he serves the role of passive observer, a task that anyone could fulfill, even a muggle. Just as bad, Dumbledore has clearly kept Harry in the dark as to what is going on. For some reason, Dumbledore feels that Harry can't be trusted and so keeps key information to himself, making it impossible for Harry to understand what is happening, and why. Instead, he's forced to stare in dumb amazement as events unfold.

During Harry's charge through Hogwarts, he does do a lot of shouting and waving his wand around, but the spells he chooses are non-lethal, and it seems doubtful that Harry takes out even a single death eater as a result. In the vernacular of muggles, Harry's gun is filled with blanks.

Harry's subsequent confrontation with Snape serves to portray Harry as childish and magically inept, but otherwise accomplishes nothing.

During all of this, Harry could in fact be replaced by an omniscient third-person point of view — the equivalent of a roaming video camera — without changing the outcome. Keep in mind that this is the climactic scene of the next-to-last book in the series. During this scene, Harry's mentor dies, leaving Harry ostensibly in charge of thwarting Lord Voldemort. And yet, Harry is effectively missing in action.

What about Dumbledore then? Even if we accept that Harry is meant to be an antihero and that by design Dumbledore has become the hero-protagonist of the series, still Dumbledore's behavior is problematic. When he lands on the roof of the Astronomy Tower, Hogwarts is under attack. Hundreds of students and staff are in danger. And yet Dumbledore seems willing to sacrifice not only himself but all those other people in order to save one kid, Draco Malfoy.

That certainly doesn't make sense, but if Dumbledore's behavior here is part of some larger plan, if his goal is to protect Professor Snape, that begs the question, why does Dumbledore value Snape more highly than himself plus, quite possibly, a large portion of the Order of the Phoenix?

Another possible explanation is that this represents an Obi-Wan Kenobi moment. Dumbledore isn't really dying, but is merely translating on to the next higher state of existence, where he will be more powerful than anyone can possibly imagine. Although this explanation fits well with events as they unfold, it remains a shaggy dog resolution. In the original *Star*

Wars movies, when Obi-Wan Kenobi lets Darth Vader kill him, he retains the ability to advise Luke Skywalker, but he doesn't directly affect events himself.

Dumbledore's situation is quite different. In Book 7, Dumbledore gives Harry information that Harry should be able to discover on his own; he formulates a plan for destroying Voldemort and leads Harry one step at a time through accomplishing that plan; and when Harry dies, Dumbledore arrives to explain that there's no need for alarm — everything has been set up so Harry can be resurrected. As such, in death Dumbledore behaves no differently than he did when he was alive. He remains the distant, watchful eye, making sure nothing bad is really going to happen.

The cheating at the end of Book 6 doesn't stop with Dumbledore's non-death. Voldemort too has a part to play.

Let us return to the top of the Astronomy Tower. Professor Snape has just killed Dumbledore. At long last, "the only one" that Voldemort feared is dead. What is more, Voldemort's next-most-dangerous enemies, the Order of the Phoenix, are conveniently grouped together inside Hogwarts, locked in a pitched battle with Voldemort's death eaters.

The most natural move for Voldemort at this point is to make an appearance himself. If he throws in with his death eaters, he can not only finish off the Order of the Phoenix, but can also take control of Hogwarts — a useful base of operation, given its many pre-existing magical defenses. As such, the flight of the death eaters is incomprehensible. At the moment of ascendancy, the enemy turns tail and runs for no discernable reason.

What we have here is yet another cheat. If Voldemort appears, he will surely be victorious. The showdown with Harry will occur here at the end of Book 6, rather than at the end of Book 7, and Harry — without the aid of the Deathly Hallows — will die for real. To avoid this sad outcome, Voldemort is forced to turn his brain off for half an hour at the most critical juncture. He is yet another widget, manipulated by the author as the spirit moves her.

Not only does Voldemort allow his enemies a chance to regroup, he's given orders that no one is to harm Harry Potter — not even to the extent of kidnapping Harry and bringing him to Voldemort should the opportunity arise, which it all too obviously does.

What makes this especially dodgy is that Voldemort has no problem ordering Draco Malfoy (and as a backup, Professor Snape) to kill Dumbledore. If Voldemort feels no need to prove he's superior to Dumbledore, then why doesn't he take the same approach with respect to Harry? Voldemort's flip-flopping on this matter isn't the sign of a deep, complex personality, but of a non-personality. In the space of a few pages, we see the story manipulating Voldemort's behavior in opposite directions, with the result that our suspension of disbelief is destroyed. We no longer accept Voldemort as someone who could logically exist in some alternate universe. He's a construct of paper and ink, nothing more.

A similar flip-flop happens with Harry. Following Dumbledore's death, Harry does in fact charge through the castle, but after the shameful events in the Horcrux cave, after his being pushed aside as useless and unreliable on the roof of the Astronomy Tower, Harry's charge makes him look not heroic, but ridiculous. This is the story changing the rules and then changing them back again. "Harry is the hero of the book. No, wait, he's a total weenie. Oops, now he's the hero again."

Compare Harry's valiant charge at the end of Book 6 to his behavior near the beginning of Book 7, *Deathly Hallows*, when death eaters attack the wedding party. What does Harry do in that situation? He runs away.

What we have here is the outline of a Monty Python skit. The death eaters are running away? Then, "Charge!" The death eaters are attacking? Then, "Run away, run away!" The story, willing to manipulate its characters unconscionably, produces a result that is unintentionally comedic.

This degenerative state was not caused by the many shaggy

dog solutions that we've seen. Rather, those cheats allow the series to progress despite a growing sickness.

11. Harry saved from Voldemort by Dumbledore, Book 7, *Deathly Hallows*.

Though dead, Dumbledore plays the same role in Book 7 that he played in the previous books. His invisible hand guides all the events of the final book and, through the godlike powers of the Deathly Hallows, Dumbledore ensures that nothing really bad will happen to Harry. If that weren't enough, following Harry's resurrection, Voldemort kicks off in response to a harmless Expelliarmus spell. While the story does attempt to rationalize Voldemort's demise, the contortions of logic required leave readers feeling cheated. The story is so busy being clever it doesn't have room left to grant Harry a meaningful role.

In spite of all the fast talking, the ending of the Potter series is a classic shaggy dog. The danger dissipates of its own accord. The deadly asteroid misses Earth even though the mission sent to deflect it has failed. The bad guy turns himself over to the police.

Voldemort might as well have dropped dead of a heart attack.

The Epilogue of Book 7 shows us a happy ending where the Big Three, now married, are sending their own children off to Hogwarts. To emphasize the cost of the inconsistency and cheating that takes place within the series, consider what would happen if we replaced the current epilogue with a different one. For example:

> An orderly in a white coat enters a patient's room. "Time for lunch, Harry."
>
> "I have to defeat the Dark Lord first!" Harry points a bit of tree branch at a stuffed doll sitting on his bed.
>
> "Hey," the orderly says, "one of these days the

'Dark Lord' is going to get you instead."

Harry grabs another stuffed doll off a shelf. "Dumbledore will just resurrect me if he does!"

The orderly shrugs. "Whatever. But hurry it up. Lunch, remember?"

Although some readers will view our alternate epilogue as sarcasm, the question it raises is a valid one. Which epilogue fits the events of the series better: one where the story is treated as something that could really happen on some shadow Earth, or one where the story could only be some form of delusion? Even if an infinitely-variable multiverse made such a reality possible, why should we care about a place where the rules change randomly and people's personalities resemble weathervanes blowing with the wind?

Harry Potter is a ward of the state. There is no Hogwarts. No Voldemort, no death eaters, never any Dumbledore. It all took place inside the head of a mental patient. And given all the clues dropped along the way, *you* should have guessed it.

Never before has there been a tomato surprise that extended over seven books. It seems doubtful that Ms. Rowling would want this particular distinction, but for some readers, this is the sad outcome.

Earned Vs. Unearned Help

To be clear, an audience can tolerate heroes receiving help at various times in their quest. However, we expect the help they receive to be earned one way or another, and that said help won't be to simply hand the protagonist the solution to a key conflict.

In the Pixar movie *The Incredibles*, the namesake family are twice helped by the villain's sidekick, Mirage. In the first instance, Mirage frees Mr. Incredible from his electronic restraints. It's worth noting that Mrs. Incredible is only moments away from arriving and performing that same feat, but even without this caveat, viewers can accept Mirage's actions because (a) Mr. Incredible spared her life earlier, (b) we have subsequently seen her growing dissatisfaction with her boss, and (c) she's merely allowing Mr. Incredible a chance to go off and save the day. She isn't saving the day for him.

The second time Mirage helps the Incredibles, she does so by giving them the launch code for a rocket ship. Once again, she isn't affecting the final battle, isn't making life easy for the Incredibles, but merely allowing them to arrive at the final battle in a timely (and more dramatic) fashion.

Thus, when we talk about unearned assistance in the Potter series, we aren't talking about Remus Lupin teaching Harry the Patronus charm, Harry receiving an invisibility cloak one Christmas, or the Weasley twins giving Harry the Marauder's Map. Rather, we're talking about the kind of help that robs the Big Three of glory, making their accomplishments seem trivial, their risks insignificant, sometimes even making us question whether Harry is needed at all.

Denouement

Would things have gone differently in that final showdown with Voldemort in Book 7 if Hermione, Neville, or even some muggle such as yourself took Harry's place? "Here, hold this stick of wood. When I give you the cue, shout 'Expelliarmus' as loud as you can and wave the stick around in the air." Think you can do that?

When the protagonist for a story can be replaced by any arbitrarily selected individual, it signals that the story has a problem. In the Potter series, this problem didn't suddenly appear in the last few pages. Rather, it took root as early as Book 1 and grew like a degenerative disease, gradually robbing the story (and Harry in particular) of strength, vitality, and ultimately even humanity.

Chapter 3:
Broken Promises

Genre-Specific Promises

A key principle of fantasy literature is that magic needs to follow rules and should have clearly-defined limits. As the title character says in Disney's *Aladdin*, "Limitations on wishes? Bleh!" But without limitations, magic would turn every tale into a shaggy dog story, because if one character or another can just snap his fingers and solve any problem, why should the reader ever sweat?

This is one area where Ms. Rowling does a good job, at least as far as Harry is concerned. Unfortunately, she does *too* good a job, keeping Harry so underpowered that he's incapable of tackling the challenges that face him in the later books. Moreover, while Harry gets demoted to peon, Dumbledore gets promoted to an all-knowing and all-powerful figure.

Luck. Luck is a form of magic, and in the Potter series luck seems to solve just as many conundrums as our hero does, maybe more. Book 6, *Half-Blood Prince*, might better be called the Book of Luck. Harry is lucky when he receives a special potions book that turns him into a genius alchemist. When he's forced to abandon the book, his ability is shown to be borrowed rather than owned. But he has the book long enough to win a bottle of ... luck. This bottle enables him to achieve his one real task in *Half-Blood Prince*, which is to obtain a memory from Professor Slughorn.

The moral seems to be that it's better to be lucky than talented or industrious.

At one point in the series, Professor Snape tells us, "There's nothing special about Harry. He succeeds though a combination of luck and more talented friends." While we realize that Snape is being tactless and mean, we also have to acknowledge that he's telling the truth.

The problem with luck, especially in the Potter series, is that it makes for an easy dodge, something the story can fall back on in hard times. Nothing is impossible to someone who's incredibly lucky. Thus, luck becomes a form of magic with no boundaries, no limitations, and no rationale as to when and where it will appear. The reader need never worry, no matter how seemingly impossible the situation. Just be patient and wait for Harry's luck to kick in.

Surely that isn't the reaction a writer wants from her readers.

Characterization. Another point to make here is that fantasy literature allows breaking the laws of physics, but it doesn't allow breaking the laws of human nature. When characters behave erratically, the result might qualify as experimental fiction, delusion, or political axe-grinding, but it falls short of being fantasy. We've already seen examples of both Harry and Voldemort flip-flopping. More examples of unreliable characterization will show up as we move forward.

Potter-Specific Promises

The Potter series makes three key promises. First, the very title of the series tells us that Harry will be the central figure. By the end of the first chapter of the first book, we expect Harry to be not only central, but the protagonist of the series — specifically, a heroic protagonist. While Harry starts off downtrodden, an insecure, oppressed orphan, we don't expect him to stay in that state. Rather, as he exits his cocoon and spreads his wings, his lowly beginnings will serve as a powerful contrast to his final form.

Second, the fixed limit of seven volumes tells us that the series won't be episodic like the typical weekly TV show, where no matter what happens, by the end of each episode everything (and everyone) is back to normal.

Finally, as the Potter series progresses, we're told over and over again that Voldemort is a Bad Man. He isn't a modern villain, a basically decent person who has gotten off track somehow. He's a genocidal lunatic capable of getting followers to carry out his murderous plans.

Each of these promises is broken by the series.

Harry as Protagonist/Hero

The first few books of the series give Harry enough strong moments to convince readers that he really is a heroic character. Other factors work to reinforce this belief, such as Harry having his name on the jacket of every book, his being nearly the only point of view character throughout the series, and his being present at the climactic moment of each book.

The human mind is capable of ignoring any number of anomalies to a fixed belief. Once we accept Harry as a hero, most of us will never change our mind. But for some of us, there are too many anomalies, too many important situations where Harry fails the test of a true hero.

To begin with, let us compare two events from Harry's life as a wizard, one event from the first book of the series, the other event from the last book.

Near the beginning of Book 1, *Philosopher's Stone*, Harry visits the zoo with the Dursleys. While there, they venture into the Reptile House, where Harry strikes up a passing relationship with a boa constrictor. When Dudley sees the snake suddenly active, he pushes Harry out of the way. The glass barrier to the snake's cage disappears, frightening Dudley and allowing the snake to escape. This bit of magic is done without Harry's conscious volition and is outside his control.

Moving forward past six years of magical education, from Harry at age eleven to Harry at age seventeen, we find Harry riding in a flying motorcycle with Hagrid, near the beginning of Book 7, *Deathly Hallows*. Voldemort pursues them and aims a curse at them. Harry's wand responds of its own accord, without his volition or control, to block the attack.

These two events, bookending the series, place in sharp relief the painful but glaring truth: Harry has failed to grow, has failed to evolve, has failed to arrive. Though Harry is a wizard, he might as well not be. If a wand can operate on its own, without requiring any skill or even quick-thinking by the user, then any of us could do as well as Harry.

But the Potter series is a big work, and we need more examples to make this particular point stick.

We start at the end of the series with Book 7. Dumbledore is dead and if Harry is the hero and protagonist, he should have stepped into his prophesied role as Chosen One. Instead, at the start of Book 7 we find Harry once again living at his aunt and uncle's house where Mother's Love can continue to protect him. When Harry becomes a legal adult, this protection will lift, and so an escort of a dozen or so wizards shows up to keep Harry safe during the trip to the Weasley home.

Whatever the reader thinks of Harry, it is clear that everyone in Book 7 feels Harry is fragile and ultimately incapable of protecting himself. To drive the point home, ask yourself, would *Dumbledore* need such an escort?

Harry is treated like an infant prince still in his crib, rather than a powerful wizard who has taken over Dumbledore's role as organizer of the fight against Voldemort.

If that weren't bad enough, Harry responds inappropriately to the security detail sent to escort him. He effectively wrings his hands and goes on about how he'll feel guilty if anyone dies trying to protect him. This behavior is perhaps meant to show us that Harry is a sweet guy who really cares about other people. Unfortunately, it fails in that task, instead demonstrating that Harry still doesn't get it. The world is at war, and he's worried someone might get hurt?

By staying with the Dursleys yet again, Harry has cut himself off from ongoing events. He relegates himself to the role of outsider and wastes the summer just as he's wasted every previous summer. This passivity is the opposite of how a protagonist should behave. But apparently Harry accepts that he's a mere passenger on this adventure.

When he departs the Dursley home for the last time, Harry rides with Hagrid in Sirius Black's old motorcycle. During that ride, he and Hagrid come under attack both from death eaters and from Voldemort. Though the death eaters are clearly trying to kill Hagrid and possibly Harry as well, Harry's response is to shout Expelliarmus. Theoretically, Harry spent much of Book 6 learning to subvocalize, but that little anomaly aside, Harry's choice of spells is inappropriate. It is the equivalent of the RAF facing the Nazi Blitz with blank ammunition in their machine guns.

Upon Harry's arrival at the Weasley home, Remus Lupin takes Harry to task for this behavior. Harry's response is to say that one of the death eaters after him was the harmless Stan Shunpike, who readers remember as the clueless conductor of the Knight Bus. Obviously, Stan has been Imperiused and isn't responsible for his actions. "You wouldn't want me to kill *him*, would you?" Harry says.

Harry has missed the point, but both Lupin and the book allow Harry to get away with this answer. The world is at war, and spells like Expelliarmus simply aren't going to cut it. Yes, Hagrid survives the flight, but he shouldn't. Harry's incompetence should have led to Hagrid's death, if not Harry's as well. Yet Harry walks away from the gunfight unscathed, though he did nothing but stick his finger out and shout, "Bang, bang."

Moving on, at the Weasley house, Mrs. Weasley prevents the Big Three from holding a planning meeting, and Harry accepts this interference without a murmur. Theoretically, the Big Three are figuring out how to stop Voldemort and thus save thousands, perhaps millions, of lives. But such a lofty enterprise can wait, in order to keep Mrs. Weasley happy? Once again, Harry doesn't get it. He is either too nice, too spineless, or too unconcerned about what is happening in the world to stand up to Mrs. Weasley.

When the wedding party is attacked by death eaters, the Big Three run away. Clearly, Harry hasn't taken on Dumbledore's role of being a counter to Voldemort, of being a power to be reckoned with.

During their race to safety, the Big Three render two death eaters unconscious in a pub. This is an acid test moment, perhaps the most telling moment in the entire series. The world is at war. Voldemort now controls both the Ministry of Magic and the wizard prison Azkaban. The Order of the Phoenix is fighting for its life back at the wedding. Muggle police would obviously be useless. There is no one to turn to, no "adult" to call upon. Mommy and Daddy are out of earshot. Now what?

At this critical moment, the reader waits to see which of the Big Three will step up to the challenge. Which one of them will say, "You two go on, I'll take care of this?" It isn't an easy situation. The two death eaters are unconscious on the floor, after all. They aren't even fighting back. And yet we know that they are serial murderers in the employ of a genocidal maniac. To leave them alive means guaranteeing they will go out and kill again.

In the end, none of the Big Three is capable of doing what the situation calls for. They simply walk out and let the two death eaters go. The worst part of this is that once again the story lets them off for free. Although at least one of these death eaters is implicated in the death of Lupin and Tonks, their death happens off stage, and so the connection is left vague. Most importantly, none of the Big Three expresses guilt or feelings of inadequacy because of this, such as, "If we weren't such wimps, maybe Lupin and Tonks would still be alive." The result is that Harry, Ron, and Hermione remain sweet, innocent children caught up in events too big for them to understand or handle.

A portion of Book 7 is spent with Harry sitting around in the woods. It soon becomes clear that while Hermione at least attempted to read up on Horcruxes during the summer, Harry spent that time as he always has: doing little or nothing. He has no idea where to look for the missing Horcruxes, no idea how to recognize a Horcrux if he stumbled across one, and no idea how to destroy a Horcrux even if it got handed to him.

This interlude reflects poorly not only on Harry but also on Dumbledore. Given the amount of time Harry and Dumbledore spent together in Book 6, *Half-Blood Prince*, how is it that Dumbledore never showed Harry how to recognize or destroy a Horcrux? If Harry is really the hero of the series, and Dumbledore is really a good guy, then this oversight is incomprehensible. It isn't as if Dumbledore's death catches him by surprise, after all.

Harry's cluelessness at this point in Book 7 reinforces events that span the end of Book 5, *Order of the Phoenix* and the beginning of Book 6 — events that suggest neither Harry nor Dumbledore consider Harry qualified to be the Chosen One.

Near the end of Book 5 we have the duel between Dumbledore and Voldemort at the Ministry of Magic. As he watches this duel, Harry must surely realize that Dumbledore was right to push him out of the way. Harry simply isn't in the same league with these two master wizards.

After the duel, Harry and Dumbledore meet in Dumbledore's office for their one big confrontation of the entire series. Harry starts off by blaming Dumbledore for the death of Sirius. This is irrational and suggests that Harry has gone from being an action hero to being passive-aggressive. All responsibility has been given to the Father figure, who then takes all the blame if anything goes wrong, whether it was something under his control or not. Harry isn't able to see that Voldemort is the true villain. His shouting is nothing but a childish tantrum that proves he isn't mature enough to be a full member of the Order of the Phoenix, never mind ready to take on the role of Chosen One.

Second, Harry has a valid reason for being upset with Dumbledore, but he says nothing about it. If Harry were truly a hero, were truly on the path of destroying Voldemort, he would be incensed over being pushed aside and kept out of the fight at the Ministry of Magic. "We had Voldemort in our hands," the heroic Harry would say. "Together the two of us could have taken him down. But no, you had to have the spotlight, and now he's still on the loose, ready to kill more innocent people."

The real kicker comes when Harry has shouted himself out. Dumbledore finally tells Harry the full prophecy, letting Harry know that he was supposed to be the one to destroy Voldemort once and for all. Dumbledore blames himself for not telling Harry sooner, admits it was a mistake to withhold the information, and explains this mistake by saying that he wanted to keep Harry safe and didn't want to pile additional burdens on the poor boy. Virtually the next scene in the book has Harry getting on the Hogwarts Express and returning to his aunt and uncle's house for the summer, where he will be ... safe.

How are we to interpret this juxtaposition? Dumbledore himself says that keeping Harry safe has been a mistake, yet now he feels that keeping Harry safe over the summer is the most important thing. Surely this must mean that Dumbledore has finally given up on Harry. Harry has failed to rise to the challenge of being Chosen One, forcing Dumbledore to switch to Plan B.

If so, Harry's response to the event is difficult to understand. He was supposed to be some kind of Chosen One but isn't up to it and never will be. Worse, Dumbledore has given up on him, a crushing blow if ever there was one. Yet Harry shows no sign of being crushed. He accepts this devastating event without a peep, without a complaint, without a tear, suggesting a level of detachment that is hard to fathom. Apparently, Harry doesn't care that he has failed to fulfill his destiny, has disappointed Dumbledore, and has possibly set the world up for domination by Lord Voldemort.

If we have any question about Harry's response to hearing the full prophecy, we get our answer at the start of Book 6. Harry's first meaningful decision in that book is to disband the Defense Association and accept the Gryffindor Quidditch captainship. Does this sound like the protagonist of the Potter series? If given a choice between preparing to face Voldemort or playing Quidditch, which path would a true hero take? Definitely not the one Harry chooses.

Stepping back further in the series, we come to the climactic scene of Book 4, *Goblet of Fire*, where Harry faces Voldemort in the Riddle graveyard. Voldemort has been restored to his body, and surely Harry must realize what that means. If Voldemort can be killed here, then untold lives can be saved. Harry knows Avada Kedavra, having been introduced to it by the false Mad Eye Moody. But what spell does he choose to cast, now that he's face to face with the murderer of his parents, the man responsible for Sirius spending twelve years in Azkaban, the man who has tried to kill Harry three times before and is about to try again? If you haven't guessed, Harry casts Expelliarmus.

Harry is no hero. In this particular scene, he isn't especially recognizable as human. He tells himself he won't just lie there and let Voldemort kill him. Convinces himself to go down swinging, if that's the best he can do. And then he immediately contradicts his brave thoughts with Expelliarmus, making himself look like an imbecile. Harry is saved by the matching wands. If not for that, he would be dead, while Voldemort would be left asking Lucius Malfoy to collect his wand for him.

Not an Episodic Series

Because the Potter series was limited to seven books, and because each book covered one year at Hogwarts, it seemed to promise a series that wouldn't be episodic. Unfortunately, this promise became the victim of a comfortable pattern.

The series keeps Harry an everyman sort of hero, unexceptional, struggling even with the simple spells they teach in class, the equivalent of a C student in high school. This makes it easy to identify with him, but it also means he won't be able to face down Voldemort. He remains the downtrodden, insecure, ineffectual wizard of his first year. A boy with a single skill: flying. A boy who in Book 7 apparently knows only a small handful of spells, all of which he must shout in order to cast.

Harry can't achieve his destiny under these circumstances, and he doesn't. By leaving Harry effectively unchanged from Book 1, the series has kept him impotent. Dumbledore must return from the grave in Book 7, bigger than ever, in order to provide a happy ending. Harry just isn't up to it.

It isn't so much that Harry has diminished during the series. Rather, as the stakes rose, as the challenges became more substantial, Harry remained the same. He failed to grow. He ended as the same sweet but vaguely incompetent boy he was in the first book. The result is that he *seems* to have diminished.

This stuck-in-the-mud fate isn't limited to Harry alone. In Book 1, Hermione is the brainy workhorse, and she retains that role through to the end. Ron is an insecure underachiever, and he never changes, never rises to the level of skill demonstrated by his brothers and sister.

The Big Three forms in Book 1 and continues on through to the end. Neville is kept at arm's length, and Harry is never given permission to embrace this other orphan who shares his dorm room. Harry saves Ginny from Voldemort in Book 2, *Chamber of Secrets*, but the next year, Ginny's trauma is forgotten as if it never happened, and she remains a second-tier character. A brief fling with Ginny in Book 6 is shut down before the book ends, and she remains a minor figure through to the Epilogue. Nothing can be allowed to upset the familiar Big Three dynamic.

Harry's relationships with Snape, Malfoy, and the other

Gryffindors are all locked in place from the instant those characters appear. Snape never wavers from his role as the sneering professor. Malfoy ever remains the malevolent snob.

Like a weekly TV show, any seeming changes that occur are undone before the end of the episode. At the start of every book, Harry is living with the Dursleys. At the end of every book, he returns there. Other than what he learns in his first year at school, the Patronus spell is a rare example of a skill that Harry retains from one year to the next. He uses the Cruciatus curse in Book 5, *Order of the Phoenix*, but his attempt is so feeble it draws laughter from the intended victim. He *never* attempts to use the killing curse, and either never perfects subvocalization or else forgets about it even before the end of the book where it is introduced.

Sirius is revealed as Harry's godfather late in Book 3, *Prisoner of Azkaban*, but forces beyond everyone's control prevent Sirius from fulfilling that role. Sirius remains a guest star through Books 4 and 5, but is never allowed to change the dynamic of Harry's life, is never allowed to interfere with the formulaic structure of the books.

Voldemort as Villain

For most of seven books, we're led to believe that Voldemort is a monster analogous to Hitler. In Book 7, though, he fails to live up to his billing. While it's one thing for Harry to spend weeks out in the woods doing nothing, it's another thing for Voldemort to mimic this behavior. If the series remained true to itself, when Harry finally emerged from those woods, everyone he ever cared about would be dead.

Let us return to the situation as it is when Harry runs off into hiding near the beginning of Book 7. Voldemort is in control of the government, is backed by his death eaters, is well on his way toward rebuilding his armies of undead and giants, and even has the dementors on his side this time. Dumbledore, "the only one he ever feared," is dead and is therefore no longer a threat that Voldemort has to worry about. (As far as he knows.) Harry has proven convincingly that he isn't up to replacing Dumbledore. His shouting Expelliarmus during the escape from the Dursley home accomplished that quite effectively, and Harry's running away from the attack at the wedding would have eliminated any remaining doubt.

As villain, what should Voldemort do? He should do exactly what we've been told he would do: he should begin wiping out all mudbloods and all blood traitors. Members of the Order of the Phoenix would automatically have a price on their heads. With Dumbledore gone, nothing keeps Voldemort from actively hunting down his enemies. What this means is that people we know by name would begin dying. Not a few here and there; they would drop like flies. The gloves would come off. The gas chambers and ovens would run around the clock.

Voldemort's failure to do this indicates that he's incompetent. Harry's laziness is a well-worn theme, but Voldemort has always been portrayed as an energetic character. If his first goal is to eliminate Harry, the logical solution would be to lure Harry out of hiding, and the best way to do that would be to package Hagrid's head in a box and owl post it to wherever Harry is hiding, or to at least run a front-page picture of it in the *Daily Prophet*.

But why would Voldemort hesitate to eliminate anyone he can get his hands on? The Weasleys, Neville, Luna Lovegood, McGonagall: all would be dead, and dead within a matter of hours of the attack at the wedding. (Actually, within hours of Dumbledore's death.) Voldemort's failure to accomplish this turns him into a shaggy dog threat, analogous to Slugworth in *Willie Wonka and the Chocolate Factory*, pretending to be a bad guy, but really in the employ of Wonka himself.

It's a cheat, and we the constant readers were the ones cheated.

Manipulation

We expect art to affect us, to make us laugh, cry, worry at the threats to characters we care for, and rejoice at their victories. Art that achieves these effects by earning them has a deeper, more lasting impact on us than that which merely manipulates us into those feelings.

Manipulation is best exemplified by the use of the laugh track in early TV situation comedies, which was used to clue in the audience that something funny has happened. Today, directors accomplish similar effects by using facial close-ups of actors to tell audiences what emotion they should be feeling. If the camera shows someone laughing, the audience will likely decide that something funny has happened. If the camera shows someone in tears or with glaring eyes, the audience will respond with sadness or anger. That is what we mean by manipulating, rather than earning, the audience's response.

The Potter books fall prey to their own form of manipulation, most often by making Harry the helpless victim of abuse. Naturally, we all hate to see someone treated that way, and our sympathies are aroused. Unfortunately, the Potter series never tires of setting up this same tableau, using it long after Harry should have grown into a powerful wizard capable of defending himself.

The real tragedy is that, by spending so much time manipulating the reader with fake emotions, the series bypasses real emotional payoffs that are piling up in the bank, waiting to be cashed in. By using cheats, by following a careful formula, by resorting again and again to the same contrived emotional scenarios, the series reneges on its promises. Ultimately, it fails to fulfill its true destiny.

Chapter 4:
Missed Opportunities

A fiction writer needs a certain capacity for cruelty, a willingness to put beloved characters in tough situations, confront them with their greatest weaknesses, and hold them accountable for their mistakes. Such cruelty leads to intense situations that heighten reader involvement and create deeper character portraits. As a wise saying has it, you can live with someone for thirty years, but you will only truly know them if you see them when things are at their worst — or sometimes, when things are at their best. Extreme situations show us who people really are.

Unfortunately, the Potter series too often bails characters out of difficult situations using luck and miracles. It seems a little too kind-hearted, a bit too eager to set things right itself rather than make the characters do so. This lack of cruelty reveals itself not only in shaggy dog escapes, but also in major confrontations between key characters that are either trivialized or else avoided altogether. The result is that many intense and dramatic moments never happen.

This, then, is the ultimate cruelty: readers are robbed of payoffs they earned by sticking around for thousands of pages.

Showdowns

Snape, Malfoy, and Voldemort are Harry's key antagonists. All three characters span the entire series, and after seven books' worth of conflict between Harry and these three, readers expect some sort of showdown for each. Unfortunately, the Potter series falls short in all three cases. But before we look at Harry's antagonists, let's look at what could have been the most interesting showdown of all, one between Harry and Dumbledore.

Harry and Dumbledore

The Potter series could easily have arranged a major collision between Harry and Dumbledore — by giving Dumbledore a role in the death of Harry's parents — but the story carefully avoids that collision. Dumbledore's involvement in their death remains blurry until late in Book 7, *Deathly Hallows*, when Snape conveniently hands Harry a memory string that explains all. The memory makes it clear that Snape only ever heard the first part of the prophecy, and that his decision to turn over a new leaf comes only when he fears that the Dark Lord will go after the girl that Snape secretly loves, Lily Potter.

This revelation conflicts with what we learn near the end of Book 6, *Half-Blood Prince*, when Trelawney makes it sound as if Snape surely heard the entire prophecy, when she tells us that Snape barged into the room where she was meeting with Dumbledore (rather than that he was thrown out of the Hog's Head part-way through the prophecy). While we have to accept Snape's memory as "how it really happened," the clarified sequence of events seems unfortunate.

Imagine that Trelawney's version of the story is the true one, and Snape heard the entire prophecy. For Snape to tell only the first part of the prophecy to Voldemort would imply that he took on the role of double agent that very night, before returning to Voldemort.

That Snape reveals only the first half of the prophecy to Voldemort serves as proof of Snape's loyalty to Dumbledore — a much more convincing proof than Snape's adolescent crush on Lily Potter, which is the one-legged dog the series currently tries to sell us.

What would Dumbledore's motivation be for having Snape tell *any* of the prophecy to Voldemort? Quite possibly, it could be his attempt to lure Voldemort out into the open, so Dumbledore can take him on.

We learn in Book 7, *Deathly Hallows*, that when Dumbledore was in his twenties, he believed (along with his friend, the evil wizard Grindelwald) that wizards had a responsibility to lord it over muggles and other lesser creatures. Dumbledore's relationship with Grindelwald led to the death of Dumbledore's sister, is presented as Dumbledore's greatest mistake, and serves as a source of agonized soul searching for Harry as he tries to come to grips with the devastating revelation.

Yawn. What Dumbledore did some sixty years ago is way past its expiry date, Grindelwald is an off-screen personage unrelated to the plot of the Potter series, and the revelation comes after Dumbledore's death, making it impossible for Harry to confront Dumbledore about what happened.

As far as providing deeper insight into Dumbledore's character, the biographical quotations we see in Book 7 are interesting, but Grindelwald is a weak choice for causing Harry to re-evaluate his relationship with Dumbledore. Imagine, instead, that Dumbledore made a decision that led to the death of Harry's parents. Now, let Harry find *that* out.

Of course, Dumbledore wouldn't *want* James and Lily to die. Their deaths would be a result of Dumbledore misjudging Voldemort's reaction to the prophecy, expecting Voldemort to go after the pureblood Neville, and being unaware that a traitor, Pettigrew, has become the Potter's secret keeper. But that is exactly the kind of backfire to a good plan that so often makes real life messy.

Having Dumbledore be at least partially responsible for the deaths of James and Lily would set up a powerful showdown between Harry and the headmaster. It would also give us better insight into Dumbledore's deviousness as a planner and a keeper of secrets.

When Harry has his hissy fit at the end of Book 5, *Order of the Phoenix*, how much better if he really had something to be angry about, something that put Dumbledore in the hot seat. In its current form, this big showdown is nothing more than a childish tantrum. Harry doesn't even come close to Dumbledore's real weak spots.

Meanwhile, the only other near-showdown between these two is at the end of book 6, *Half-Blood Prince*. Harry has discovered that Snape overheard the Chosen One prophecy. He puts two-and-two together, decides that Snape is implicated in the death of his parents, and confronts Dumbledore about it. Unfortunately, rather than a knock-down, drag-out argument resulting in a major break between these two key characters, Dumbledore dodges the conversation altogether in the name of more pressing business, and Harry lets him get away with it. Within another chapter, Dumbledore is dead, the opportunity forever lost — both to Harry and to fans of the series.

Dumbledore and Harry have an archetypal mentor/gifted pupil relationship, a relationship that could easily have a train wreck built into it. But the series carefully keeps the trains on separate tracks, and makes it clear that Dumbledore had no responsibility at all for the events at Godric's Hollow. What a shame.

Dumbledore is never forced to explain to Harry what he did and why. Harry is never forced to understand how Dumbledore could make decisions that put people's lives at risk, nor is Harry forced to forgive Dumbledore for his involvement in a tragic event. As a result, readers are left with an incomplete portrait of two characters who fill the pages of seven books.

Harry and Snape

Snape is one of the most important characters in the Potter series. When Dumbledore sacrifices his own life at the end of Book 6, the best explanation for his behavior is that he wants to save not Draco Malfoy, but Severus Snape. Snape is on the inside of Voldemort's organization. As a result, Dumbledore apparently views Snape as more important to Harry's ultimate success than Dumbledore himself is.

While this is merely one possible interpretation of events — the series is again vague, this time with regard to Dumbledore's motivations — it makes more sense than if Dumbledore sacrificed himself to save Malfoy. With the world at war and many thousands of innocent lives at stake, Dumbledore can't afford to cash it in for some kid who got in over his head with the bad guys.

Thus, the best explanation for Dumbledore's sacrifice is that it keeps Snape in his role as double agent. Yet, when we get to the end of Book 7, Snape's role is to effectively say, "I was a good guy all along," and then die.

For six books, readers endure the endless antagonism between Snape and Harry. Snape plays his own part in the death of Harry's parents and kills Dumbledore in front of Harry's eyes. In Book 7, Harry and Snape are (according to Dumbledore, anyway) the two most critical players in bringing about the end of a terrible war. And then ... nothing. Snape dies. Harry doesn't kill Snape, nor does he have an opportunity to prevent Snape's death. Instead, Harry acts as a video camera, recording the event and taking from Snape key bits of expositional video footage that explain everything.

On a scale of one to ten, the intensity level here is about a three. Yes, Snape dies, so break out your hankies. But this sequence robs Snape of any meaningful part in Voldemort's downfall, while simultaneously turning Harry into a passive entity. Above all, it fails to repay the reader for enduring hundreds of pages of tedious sniping. The long feud ends with a whimper, influences nothing, leads to nothing, and therefore means nothing.

Harry has it far too easy. He isn't forced to decide whether to trust Snape or not — preferably with something important on the line such as Harry's life and the final defeat of

Voldemort.

How much better if Harry had found Snape alive and well, now Voldemort's closest lieutenant. Harry realizes that he doesn't have to kill every piece of Voldemort's soul, he merely has to bring about Voldemort's final destruction. What if Harry says as much during his last confrontation with Voldemort? He could turn his back on Voldemort in order to destroy Nagini (the last of the Horcruxes), leaving Snape to destroy the piece of Voldemort's soul that still resides in Voldemort's body.

That would require bravery, forgiveness, insight, and trust on Harry's part. It would make Dumbledore's self-sacrifice at the end of Book 6 seem reasonable rather than inexplicable. It would make for a much more dramatic climax to Harry's relationship with Snape, while also injecting additional tension into Harry's final showdown with Voldemort.

Most importantly, giving Snape and Harry some kind of meaningful showdown in Book 7 would at least partially repay the reader for putting up with six books of otherwise pointless bickering between these two characters.

Harry and Malfoy

One unfortunate aspect of the Potter series is that so few characters change. Eleven-year-old children arrive with their personalities fully set. They might get older, but who they are remains carved in stone.

Draco Malfoy is one of those characters who seems to call out for a meaningful change. He certainly shows signs that he isn't happy being a death eater. Pure-blood wizards crawling on hands and knees to kiss Voldemort's robe? That seems a bit demeaning, and surely Draco is proud enough to resent it. He obviously doesn't like the threat of death constantly hanging over himself and his parents. The murder of a Hogwarts professor in Book 7 clearly upsets him. And Draco ultimately can't bring himself to kill Dumbledore.

But even with all these forces in play, Draco remains

locked inside his role as a minor antagonist to Harry. While Book 7 does give us a fight between the Big Three and the even-bigger three of Malfoy, Crabbe, and Goyle, that fight is simply more of the same. No one demonstrates insight, and though Crabbe dies, he isn't killed by one of the Big Three but rather by his own stupidity. (Once again, an unwillingness by the series to assign responsibility to any of the key characters.)

What if Malfoy decided at some critical moment in Book 7 to switch sides? Malfoy need only realize that Voldemort is as big a danger to pure bloods as he is to muggles and mudbloods. His switchover might reveal itself when Malfoy rescues not Harry, but Hermione from some dangerous situation. What a powerful moment that could be!

But if Draco chooses to continue supporting Voldemort, we'd at least like to see Harry confront Malfoy, talk sense to him, argue the real issues, and generally move beyond petty schoolboy bickering in the face of larger events. As a result, their relationship would include a confrontation in the deeper sense of that word, rather than simply another tussle.

By the time we reach Book 7, readers have already seen enough fights that leave both Harry and Malfoy unchanged in terms of their beliefs and behaviors. How about giving us something a bit more substantial, a bit more meaningful, rather than simply covering the same old tired ground yet again? We can get "different day, same stuff" from any TV channel or simply by waking up and going about our business. We expect more than that from the Potter series.

Harry and Voldemort

In the biggest showdown of them all, the stakes are skewed. Voldemort's life is on the line while Harry's isn't. Convoluted rationalizations don't change the fact that Harry's return to life after being zapped by Avada Kedavra robs the climactic confrontation of its adrenaline. It's a cheat, and a big one.

Meanwhile, the very complexity of the ending detracts

from the reader's sense of satisfaction. Too many of us were left blinking our eyes like stunned rabbits, going "Huh?" Whether all the pieces line up and make sense doesn't matter. The pieces are clearly arbitrary, shuffled about like in a shell game, and lead to one conclusion: the story refused to give control over to its characters. Things work out just as planned, never mind how much smoke and mirrors it takes.

Did Harry kill Voldemort? Well, he certainly never cast the killing curse. He never *overtly* tried to take anyone's life. So the groovy thing is, Voldemort is dead without Harry having any blood on his hands, without his having any direct responsibility for killing the guy.

Unfortunately, Harry doesn't get any direct glory for killing Voldemort either. If somebody decided to give out a medal for this final victory, clearly it would have to be pinned to Ms. Rowling's word processor. To paraphrase the Wizard of Oz, "Pay no attention to that woman behind the computer screen."

The ending of the Potter series is clever. Too clever. Instead of readers closing Book 7 with the warm feeling that comes from a nice, tight resolution, we closed it and raced for some aspirins to ease our aching heads.

Harry's Relationship with Dumbledore

Showdowns aren't the only missed opportunity in the Potter series. Relationships are another place where the opus lets readers down. Friendships and romantic attachments are often left in an idealized or half-realized state, with the relationship between Harry and Dumbledore being an especially critical example of this.

As readers, we long to participate vicariously in the affection between two likeable characters. That kind of relationship helps balance the hate and violence that arise elsewhere in a story, reminding us that the world isn't an entirely hostile place.

At the end of Book 5, *Order of the Phoenix*, Dumbledore

explains his aloofness during the previous year by telling Harry, "I didn't want Voldemort to think there was anything but a normal Headmaster to pupil relationship between us." That should have been easy, since there never *was* any special relationship.

Harry naturally idolizes Dumbledore and perhaps has more interaction with him than the typical student, but when do they spend any amount of time together? Here and there, Dumbledore dispenses words of wisdom and hands out a few bits of praise. Given Harry's background and the scarcity of such experiences for him, those brief moments must have glowed especially bright. But only in Book 6, *Half-Blood Prince*, does Harry spend more than a few minutes at a time with Dumbledore. The lack of time spent with Harry reflects poorly on the old man and is a significant deficit in the series. Not a single summer spent tutoring Harry. No special classes on advanced magic. No lessons on how to treat with centaurs and giants.

Even during Book 6, Dumbledore contents himself with showing Harry various memories in the Pensieve. While those memories give us Voldemort's backstory, they are effectively TV time for Harry. He's a passive observer, the beneficiary of Dumbledore's detective work. The knowledge he gains is interesting, but what's missing are the lessons Harry really needs to learn: leadership, the importance of secrecy, the subtleties of magic, how to recognize and destroy Horcruxes, how to set up a defensive perimeter — maybe even how to make friends with a phoenix.

By Book 6, it is already too late for Dumbledore to take Harry under his wing, just as it is too late for Harry to clue in. However, suppose that at some earlier point in the series, Harry rebelled at the idea of returning to the Dursley's home. Dumbledore interprets this as a sign that Harry has taken on the mantle of Chosen One, and during the following summer, Harry studies intensively one-on-one with Dumbledore.

As a reader, which would you rather be party to: yet

another summer with Harry at the Dursleys, or a summer with Harry at Hogwarts, being taught by Dumbledore?

This would not only help the series break out of its episodic "summer with the Dursleys" rut, but would create an opportunity for Harry and Dumbledore to develop a real relationship, one based on knowing and understanding each other, rather than one based on idealized childhood adulation.

With such a relationship in place, later events take on greater importance. Dumbledore's death is an obvious example. But another example is Dumbledore's aloofness during Book 5. As it stands now, Harry is annoyed, but it isn't as if his day-to-day life is affect by Dumbledore's preoccupation. Now, imagine that after spending the summer with Dumbledore between Books 3 and 4, Harry is *then* given the cold shoulder by Dumbledore.

Harry spending time with Dumbledore would also allow the series to reveal Dumbledore's history in a narrative, interactive fashion, rather than dump his backstory on us via dry quotes from a biography. Dumbledore is such a strong character, yet he remains a distant, vague, mystical presence, his full potential unrealized.

Having Dumbledore fulfill his role as mentor would also ramp up the dramatic tension between Harry and Dumbledore. With the death of Harry's parents partly Dumbledore's fault, the reader will recognize that, the stronger this relationship grows, the greater the eventual explosion will be when Harry learns the truth. Not only is there a head-on collision coming, the two trains are picking up speed with every passing page.

Emulating Dumbledore

A good pupil will emulate his mentor, but Harry does a poor job of this, a further indication that the mentor/pupil relationship has been left unrealized and that Harry has failed to arrive as a capital-H Hero.

(a) In school, Dumbledore was not only a star student, he

corresponded with adult wizards outside school as a means of advancing himself. He has all kinds of cool gadgets in his office, some of which he apparently designed himself. This indicates native talent, both academic and magical, combined with a solid work ethic. By comparison, Harry not only struggles with the simple stuff they teach in class, he doesn't seem to care that his performance is substandard. Unless his life depends on a spell in the next 24 hours or so, he can't be bothered to take it very seriously.

(b) Dumbledore has a big network, as muggles would say. He's on terms with the centaurs in the woods, the ghosts in the school, the merfolk in the lake, and at least knows how to treat with giants. He organized the Order of the Phoenix and makes liberal use of it during periods of strife. He's head of the Wizengamot. All of this on top of being Headmaster of Hogwarts.

And Harry? He disbands the D.A. as soon as it conflicts with his schedule. He snubs Moaning Myrtle even after she has helped him twice. Though he has a relationship with Dobby, it isn't something he does much to foster. Certainly, when Winky shows up in distress, Harry doesn't even attempt to help her. It slips Harry's mind that Hagrid needs help with Buckbeak's defense. And though Harry has close ties with Ron and Hermione, everyone else remains virtually a faceless, uninteresting nobody as far as he is concerned. Colin Creevey and his brother get the cold shoulder. Neville gets almost totally ignored, as does Harry's date to the Tri-Wizard ball. Harry demonstrates sympathy for Luna Lovegood when she has had some of her things stolen, but that is a transient emotion and doesn't lead to any long term change in their relationship.

(c) Dumbledore is able to make difficult decisions, including those that put other people at risk. He asks Snape to take up and then resume his role as double agent. He asks Remus Lupin to act as representative to the werefolk. In Book 3, *Prisoner of Azkaban*, Dumbledore sends Hermione and

Harry on a dangerous mission to free Sirius before the dementors can administer their kiss. Plus, most of Harry's potentially deadly adventures occur with Dumbledore's at least tacit approval.

And people *do* die, among them Harry's parents and his godfather Sirius. Of course, if Dumbledore had done nothing, many more people would have died, Harry's parents among them sooner or later. Still, the high cost of making a mistake is exactly why these decisions are so difficult, and why so few people are willing to take on such responsibility. Dumbledore is one of the few.

Harry, in contrast, is a hand-wringer. "What if someone got hurt because of me?" is an attitude he falls prey to more than once.

(d) Dumbledore has a long-range goal of defeating Voldemort. He gathers information on the Horcruxes, assigns tasks to members of the Order of the Phoenix, sets a guard on the prophecy. Meanwhile, Harry has no discernable long-range goal at all, unless it's to be a professional Quidditch player. His obsession in Book 6, *Half-Blood Prince*, is "What is Draco Malfoy up to?" Even in Book 7, *Deathly Hallows*, Harry's plan amounts to sitting around and waiting for inspiration to hit.

To summarize, it seems reasonable that Harry, through intense exposure to Dumbledore, would both consciously and subconsciously begin to embody at least some of Dumbledore's key traits. (If Harry embodies some of Voldemort's traits as well, so much the better.) Unfortunately, Harry is virtually the opposite of Dumbledore in every way — a clear indication that the mentor-pupil relationship has not been fully realized.

Readers have been given the short end of the wand once again.

Snape

While Professor Snape is potentially one of the most complex characters in the series, unfortunately he fails the test of believability.

Snape's importance to the Potter series isn't to be underestimated. Late in the series, Snape emerges as Dumbledore's lieutenant. If Dumbledore has confided his full plan to anyone, he must have confided it to Snape. Given that Dumbledore never so confided in Harry or any other member of the Order of the Phoenix, we're left with Snape as someone that Dumbledore trusts and respects above everyone else.

Snape's assignment as double agent requires bravery, a well-developed acting ability, and magical talent. As an Occlumens, Snape must be strong enough to keep even Lord Voldemort from discovering his true role. His knowledge of alchemy is impressive. And in the treating of certain maladies, he's more qualified even than Madam Pomfrey.

As a teacher, however, Snape is entirely incompetent, making Professor Trelawney seem like a master instructor by comparison. Snape doesn't teach. While he lets his pets get off with substandard work, those he dislikes are brutalized, and anything they do that might be praiseworthy is destroyed or sneered at.

This isn't Snape as the scary, tough-but-fair teacher. This isn't the stern coach. This is an abusive jerk. For an example of the stern coach, we need only look at the fake Mad Eye Moody in Book 4, *Goblet of Fire*. During one class, Moody introduces the Cruciatus curse. When he realizes that this lesson has traumatized Neville, Moody calls the boy into his office and builds him back up.

Of course, Moody has an ulterior motive, but still, here we have a murderous lunatic showing us how the stern coach role is properly played. The coach's goal is to introduce kids to the real world, to convince them that he isn't there to coddle them. They pay attention, they work hard, they produce, or there *will* be consequences. But if the coach goes too far, if he discovers that instead of helping to crack open an egg shell or snip a pair of apron strings, he has instead injured one of his charges, then he looks for a way to make it up. He doesn't continue on until nothing is left but a bloody mess. To do so means he isn't an actor playing a (possibly quite comfortable) role, he's a mindless machine, a monster.

Snape is, in fact, that very sort of monster, and it reflects poorly on Dumbledore that he would keep Snape on the staff for more than fifteen years. Let Snape find a job at the Ministry of Magic, because this man has no business around children.

As with other non-sequiturs in the Potter series, Snape's incomprehensibility is a result of his not being a true character. He is a widget that the series uses as needed, whether the result is recognizably human or not.

In Book 1, *Philosopher's Stone*, Snape makes for a convenient red herring, helping to keep the reader's suspicions off Professor Quirrell. Having Snape sneer, bark, and generally cut into Harry serves this purpose, and the question of why Snape would really act this way becomes a minor issue in comparison to the need for keeping Quirrell's secret under wraps (literally) until the end of the book.

Let us consider how Snape might be made into a more believable character. In Book 1, Snape could still bark and sneer, could still give Harry a good working over, so long as his favoritism is abandoned. Rather than being totally arbitrary, Snape would thus merely be one of those naturally-scary teachers. If this sounds too much like Professor McGonagall, no matter. It should be possible to differentiate the two sufficiently, particularly if Snape does, in fact, go extra hard after Harry.

Why would Snape do that? Not because of schoolboy antagonism between Snape and James Potter, but because Dumbledore has asked him to! "We have to bring this kid along, Sevvy," Dumbledore would say. "And you have to play the bad cop, at least for a while."

Even so, a believable Snape wouldn't cross the line from stern coach to abusive jerk. Rather, it would be Harry's *perception* of Snape that colors the man as evil. Older students could tell Harry, "Snape's okay so long as you do all your work and don't screw around in his class." But Harry wouldn't be listening. His experiences as a child would have him projecting Vernon Dursley onto Snape, converting the man's imperious nature into something sinister.

This approach offers two benefits. The first is that Snape can remain a human being, someone deserving of a professorship at Hogwarts under Dumbledore, someone deserving of Dumbledore's trust, and above all, someone readers can accept as a believable character.

The second benefit is that Harry could be seen to evolve and learn. At the end of Book 1, if Harry is able to recognize in Snape not someone who hates him, but someone trying to help him grow up, it would show that we haven't returned to square one after the events of the book. Harry has learned something about human nature, about looking beyond the surface. And what he has learned will help him accomplish some of the tasks that he faces in years to come.

Imagine, a relationship between two people in the series changing!

Would such a change create problems for the rest of the series? Yes, but minor problems only. Snape's attempted capture of Sirius Black at the end of Book 3, *Prisoner of Azkaban*, for example, could still happen. The difference would be Snape's demeanor, his actual belief that he's saving Harry, Ron, and Hermione, rather than his actions being petty and motivated by pathetic vindictiveness. The man can certainly be hard-headed without having to be either shallow, stupid, or a nutcase.

In Book 5, *Order of the Phoenix*, why not let Snape do an admirable job of teaching Harry Occlumens? Snape could smile and pat Harry on the back. "You're really something. This is difficult stuff, but you take to it like a duck." What about the dream that leads Harry to the Department of Mysteries at the end of Book 5? Harry still has it, not because Snape was a lousy teacher, but because Harry's curiosity has been aroused, he's feeling his oats, and — contrary to

Dumbledore's wishes — isn't employing Occlumens when he sleeps. Or, perhaps he *is* employing it, only his connection to Lord Voldemort is such that Occlumens has no effect on it.

The point is, Snape can be portrayed as a recognizable human being and an admirable character without invalidating key plot events. The loss of bickering between Harry and Snape would actually be an improvement, as it would force the series to replace that empty noise with tension and conflict arising out of Harry's evolving personality and his reckless pursuit of his role as Chosen One.

Other Characters

Ron Weasley is perhaps the most egregious example in the series of an underdeveloped character. As part of the Big Three, he appears in a majority of the scenes in the series, and yet he remains two-dimensional. What exactly does Ron bring to the Big Three? The chess game in Book 1, *Philosopher's Stone*, is a substantial contribution, but other examples are hard to find. Though Ron comes from a family gifted both magically and intellectually, he demonstrates none of those traits.

If Ron were to take after his father, for instance, he could become the Magical Tinker, as a complement to Hermione's role as the Big Brain. Unfortunately, nothing like that happens. Even after seven books, if we were to describe Ron's personality and key skills, we would have little more to say about him than about Neville, Luna Lovegood, or some other second-tier character. By giving Ron skills that actually become useful later on in the series, by giving him a more rounded personality and goals of his own, the Big Three dynamic would also be enriched.

Neville Longbottom and Ginny Weasley, meanwhile, are two supporting characters who seem to cry out for more screen time and larger roles. Whether or not they become part of Harry's inner circle, thus transforming the Big Three into the Big Five, leaving these two characters in such minor roles seems an incredible waste.

Dangers for Harry

While Harry faces physical harm in every book, there are other dangers to which he seems immune. Arrogance, monomania, uncontrollable rage, murderous tendencies, depression, post-traumatic stress, cynicism, loss of humanity.... If the Potter series did more with these sorts of internal dangers, it would make Harry a more believable character, and would do a better job of keeping readers sweating.

What if Harry began practicing Avada Kedavra once the false Mad Eye Moody has shown it to him, perhaps using it on helpless forest creatures? Couldn't there be some worry in our hearts that Harry is emulating Voldemort as much as he is Dumbledore? Or that Harry will become like Barty Crouch, Sr., barely distinguishable from the death eaters he hunts down?

If we saw more examples of Harry's anger getting the best of him — and if current examples such as the blowing up of Aunt Marge were turned into overt acts, rather than presented as accidents outside Harry's conscious control — it would make Harry more believably human, and would heighten the tension in various scenes. Here's a kid raised in a neglectful environment. He's been attacked over and over again. He lives every moment with the realization that another attack could happen at any time. The question isn't whether Harry would have anger-management issues, but rather, will he be able to avoid lashing out inappropriately, perhaps killing Dudley or Malfoy in response to an ill-timed snide remark?

As for the sin of pride, what if Harry's proposed summer with Dumbledore left him a bit cocky? His arrogance could be displayed in reckless behavior, in his using Colin Creevey as a gopher, or in his taking Ron and Hermione for granted.

An attraction to the dark side, uncontrolled rage, arrogance: these are just a few of the potential threats to Harry that get bypassed in the series. As for the primary threat to Harry, the series could certainly do more with Lord Voldemort. In Book 5, *Order of the Phoenix*, Voldemort has discovered he can send images and thoughts to Harry, yet Voldemort fails to use this connection to its fullest extent. He doesn't try to drive Harry insane. Doesn't try to push Harry into lashing out at someone. Doesn't tell Harry about Snape and Dumbledore's role in the death of Harry's parents. In fact, Book 5 presents not Voldemort, but Dolores Umbridge, as Harry's primary nemesis. Ridiculous!

The Potter series keeps Harry from both lasting harm and lasting change, preferring a Harry who is impotent, innocuous, and ultimately bland. The result is a missed opportunity of epic proportions.

Chapter 5:
Alternate Interpretations

We have to consider the possibility that the Potter series in its current form isn't accidental but intentional. When we look at the books in this way, it forces us to find new explanations for what we see. For example, given that Harry isn't the hero of the series, does that mean Dumbledore *is*?

Most of the alternate interpretations offered below all seem unlikely, yet it's important to take the books as they're written, rather than base our opinions on what we *assume* the intent was. After all, as time goes by, that is how the series will be judged. Not in the warm glow of Potter-mania, but by cold evaluation of the text itself.

The sometimes hateful interpretations that result from such an objective reading are another incentive for Ms. Rowling to undertake an alternate edition.

The most obvious conclusion from reading the Potter series is that Dumbledore is the protagonist-hero and Harry is either a champion of pacifism or else some form of antihero. While these interpretations seem safe and tame enough, if we look closer, we find that they take us to places that are demoralizing, hateful, and even sick.

Dumbledore as Protagonist

The war against Voldemort is Dumbledore's fight more than anyone's. He resists Voldemort during the first wizard war (which we'll call WW1), and once he realizes Voldemort isn't truly dead, Dumbledore begins making plans to destroy the Dark Lord completely and irrevocably.

During WW1, Dumbledore forms the Order of the Phoenix to combat Voldemort. Unfortunately, the Order isn't strong enough. Voldemort has his own followers and they outnumber the Order. The only way to stop Voldemort is to neutralize the man himself. Without that, the outlook is bleak.

One problem of never being inside the protagonist's head, never being fully in the protagonist's trust, is that we're forced to fill in certain blanks, but it seems likely that during WW1, Dumbledore hopes for a chance to face Voldemort one-on-one. Having defeated the evil Grindelwald several decades earlier, Dumbledore now wields the Elder Wand, a wand that can't be beaten, and so Dumbledore feels he has a good chance of ending the war (and enhancing his own prestige in the bargain) if he can just catch up to the slippery Voldemort.

But Trelawney's prophecy sets in motion a sequence of events that leads to Voldemort's undoing — the point at which Book 1 takes up the story from Harry's point of view.

Unfortunately, we have no idea what Dumbledore's response was to this event. Did he feel robbed of another chance at glory? Did he harbor bitter resentment toward the young child whose fame might one day eclipse his own?

Consider Dumbledore's behavior at the beginning of Book 1, *Philosopher's Stone*. First, he puts Harry in Hagrid's sole care following the death of Harry's parents. He then leaves Harry lying entirely unprotected on the Dursley's doorstep, with the expectation that — even if Harry isn't picked off by a death eater — he will be raised by his Aunt Petunia who hates everything to do with the wizarding world, a fact Dumbledore must surely know.

These actions on Dumbledore's part only make sense if Dumbledore is hoping either that Harry will be killed in the aftermath of Voldemort's demise or, failing that, will grow up a downtrodden waif incapable of challenging Dumbledore's place in the history books.

At the start of Book 1, Professor McGonagall questions the wisdom of leaving Harry in Hagrid's care. Dumbledore's response is that he fully trusts Hagrid, but this elusive answer sidesteps the real issue. Though Voldemort is gone, all of his death eaters are still at large and they outnumber the Order of the Phoenix. There is also an army of full-blood giants and an army of the undead to be dealt with. If ever there was a time when Harry shouldn't be allowed out of Dumbledore's presence, it is here, at the beginning of Book 1.

If Dumbledore really cared about Harry's safety, that is.

That Hagrid arrives on Sirius Black's motorcycle is a clear indication that Hagrid isn't a safe choice for watching over Harry. As far as Dumbledore knows, Sirius Black is the traitor, the keeper of the Fidelus charm, the one who turned the Potters over to Voldemort. That Sirius met Hagrid, saw Harry, and yet failed to kill the boy must have struck Dumbledore a great shock, but he manages to hide his disappointment. So the oaf Hagrid kept the boy safe? The traitor Black wasn't up to killing an infant? Too bad, but we have other means at our disposal....

Of course, it's possible that Dumbledore's intentions are good, but with so many death eaters at large, leaving Harry on a doorstep is hard to fathom. When Professor McGonagall questions the wisdom of leaving Harry with the Dursley's at all ("They're the worst sort of muggles" she tells him), it requires a bit of fast footwork on Dumbledore's part. "It's, um, a way to keep him safe! Yeah, that's it."

Only, surely a magical contract must require some form of overt agreement. A contract formed via mere tacit approval or outright subterfuge couldn't possibly be as powerful or binding as something done willfully.

In this light, the baby on the doorstep gag just doesn't add up. Surely Dumbledore knows that Lily Potter's sister Petunia isn't going to welcome a wizard child in her house. The note Dumbledore pins to Harry's blanket, however eloquently written, could never guarantee that Petunia would keep Harry rather than send him straight off to an orphanage, as Aunt Marge later suggests should have been done.

If Dumbledore were serious about the whole "you will be kept safe by your mother's blood" business, he would take Harry up to the door, ring the bell, and have a sit-down with Petunia, explaining to her what is expected of her — leaning on her if she tries to wiggle out of the responsibility. "If you don't take him, I'll curse your house so the shutters are always neon purple and the siding a bright orange."

Given Dumbledore's failure to do this, we have to accept that there never was any protective spell. It was simply a ruse, Dumbledore doing everything he could think of to get Harry killed and, when that failed, at least to subject Harry to a childhood full of abuse, thus minimizing the risk to Dumbledore's own fame.

Dumbledore's aloofness toward Harry at school, his failure to ever tutor Harry one-on-one in magic, his sending Harry home every summer rather than letting him stay at Hogwarts, his failure to confide the most critical bits of information to Harry about the plan to kill Voldemort, his not involving Harry in the destruction of the ring Horcrux: these actions all take on a sinister quality.

Why should Professor Snape be so harsh with Harry from the very beginning? Wouldn't he have tried to connect to Harry as Lily's son? But what if Dumbledore told Snape to take this hard line with the boy, as another means of keeping Harry beat down? Snape might object, but Dumbledore would rationalize the approach with, "We need to toughen him up, Sevvy."

Though Voldemort spends one entire school year riding around on the back of Professor Quirrell's head, Dumbledore remains unaware of this — or does he? He not only gives Harry the invisibility cloak, but returns the cloak to Harry late in the school year after it was misplaced. This suggests that Dumbledore *does* know about Voldemort's presence and is hoping the dark wizard will succeed in finishing Harry off when the boy goes poking about.

Dumbledore's kindly appearance is merely his mask. In truth, he's a selfish, heartless monster, consumed with his own press clippings and playing a private game of "who's more famous than whom," a game he'll stop at nothing to win.

Plan B. All of the above seems plausible until we get to Plan B. In the end, Dumbledore arranges it so that Harry will get credit for destroying Voldemort. How to explain this? Perhaps Dumbledore does it out of guilt. At the end of Book 5, *Order of the Phoenix*, Harry throws his little tantrum in Dumbledore's office, smashing things that Dumbledore can reconstruct with a wave of his wand, ranting about Sirius being dead while remaining oblivious to the terrible threat the entire world faces.

Does Dumbledore suddenly feel ashamed of what he's done? James and Lily were both talented wizards and brilliant students at the top of their class. Perhaps they were even Dumbledore's friends. Yet here is their son, almost sixteen now but acting more like an eight year old, a stunted and pathetic shadow of what he could have been, all because of Dumbledore's thirst for personal glory.

At the beginning of Book 6, *Half-Blood Prince*, Dumbledore chides the Dursleys for the terrible damage they have done to Dudley, spoiling him and turning him into an obese bully. We can only wonder if this is Dumbledore's projection mechanism at work, his words rebounding doubly upon him, given his orchestrated abuse of Harry over the years.

Whatever his unknown motivations, whatever agonies of indecision Dumbledore goes through as he plays puppet master, in the end Dumbledore lets Harry have the glory. Perhaps he feels safe in doing so, since Harry will be a mere lure. A sacrificial lamb. Shark bait. Thus, even though Harry gets the credit for destroying Voldemort, Dumbledore will rest easy knowing the truth.

But it seems more likely, and more uplifting, if Dumbledore finally renounces his lust for glory. Though this is his greatest challenge because it hits him at his weakest spot,

Dumbledore finally accepts what must be done. Not only must he sacrifice his life, he must sacrifice his press clippings. This is the change he undergoes as a character.

Even inside this moment of triumph over self, however, a dark shadow lurks, because Dumbledore will (once again) use an innocent, helpless child as a lure to bring Voldemort into killing range. A boy incapable of learning to subvocalize. A boy who would have flunked out of school if not for Dumbledore's leaning on teachers to give him passing grades. A boy who, even at age seventeen, needs Hermione to lead him around by the hand and keep him safe — a tall order, since Harry himself doesn't seem to realize that he is mentally challenged.

Did Dumbledore ever call the Hogwarts staff in, Snape especially, and say, "Voldemort must never suspect the boy is deficient. Must never realize what kind of 'special' he is"?

Using a mentally handicapped boy as bait! But Dumbledore has shown he's capable of making hard decisions when they're needed. This terrible solution will save thousands and thousands of lives. However hateful the approach may seem, it's the best, and possibly only, hope of destroying Voldemort for good.

This sort of dedication to a goal is the mark of a true protagonist. Unfortunately, this particular protagonist leaves readers feeling demoralized and with a sour stomach, rather than uplifted and encouraged.

Ambiguity

In the theatrical release of the movie *Blade Runner*, the audience is left to wonder whether Deckard is a replicant or not. That ambiguity was removed in one alternate version of the movie. Via the inclusion of a single short scene, the infamous unicorn dream, the alternate version left little doubt but that Deckard *was* a replicant. The loss of ambiguity in this case was unfortunate, since the question, "Is Deckard a replicant or not?" makes us wonder, "Does it matter?" Bigotry is an underlying theme of *Blade Runner*, and the ambiguity surrounding Deckard works to support that theme.

The Potter series moves beyond ambiguity into confusion and muddle, but even if we ignore the many inconsistencies and non-sequiturs, even if we grudgingly apply the term ambiguity to the unanswered questions left behind by the series, still it is a harmful form of ambiguity, precisely because the question, "Does it matter?" must be answered, "Yes it does!"

Does Dumbledore truly care about Harry's safety, or does he hope the kid will kick off so as to remove a threat to Dumbledore's prestige? Is Harry a pacifist, mentally handicapped, a total jerk?

After seven books, to have these sorts of questions unanswerable feels like a pretty big oversight.

"Don't give the reader any piece of information until they absolutely need it" is a good bit of advice for fiction writers, as it helps maintain suspense and discourages the dreaded information dump (large blocks of exposition or backstory that come out, all too often, in dry and undramatic fashion). The Potter series is masterful at keeping information back until the very last moment, but at times it goes too far. While we like surprises, readers become unhappy when a surprise is pursued at the expense of reliable characterization or at the expense of what makes sense, and we resent being left with important questions unanswered.

One key character shrouded in secrecy is Dumbledore. His backstory comes to us in Book 7, *Deathly Hallows*, but it comes in the form of long, dry quotes from a posthumous biography. (a) This is the least dramatic way to get information across to the reader. (b) Coming as it does after Dumbledore's death, it fails to give Dumbledore a chance to defend himself or to clarify his motivations, and it robs Harry or anyone else of a chance to confront Dumbledore about various issues. (c) It fails to deal with recent history. Dumbledore's biographer is no more privy to Dumbledore's plan for defeating Voldemort than anyone else is. Nor does the biographer have any unique, personal insight into Dumbledore's character; she's a journalist (and a muck-raking one) that Dumbledore tended to avoid when he was alive.

Dumbledore's secrecy not only leaves his motivations murky, it implies either that he distrusts Harry or else that he has some sinister ulterior motive. It is one thing for the reader to be excluded from private meetings that Harry and Dumbledore have along the way, and even for Harry to withhold from Ron and Hermione (and thus from the reader) certain details of what is in the works. But if Harry is the protagonist, the hero, the Chosen One, it is wrong for Dumbledore to keep Harry in the dark, and the Dumbledore I want to believe in would know as much.

Like anyone, Dumbledore is capable of making mistakes, but leaving Harry out of the loop with regard to the Plan goes beyond mistake and enters the realm of the malevolent.

Show and Tell. The biographical information about Dumbledore that we receive in Book 7 is exposition. The same is true of the memory clip that Snape hands Harry at the end of Book 7, and the sequence of memory clips that Harry passively watches in Book 6, *Half-Blood Prince*. In Book 6 especially, we become TV viewers watching a show about people who sit around watching TV....

In asking for less ambiguity, we aren't asking for more exposition or more TV time. Nor are we asking for an article, web page, or book that explains away the various inconsistencies and gaps. As fans of the series, like all other readers of fiction, we pray that pertinent information will be revealed dramatically, that those revelations will be earned by the protagonist rather than merely given to him, and that the revelations will come at a point in the storyline where they make the most sense and can have the greatest impact.

Harry as the Foundling Prince

The prince-in-hiding is an archetypal image inherent in the Potter series. Harry is the future King Arthur, spirited away as an infant to a safe place where he will be raised anonymously. Dumbledore plays Merlin, the wise wizard who alone knows Harry's true identity. All that's missing is a sword for Harry to free from a stone!

Sadly, all that's missing is a sword for Harry to free from a stone....

While there are moments that could serve as Harry's equivalent, those moments pass by without fanfare and without producing any change in Harry's stature or situation. Though he moves through phases of being revered and mocked by the masses, though he's famous for the duration of his life, Harry never becomes the sort of leader or the sort of powerful wizard that Dumbledore is. Instead, Harry forever remains the lackluster step-brother, overshadowed by those more talented than himself.

Harry never takes over leadership of the Order of the Phoenix. He disbands the D.A., which could have been his personal Knights of the Round Table. He never shakes off his orphan persona, a fact made unmistakable by Harry's annual return to the Dursleys. Whatever Harry does during the year, it never earns him a castle or a throne; his true home remains that place where he's the unwanted stepchild.

Even in Book 7, *Deathly Hallows*, Harry isn't regarded as the leader of the resistance movement. At a time when the world is spinning out of control, Harry isn't sitting at the head of the table, he's doing chores for Mrs. Weasley.

It doesn't get much more demoralizing than that.

Harry as Pacifist

One way of interpreting Harry's actions in the later books is to see him as a pacifist. However, not only is Harry's attitude toward violence left muddled, the happy ending of the series turns this interpretation into a truly hateful one.

The first clear example of Harry's pacifism comes near the end of Book 4, *Goblet of Fire*, when Harry faces the revived Voldemort in the Riddle graveyard. Harry knows the killing curse. However, he makes no attempt to use it and instead uses his trademark Expelliarmus, an entirely harmless spell that merely knocks the wand out of the opponent's hand.

At the end of book 6, *Half-Blood Prince*, following Dumbledore's death, Harry has an opportunity to kill several death eaters that he encounters during his chase after Snape. Though he does make use of spells more violent than Expelliarmus, at no time does he use the killing curse.

Finally, Book 7 is littered with examples of Harry passing up opportunities to thin the enemy ranks. Even in the final duel with Voldemort, Harry makes use of Expelliarmus. No doubt, he's as surprised as anyone when Voldemort drops dead.

Does Harry feel he's been lied to, hoodwinked? "You never told me it was going to kill him!" Would he take it back?

We're left with these questions unanswered. Harry's position on non-violence is never stated overtly. We see only his actions which, though they do speak louder than words, would be made clearer if a few appropriate words accompanied them. "Death to violence!" Or something like that.

Ambiguity aside, several problems arise from the Harry-as-pacifist interpretation. First, Voldemort's death is entirely his own fault. This is a cheat, plain and simple. The bad guy is dead but, wait, our pacifist hero emerges without blood on his hands? Wrong answer. This is the series wanting to have its cake and eat it too. Harry must remain sweet and innocent, but we also need a happy ending. So Voldemort shoots, misses, and is killed by the ricochet.

Better if Voldemort had laughed himself to death when Harry cast that final Expelliarmus.

Second, we have the problem of a book that ends with a

few extras dead while the bulk of the cast emerges unharmed, cheeks aglow. With Dumbledore dead and Harry spending months Book 7 hiding (either with his aunt and uncle or in the woods), this is an offensive outcome, the equivalent of saying that Hitler wasn't such a bad guy, that the Holocaust never happened or else that it wouldn't have happened if Chamberlain had been kept in office and Churchill kept out.

Gandhi vs. Neville Chamberlain. The reason that history views Gandhi as a genius is because he used passive resistance against the British Empire. Now, the Brits weren't behaving well in India at that time. There was bigotry, greed, and love of power, all in abundance. But underneath that, there was a country with a conscience. For sure, no one was out to commit genocide. Thus passive resistance was a viable, and in fact a perfect solution for dealing with the situation.

The reason Neville Chamberlain is viewed as a dunce is because he tried to use passive resistance against Hitler and the Nazis. Underneath the Nazi bigotry was insanity. "You want to lay down in front of the tanks? That's great, just spread out a little so you don't gum up the treads, okay? Thanks!"

Using passive resistance isn't something you can do mindlessly. You have to understand who your enemy is. Is there a conscience there, or will they simply run over you?

For most of seven books, we're told that Voldemort is a Hitler-type character who wants to commit genocide. Then suddenly, when there's no one to oppose him, when he holds all the high cards, he goes on holiday. Apparently, Voldemort isn't such a bad guy after all. "He's not going to kill anyone so long as everybody cooperates." Ever heard that one before?

Embracing Sanity

Well, enough of that. Unfortunately, these sick interpretations aren't just possible, they're terribly easy to arrive at. Could we find counter-examples to these interpretations? Certainly. Then again, because of the many inconsistencies within the Potter series, happier interpretations are just as easy to refute as these not-so-nice ones. Which answer you pick becomes a matter of personal preference, rather than something that can be solidly based on the evidence at hand. *Every* foundation is built on quicksand.

How did things get so messed up? Most likely what happened was, the series followed its plot outlines faithfully, outlines that may have existed even before the first book appeared. Those outlines contained several common mistakes that plague fiction writers.

(a) They treated plot as "the sequence of events that make up a story." While that serves well enough to describe plot for readers, for writers a better definition is, "The actions a protagonist takes to achieve his goal." Ultimately, Harry has no goals outside what the current book wants him to accomplish. This leads to another common problem.

(b) Key characters became mere extensions of the author's will, rather than recognizable people with their own motivations. As we've seen in the Potter series, the resulting inconsistencies can create a story both unconvincing and open to almost any interpretation.

On the other hand, if it really is Ms. Rowling's intention to deliver a pacifist message, fine. But surely her own parents or grandparents were part of the muggle WW2 generation. Does she really want to trivialize what they went through? Let her play fair, let her be honest. Yes, let people climb passively into the freight cars and walk passively into the showers. Yes, let America/Harry remain isolationist until the last minute. But then show us the piles of corpses that result. Not just nameless, faceless corpses, but corpses of people we know. Let us, let *Harry*, see Ginny's head sticking out the middle of one of those piles. Let a death eater kill Hermione in front of Harry's eyes — a death eater that Harry let go earlier. Then this pacifist message will be a realistic, believable one, rather than an idealized daydream that is ultimately offensive to the memory of millions of people.

Harry as Antihero

One way to interpret the Potter series is to see Harry as a modern antihero. As such, Harry has a number of traits that fit the bill.

Loner. Harry has many opportunities to reach out past his tiny clique of friends, but mostly he fails to take advantage of them. Neville Longbottom is a particular example, and the reader has to wonder, why *couldn't* Harry reach out to Neville through all those long years of sharing a dorm room with him? Harry brushes off both Dobby and Moaning Myrtle as "odd." He makes a brief connection with Luna Lovegood over her lost possessions, but nothing comes of it.

Harry's view of the D.A. is another case in point. He waxes eloquent in Book 5, *Order of the Phoenix*, about how nothing is more important than preparing for the coming storm. He spends quite a bit of time teaching members of the club Expelliarmus and other non-violent ways of dealing with death eaters. But when several members of the D.A. volunteer to help Harry save Sirius toward the end of Book 5, he rejects their offer. They will just get in the way. Some of them might get hurt. Then, in Book 6, *Half-Blood Prince*, Harry disbands the group entirely. Apparently he prefers the Rambo approach, and the fewer tagalongs he has to mess with, the better.

Lazy. Summers spent goofing off. Holiday vacations spent goofing off. Long hours in front of the Gryffindor fireplace with Ron, making fun of Hermione because she has a work ethic.

Harry is like one of those kids who doesn't come to practice, but still expects not only to play on game day but also to be a starter, a star. Bobby Knight, a basketball coach whose teams won three NCAA championships, once said that he wasn't especially interested in having players with the will to win. He preferred players with the will to *prepare* to win. Once you get to a certain level, no amount of native skill can make up for laziness, because everyone is talented. At that point, the difference between good and great is hard work. Unfortunately, this is a message that Harry never gets.

Clueless Fumbler. In Book 2, *Chamber of Secrets*, Harry forces the incompetent Professor Lockhart to accompany himself and Ron down to the Chamber, a decision that nearly ends in disaster. Once in the chamber itself, Harry's approach to the situation involves yelling for help — a mile underground.

In Book 5, Harry fails to master Occlumency, which then makes him a pawn that Voldemort manipulates into visiting the Department of Mysteries. In Book 6, Harry has to be told that heat and light imply fire, and a few minutes later he forgets what he's just been told, nearly getting both himself and Dumbledore killed in the Horcrux cave. In Book 7, *Deathly Hallows*, Harry doesn't know how to destroy a Horcrux or even how to detect one. He runs off into hiding without his invisibility cloak. He doesn't know how to set up a defensive perimeter. He continues to shout spells at the top of his lungs, despite having been laughed at by Snape for that the year before.

Character Commentary. As the Potter series progresses, various characters comment on Harry's unexceptional nature. Harry himself states that he has but a single skill, flying. The false Mad Eye Moody chortles over how he had to practically lead Harry by the hand through the Tri-Wizard tournament, that Harry could never have finished or kept up with the others if not for Moody's help — that, in summary, Harry is nothing special. Snape explains that Harry's success is due to luck and more talented friends. In Book 7, Ron gets so fed up with Harry's incompetence that he walks out on him.

Most tellingly, Dumbledore's comments to Harry at the end of Book 5 make it clear that Harry isn't ready to play the role of Chosen One. Though Dumbledore tells Harry the full prophecy at this point, he first explains that Harry should have heard the prophecy years earlier, that it was a mistake to withhold the information so long. One interpretation of "I waited too long to tell you" is "Now it's too late to really do any good." When, a few pages later, Dumbledore sends the "Chosen One" home to spend the summer with the Dursleys, it's a silent commentary that speaks volumes. Whatever role Harry is to play in the destruction of Voldemort, it won't be as someone intimately involved in the planning, much less as someone leading the effort.

At no point does Dumbledore groom Harry to take over as head of the Order of the Phoenix. Dumbledore doesn't even trust Harry with the details of the Plan.

Given Dumbledore's revered status in the Potter series, his behavior toward Harry is especially damning. While we might be able to brush aside Harry's self-commentary as false modesty and the comments of Snape and the fake Mad Eye Moody as lies designed to tear Harry down, Dumbledore's judgment cannot be so easily ignored.

Department of Mysteries. One of the most devastating scenes for Harry in the entire series comes near the end of Book 5. For several hours, Harry has been telling everyone who will listen that nothing in the world is more important than rescuing Sirius. Finally, along with several members of the D.A., Harry manages to reach the Ministry of Magic, and they make their way into the Department of Mysteries. Sirius is close now.

Then Harry spots a curtain hanging over a table in one of the rooms. "Wait," he says. "Let me go look."

Hermione asks him, "What about Sirius?"

But suddenly Harry isn't concerned about Sirius. Voldemort is merely using the Cruciatus curse, after all. Sirius can surely handle another couple minutes of that before being reduced to an insane shell of his former self. Meanwhile, what about this curtain!

Even in a zany comedy, this wouldn't work because a person's life is at stake. Imagine a woman running down the street screaming, "Stop that man. He has my baby!" Then suddenly she stops. Her friend bumps into her and says, "Why are you stopping?" And the woman replies, "Margaret, look in the window. Next season's shoes! Oh, aren't they darling?"

This isn't antihero, it is dementia. If the man had stolen the woman's purse, it might be funny. Or if we knew the man wasn't dangerous, that he wasn't going to dismember the kid and bury the body parts in his back yard. But barring that, how can we relate to people like this, never mind respect them?

When Harry makes his detour to view the curtain in the Department of Mysteries, our opinion of him is forever tarnished. Is Harry a total airhead? Does he have short term memory deficit? Is he that insensitive? Is he insane? Some kind of incomprehensible alien?

If Harry is meant to be an antihero, this scene takes things a step too far. Perhaps the goal was merely to stretch the tension prior to actually finding the prophecy room, following the standard writer's dictate of making the reader wait for a payoff. If so, then the tension got stretched at the cost of breaking the reader's connection to Harry.

It isn't that Harry acts like an antihero in this scene. Rather, he doesn't behave like any variety of human being at all.

Religious Allegory

In the last book of the series, Harry becomes a metaphorical Jesus, the sacrificial lamb willingly led to slaughter who, by virtue of knowing people in high places, comes back from the dead. His sacrifice sets up the mechanism for Voldemort/Satan's downfall and the salvation of the human race.

One important difference here is that Jesus didn't have to die. He had the power to call on ten thousand angels to rescue him. Moreover, Jesus wasn't simply a passive character blindly following a trail of breadcrumbs. He knew the score right from the beginning and actively played his part.

Harry on the other hand was totally outgunned by Voldemort and couldn't have defeated him or his death eaters in a straight-up fight. Nor was Harry ever in on the full plan. He went where he was told to go, moving one step at a time, operating mechanically and blindly.

Finally, no one else could have played the part that Jesus played. Nailing one of Jesus' disciples to the cross wouldn't have worked. Harry, on the other hand, brought nothing special to his role. Hermione could just as easily have taken his place. Or Ron, Neville, Luna Lovegood. Heck, even a muggle could have stepped in. You don't have to know magic, just be able to hold a stick of wood and shout Expelliarmus.

Returning to Earth

What did Ms. Rowling intend? Unfortunately, readers can only guess. But whatever her intent, the confusion within the Potter series must be treated as accidental, as a mistake.

Given the amount of planning that Ms. Rowling did (apparently she had boxes full of notes and ideas for the Potter series), it seems possible that all seven books were outlined before the first one got written. But even if not, given the pressure put on Ms. Rowling to produce a new book virtually every year, it makes sense that any bad habits she had as a writer would taint not just the first book but all of them.

Who was going to stand up and tell Ms. Rowling she was getting stuck in a rut; falling prey to a formula; cheating the reader, the series, and ultimately herself out of the full potential of what she had invented? The publisher sure as Azkaban wasn't going to do it. In all fairness, even an independent professional editor — someone with no vested interest in anything other than literary quality — might not have seen the inconsistencies and symptoms of episodic fever when they first began to appear.

Even now, when we dare suggest that the Potter series contains mistakes, an army of fans are ready to stand up and say, "It isn't a mistake. This is what Ms. Rowling intended!" Meanwhile, even disinterested parties will accuse us of errant pedantry. "Who cares what it says in some stupid writing book about a protagonist needing to protag or deus ex machina being naughty? This is art. There are no rules!" Finally, the success of the series speaks for itself. Can a bajillion people all be wrong? Can the most successful author since Charles Dickens be guilty of serious mistakes? Ridiculous!

Without any special insight into Ms. Rowling's thought process, and with a view to what the cold future has in store, we're forced to play devil's advocate. I like to think that Ms. Rowling would reject unequivocally most, if not all, of the nonsense raised in this chapter. I don't want to believe these things myself. And yet, if the word "mistake" is forbidden to us, we must look at what is actually in the books, what is actually on the page.

Mistakes of a Genius

As Dumbledore says, even geniuses can make mistakes, and when they do, those mistakes are often prodigious. Let us be clear, then, that when we use the word mistake, it has no implications regarding Ms. Rowling's abilities as a writer.

Even a combination of natural talent and hard work doesn't always result in a well-rounded master artist. In his early career (as a body-builder rather than as governor), Arnold Schwarzenegger had a self-acknowledged weakness; his legs were underdeveloped compared to the rest of him. Then Arn injured one of his knees. By the time his injury had healed, his legs had gone from a minor weakness to a major one. Rather than throw away his steroids in despair, rather than press on with business as usual, he dedicated himself to work on his legs until they caught up to the rest of him. The result was a more rounded physique that allowed him to dominate the sport of bodybuilding for years to come.

Magic Johnson is another example. At the height of Magic's career as a basketball player, when he was already a superstar and the leader of the L.A. Lakers, with several championship rings in his possession, Magic dedicated himself to overcoming his one weak spot: his free-throw shooting. As a result, he emerged as an even more formidable player than before.

If Ms. Rowling has a weakness as a writer, it's a disregard for the importance of character, especially the true role of a protagonist within a story. Given Ms. Rowling's many strengths and her rapid rise to prominence, it makes sense that this weakness would go unnoticed and unaddressed. However, this single weakness left the series open to some very unhappy interpretations.

Chapter 6:
Mechanics

Evolution of a Story

In an interview, Ms. Rowling once said that her first idea for the Potter series was of a boy who was a wizard but didn't know it. Does that lead inevitably to Hogwarts? To Hagrid, Dumbledore, and Voldemort? Heck no. The Potter series is only one possible outcome, and arriving at that universe required that Ms. Rowling make many, many choices along the way, as her imagination contributed additional ideas, each of which she had to fit into the growing framework.

How does a writer decide which path to follow? A few criteria show up frequently in books on writing: look for the path that seems the most dramatic; the one that feels the least over-used; or the one that suits the characters who inhabit the story. But beyond all this, a writer needs some sense of who her audience is.

If hearsay is to be trusted, Ms. Rowling used herself at age ten as the target audience for the Potter series. This is fine, except that Ms. Rowling's choice of audience was soon at war with her subconscious, and that war was allowed to scar and ravage the pages of the series.

Fantasy writers like to joke about leaving out milk and cookies for the elves at night in return for finished pages of manuscript in the morning. That seems like an apt metaphor, given the magical way the subconscious works.

When the conscious mind says, "I'm going to write another Narnia story, the sort of thing I would have loved as a ten year old," that may be enough to guide the elves to provide appropriate images and ideas. But if the elves provide, instead, a genocidal wizard who takes possession of a teacher at a children's boarding school, drinks unicorn blood, and tries to kill our eleven-year-old protagonist, then we have a disconnect.

This disconnect isn't fatal, so long as the writer spots it and adjusts accordingly. Is she more interested in maintaining her initial conceptual framework, or is she willing to adjust in light of what the subconscious is handing her? This is merely being alert to the subtle messages of the elves. Writers often experience this sort of thing. "The story took on a life of its own." Nothing to be ashamed of there. In fact, most authors seem to bear such a scar as a badge of honor.

Ms. Rowling has tapped into something monumental with the Potter series, but what has emerged is confused, and one possible explanation for the confusion is that her conscious choice of audience was at odds with her subconscious voice. Accepting that hypothetical explanation, what we see is that, rather than let the story take its own path, the author constantly reined it in so as to make it fit her conscious goal, thereby undercutting the work the elves were doing.

At the end of Book 1, *Philosopher's Stone*, Harry kills Quirrell in order to drive away Voldemort. At the end of Book 2, *Chamber of Secrets*, Harry destroys the part of Lord Voldemort's immortal soul stored in the diary Horcrux. In Book 3, *Prisoner of Azkaban*, Harry says he will kill Sirius Black if he gets a chance. At the end of Book 4, *Goblet of Fire*, Harry faces Lord Voldemort in the Riddle graveyard and shouts ... Expelliarmus?

Something is broken here.

In fighting the subconscious voice, the Potter series wound up not only schizophrenic, but shallow. During his childhood, Harry is made to sleep in a closet by the Dursleys. This abuse is treated as a joke — typical of children's books, which don't want to unduly alarm their target audience. But given how cruel children can be, might it be better (for once) if a children's story showed what this kind of abuse can do to someone?

> "Who locked Jeffery in the closet?" Mother says.
> "I did," Timmy says.
> "Good work, Einstein. Now he won't talk, he can't sleep without the light on, and he's wetting the bed."
> "He's a weenie," Timmy says. "Harry Potter spent ten years in a closet and it never bothered *him*."

Perhaps if, instead of sugar-coating things, children's authors told the truth, some children might learn empathy, might understand that, far from being funny and silly, cruelty hurts others. Meanwhile, victims of abuse might gain some hope from the story, rather than feel weak and inferior because they didn't just shrug off their abuse like Harry Potter did.

Our hope is that Ms. Rowling will undertake an alternate version of the Potter series, and that as she does so, she will abandon the vision of a ten year old reading through all seven books. This will free her to follow the guidance of her elves, rather than constantly beat them into submission with predefined plot outlines. Discarding a fundamental goal can't be easy, but we earnestly believe that doing so in this case would allow the Potter series to achieve its full potential.

Character-driven vs. Plot-driven

The Potter series is clearly plot-driven. Events form the focus of every book, and characters become mere widgets who do whatever the plot outline needs them to do.

For now, let us focus on Harry himself. After ten years of abuse and neglect, Harry discovers that he is not only a wizard, but a famous wizard. How does he respond to this? He quickly accepts the situation, and then takes it for granted. At Hogwarts, he goes through the motions, quite comfortable with his mediocre performance in class. He accepts Ron and Hermione as his friends as if having friends is no big deal. His laziness and apathy are presented not as debilitating illnesses resulting from insecurity and depression, but as harmless attributes. As a result, Harry's years with the Dursleys are revealed as nothing more than manipulation of the reader's sympathies. Harry's childhood ultimately has no effect on Harry's personality.

Harry kills Quirrell, then effectively goes on about his business as if nothing had happened. He destroys the Horcrux diary and a magical basilisk, but experiences no guilt. After years of being constantly attacked, he shows no signs of post traumatic stress.

The result of all this is that Harry begins to seem inhuman.

When the story needs Harry to investigate a mystery, he does so. When it needs him to sit quietly and twiddle his thumbs, he does so. When it needs Harry to demonstrate murderous tendencies toward Quirrell, Riddle's diary-ghost, and Sirius Black, he does so. When it decides he needs to remain pure of heart, with a soul untainted by murder, Harry effectively becomes a pacifist.

These changes in Harry are never fully explained and are often contradicted by Harry's words or thoughts. He decides to go down swinging at the end of Book 4, *Goblet of Fire*, then immediately reverts to pacifist mode by casting Expelliarmus. As we've seen, Harry flips back-and-forth between hero and helpless dolt several times at the end of Book 6, *Half-Blood Prince*, and the beginning of Book 7, *Deathly Hallows*.

And Harry isn't alone in this respect. Other characters, including Voldemort, Snape, and Dumbledore, are all forced to behave out of character during the course of the series, something that Part 2 of *Destiny Unfulfilled*, the book-by-book discussion, will cover in greater detail.

Character Change

One sign that the events of a book are significant is that they cause key characters to change. Near the end of Book 3, *Prisoner of Azkaban*, Harry says, "None of it made any difference." Dumbledore disagrees with him, but there's a lot of truth to what Harry says. While Sirius Black is free and Wormtail is off to get Voldemort, Harry shows no sign that the events of the book have changed *him*.

In fact, none of the books cause Harry to change. By Book 5, *Order of the Phoenix*, Harry is taller and no doubt (cough) hairier. However, this is a natural result of aging, rather than a result of his life experiences.

Does Harry overcome his insecurity? Does he gain some insight into human nature that causes him to treat people differently? Does he learn to be a leader? Does he take on a life-directing goal?

Early in Book 5, we see Harry being quite cruel and Snape-like to Dudley. While this indicates he's learned some new skills, and shows him acting out the abuse he's received, it's also an isolated incident that doesn't redefine Harry's character. It isn't that Harry has been turned into a predatory monster. Rather, as with so many things in the series, his behavior toward Dudley is merely a convenient way to inject additional stress into the scene. Once the dementor attack is over, Harry cycles over into another one of his stock moods. The result isn't a linear progression toward some truly new version of Harry, but merely a flipping back and forth between a set of transient states.

Also in Book 5, while running the D.A., Harry discovers he is a good teacher. Unfortunately, this discovery goes nowhere. Harry never focuses on Neville or even Ron, in an attempt to help lift those two out of their mediocrity. The D.A. is a convenience for the author in Book 5, but once it has served its purpose, it gets trashed, and any impact it might have had on Harry is allowed to dissipate.

Most importantly for the Potter series as a whole, there is never a breakout moment for Harry. In the movie *Forrest Gump*, the young Gump is being chased by a group of local bullies. Gump's friend Jennie yells, "Run Forrest, run!" Gump runs, and as he does so, the metal braces on his legs come flying off. It's the climactic moment of the first half of the movie, and is a dramatic way of showing that Gump has discarded the unnecessary hindrances of a childhood handicap. Without this change, which affects Gump not only physically but emotionally, it would be impossible for him to have the many adventures that fill the remainder of his life.

The Potter series is missing a "Run Forrest, run!" moment. We'd like to see *every* book in the series cause some sort of noticeable change in Harry, but it seems reasonable that he would also have one of these breakout events, a specific place the reader could point to and say, "Here Harry threw off his false handicaps and stepped onto his true path."

Because Harry needs time to adjust to his role as Chosen One and needs time to prepare for the challenges ahead, this breakout moment wouldn't be especially believable if it came at the end of the series. As in the story of Goldilocks, somewhere in the middle of the series seems just right. As we'll see in the book-by-book discussion, the end of Book 3 offers a ready-made spot for Harry to have his "Run Forrest, run!" moment.

Enid Blyton and the Group Protagonist

Some aspects of the Potter series are reminiscent of Enid Blyton's work. Blyton wrote hundreds of children's books in the early-to-middle 1900s and may still be the best-selling author of books for children under age twelve. Her stories frequently involve a mystery that the protagonists solve, and she made use of group protagonists such as the Famous Five and the Secret Seven.

In a Blyton book, however, the children themselves resolve

the relevant conundrum. Even though these children tended to be younger than the Big Three, still they were able to succeed by a combination of bravery, cleverness, and teamwork. It would be hard to find a Blyton book where Mommy, Daddy, or anyone else suddenly arrived to save the day. Although the police might well become involved at the end of a mystery, they do so only because the children actively go to the police and hand over the evidence they collected — being smart enough not to try apprehending a gang of criminals themselves.

Divine intervention aside, we see indications that the Potter series is aiming at the same audience Blyton wrote for, most notably in the way it skates over the emotional and psychological implications of major events. Unfortunately, the Potter series unleashes true villains. Our heroes aren't trying to outwit a few greedy but clueless jewel thieves, as in a Blyton adventure. Rather, they're going up against the equivalent of Hitler, Sauron, or Jack the Ripper.

As a result, it seems like the Potter series can't quite make up its mind what it wants. Is it aiming for a Blyton-style children's story? If so, better if Voldemort and his death eaters got replaced by Mundungus Fletcher and a few more blokes like him. The Big Three could track down the missing Horcruxes for a museum and have amazing, scary, and silly adventures along the way. But if Voldemort stays, then keeping the Big Three innocent, weak, and psychologically unscarred will also leave the series feeling shallow and false.

Naturally, there's no reason why we couldn't have *both*. One version of the Potter series could be aimed at younger readers, featuring Dung Fletcher as the key antagonist. And another version could be aimed at older readers, featuring Voldemort. Heck, most of us would wind up owning both versions! Unfortunately, what we have now is a single version that tries to chase two rabbits at once, with the result that both get away.

The Big Three

Enid Blyton made regular use of group protagonists. The Famous Five was one such. The children (and their dog) shared a common goal and, petty internal strife aside, worked as a team to achieve success.

At times it seems this is a path the Big Three will follow, but ultimately nothing much comes of it. Because so many problems are solved by a mysterious entity called the word processor, the Big Three are never forced to reach their true potential. Ron and Harry never even emerge as distinct personalities.

Ron is the emotionally-stunted, not very talented, but faithful sidekick? Cool. Only, that's a pretty good description of Harry as well. Look at Harry's callous handling of Moaning Myrtle, Cho Chang, Winky, and Kreacher. Who's emotionally-stunted and insensitive? Watch Harry accompany Dumbledore to the Horcrux cave, and then watch Hermione leading Harry around by the hand in the final book of the series. Who's the not very talented sidekick?

Hermione is the only member of the Big Three that we can get a solid handle on. She's the brain, the planner, the sensitive one, the hard worker. While long winters in front of the fireplace have turned Ron and Harry into flabby couch potatoes, Hermione has emerged as a competent witch and a goal-oriented character. Fighting for elf rights, developing the polyjuice potion, helping Hagrid with the defense of Buckbeak, creating a cursed signup sheet for the D.A., putting a Protean charm on the D.A.'s summoning coins, studying up on Horcruxes, and constantly working her butt off to improve herself: Hermione isn't going to waste weeks at a time sitting around trading chocolate frog cards or feeling sorry for herself. She's going places.

But even with Hermione, we come away feeling like something is missing. If Hermione were allowed to step into the role of Chosen One when Harry fails to rise to the occasion, then perhaps we would see Hermione reach her full potential. As it stands, she's more like a really strong Chaser on a Quidditch team that's otherwise made up of klutzes. We can see that she's good, but we can't see just how good she could be, if only she had some strong people around her. People to back her up, cover her weak spots, and push her.

Some people will argue that Harry never rises to the same heights as Dumbledore and Voldemort specifically because he's merely one-third of the solution, that it is the Big Three which collectively counterbalances Voldemort. That argument has a problem, as the Potter series singles Harry out. The first book isn't *The Big Three and The Philosopher's Stone*, after all. But if we hypothetically accept that Ms. Rowling intended to use the Big Three in this way, we still have to admit that the three of them put together wouldn't last long against Voldemort. Ron and Harry, especially, are both too weak and talentless to fulfill even a one-third portion of such a team.

Fenimore Cooper's Literary Offenses

In 1895, Mark Twain wrote a critique of the author James Fenimore Cooper's work. Though Twain wrote his article more than a century ago, and much of what he said was specific to Cooper's opus, Twain's "rules governing literary art in the domain of romantic fiction" are still considered valuable by modern writers and editors. Here, we repeat those rules and apply them to the Potter series.

1. A tale shall accomplish something and arrive somewhere.

We give the Potter series a 50% rating on this one. The books each have a central conflict or mystery that provides a purpose to the tale. However, the seven books taken together leave the Big Three and the world around them changed only superficially.

If we were to take the Big Three as we find them near the middle of Book 1, then have their lives be uneventful from there on, would the Epilogue of Book 7 read differently? Dumbledore dies of old age in their sixth year, Fred Weasley dies from a prank gone wrong in their seventh year. Voldemort was truly killed when he attacked Harry the first time, so there is no comeback. Just seven years of school and getting older.

How would things be different in the end?

Has there been any change in elf rights? A detente between Slytherin and Gryffindor houses? Has the muggle world learned of the existence of the magical one? Is there any emotional, post-traumatic impact on any of the Big Three? Has anything of significance changed, other than that the world and those in it have gotten older?

If mowing the grass is to accomplish something and to arrive somewhere, then the Potter series succeeds. But as for a less evanescent sort of accomplishment, it comes up short.

2. The episodes in a tale shall be necessary parts of the tale and shall help to develop it.

The Potter series contains quite a few scenes that neither connect to the plot nor increase our understanding of the characters. Some of these scenes immerse us in Harry's world, helping us imagine what it would be like to live as a wizard in the Hogwarts universe, and readers appreciate such scenes as well. But that still leaves hundreds of pages spread throughout the Potter series that merely kill time, bury a forward reference to a later book, or hide some clue for the current tome.

Slipping in a clue here and there is a good practice, as it rewards readers for paying attention. However, justifying tedious sections of prose by saying, "There's a clue hidden in there," is a bad business. Readers show up outside a book to be entertained, and once they step inside, they want every section of a story to meet that minimum requirement, clues or no clues.

3. The personages in a tale shall be alive, except in the case of corpses, and always the reader shall be able to tell the corpses from the others.

In a work of fantasy, this particular dictate can make your head hurt, but let us point only to Dumbledore in Book 7, *Deathly Hallows*. Though dead, he behaves little differently, and is generally indistinguishable from his earlier, fully-alive self.

4. The personages in a tale, both dead and alive, shall exhibit a sufficient excuse for being there.

Ms. Rowling does a good job of this. However, Harry becomes effectively unnecessary in Books 6 and 7. As we have pointed out already, at times he could be replaced by any arbitrary person, and sometimes even by a video camera. In Book 7, Harry and Ron *both* feel superfluous, and the reader wonders why Hermione needs those two losers tagging along after her.

5. When the personages of a tale deal in conversation, the talk shall sound like human talk ... and have a discoverable meaning, also a discoverable purpose, and a show of relevancy, and ... help the tale out.

Most conversations in the Potter series are relevant, so long as the scenes they occupy are relevant. Some of the talk feels a bit formal, a bit long-winded, but overall we feel that Ms. Rowling does a good job here.

6. When the author describes the character of a personage in the tale, the conduct and conversation of that personage shall justify said description.

Good job.

7. When a personage talks like a giant at the beginning of a paragraph, he shall not talk like a goblin at the end.

Good job.

8. Crass stupidities shall not be played upon the reader and passed off as "luck" by the author or the people in the tale.

We've beaten this particular fault to death already.

9. The personages of a tale shall confine themselves to possibilities and let miracles alone; or, if they venture a miracle, the author must so plausibly set it forth as to make it look possible and reasonable.

It's unfortunate that Mr. Twain decided to add the "or" clause above. Let us amend his august words with yet another clause, "And no more than one miracle shall ever be allowed to any one personage, not even across multiple volumes."

In Harry's case, his one miracle is that his mother's sacrifice saved Harry from being killed at the opening of Book 1, *Philosopher's Stone*. Her lingering protection at the end of that same book is a questionable dodge, but the miraculous arrival of Fawkes at the end of Book 2, *Chamber of Secrets*, Harry's resurrection and Voldemort dropping dead in response to Expelliarmus at the end of Book 7, to name but a few cases: these all constitute one miracle too many for our brave hero.

10. The author shall make the reader feel a deep interest in the personages of her tale and in their fate; and she shall make the reader love the good people in the tale and hate the bad ones.

This particular rule has been slightly overtaken by events, since our enlightened, politically-correct times allow us to sympathize even with the bad guys. However, the gist of the rule is still valid, and here we again give Ms. Rowling 50%. Fans earnestly want to feel a deep interest in what is going on in the Potter series, we desperately want to love Harry and the other good guys, and we really want to hate Voldemort.

But when a story cheats us so many times — pulling people out of danger without sufficient explanation, changing the rules then changing them back, and forcing even main characters to behave inconsistently in the name of surprise or plot expediency — then we find it hard to be deeply interested in the fate of the characters. We know they aren't really in any danger. Some people die while others live only because that is what it says in the author's plot outline, not because it makes sense given the universe of the story. As such, why *should* we care?

11. The characters in a tale shall be so clearly defined that the reader can tell beforehand what each will do in a given emergency.

We have already covered this particular failing already and will do yet more in Part 2. However, let us again append a clause to the previous rule, namely, "Important characters in a tale shall be made to seem like real, three-dimensional human beings, rather than flat cardboard cutouts or incomprehensible aliens."

Let us merely point to Harry himself. What is especially disturbing about Harry is that he can pass through traumatic events without showing any effects at all. Imagine if you were at school and a man took you down into the basement at gunpoint and told you he was going to kill you. You manage to get the upper hand and kill him instead. Would this be something you just shrug off, regardless of your age?

A year after that first attack, you open your school locker and a rattlesnake jumps out and bites you. At that point, in comes the guy who tried to kill you the year before. You manage to kill him by stabbing him in the neck with the rattlesnake, and then you ask yourself how many more times you'll have to kill him before he stays dead.

Now, are you just going to go back to school like nothing happened? Would you be having nightmares? Develop agoraphobia? Would you experience panic attacks every time you hear a strange sound at night?

Harry not only endures ten years of abuse with the Dursleys, but he is attacked over and over again, and spends every moment of his adolescence aware that Voldemort wants to kill him and will do so if the chance arises. Yet none of this has any effect on him. The best explanation for this is that Harry is a two-dimensional character in a book and isn't remotely human.

James Fenimore Cooper died 50 years before Mark Twain wrote his critique of Cooper's opus. This seems a bit unfair, as Cooper then had no chance to either defend himself or, if he was so inclined, to fix some of the problems that Twain pointed out.

Cooper's books were very popular in their time, are still available, and some (ex., *The Last of the Mohicans*) have been made into motion pictures. This shows that even a story that is full of so-called "flaws" can sell well and continue to be read hundreds of years later. Whether such works leave behind a legacy the author would be comfortable with is another matter.

Chapter 7:
Strengths of the Potter Series

In the original version of *Destiny Unfulfilled*, I made no attempt to discuss the strengths of the Potter series in any detail. At the time, I rationalized this by pointing out the success of the series. Its commercial success shows beyond a doubt that Ms. Rowling's magnum opus is a powerful work of fiction that appeals to a wide range of readers, while its critical success has resulted in books, websites, reviews, and articles that address the strengths of the series more thoroughly and with more skill than I could manage.

Though none of this has changed, in the fullness of time I recognized my approach for what it was: laziness. Criticizing will always be easier for me than offering praise. But personality flaws aside, in failing to analyze and meditate upon the strengths of the Potter series, I had missed half of the equation. A writer, to be successful, has to do more than avoid making mistakes, she must also imbue her work with positive characteristics.

Critics occasionally complain that a particular bestseller is poorly written. Assuming that some of those complaints are valid, this suggests that certain positive qualities in fiction are so powerful that they can overshadow various weaknesses. In the case of the Potter series, the positive qualities are such that they cover a multitude of sins — enough sins, in fact, to fill an entire book, as *Destiny Unfulfilled* shows.

Is it possible that certain positive qualities are so powerful that a writer dare not ignore them? After considering a wide range of bestselling commercial fiction, it seems clear that only one quality can be called an absolute requirement: story. Control of point of view (POV), clean prose, a solid protagonist: we can find bestselling novels lacking one or more of these qualities. We can find bestselling novels that start with long expositional blocks (ex., some of James Michener's epics). But all such books have a story to tell, and they tell it.

Telling A Story

In a work of commercial fiction, the one inescapable positive trait is *story*. This may sound too obvious for words, and yet the world's slush piles are filled with novels that fail this test.

Not only must a writer have a story, she must tell that story (not get sidetracked) and must tell that story effectively. Most of this chapter will focus on these two addendums, because many factors play into them. For now, however, let's consider the Potter series and the story it tells.

In a single sentence, the Potter series is about a young wizard who struggles to fulfill his destiny while also retaining his humanity.

This summary is certainly vague and would benefit from a few specifics. However, it also encompasses the overarching plotline of a seven-book series. To prove that our one sentence summary represents a story, we need only compare it to the generic description of a story: A protagonist ("a young wizard") overcomes various obstacles ("struggles") in order to achieve his goal or goals ("fulfill his destiny" and "retain his humanity").

For each book in the Potter series, we can play this same game. The summary of Book 1, *Philosopher's Stone*: In order to protect the wizarding world that he has so recently inherited, Harry must prevent the Philosopher's Stone from falling into the wrong hands. For Book 2, *Chamber of Secrets*: In order to keep Hogwarts from being closed forever, Harry must solve the mystery of the Chamber of Secrets. For Book 3, *Prisoner of*

Azkaban: In order to come to terms with the death of his parents, Harry must track down their killer. And so forth.

Would Ms. Rowling provide an identical one sentence plot description for the first three books? Probably not, but the point here is that each book can be boiled down to such a degree precisely because they each have a definite story to tell.

Caveats

But can't *every* work of commercial fiction be similarly condensed? Unfortunately, no. The slush piles and remaindered warehouses of the world are full of novels that fail the one sentence stress test.

Honesty (and our earnest belief that there *are* no rules) requires that we pause to consider successful works that resist a one sentence summary. *The Stand* and *Under the Dome* by Stephen King are both epic works with involved plotlines that encompass a wide range of POV characters. George R.R. Martin's *Ice and Fire Cycle* is similarly complex and therefore difficult to capture effectively in a single sentence. Books like *Centennial* and *Hawaii* by James Michener are perhaps even more difficult to summarize.

We could certainly make a stab at a single sentence summary for epics like those by King and Martin, and we could wave off Michener's novels as being collections of related stories, but in this case, discretion seems preferable to valor.

For most first-time novelists, however, pursuing a story that resists the one sentence stress test is perilous. Stephen King didn't start off with *The Stand*; his first book was *Carrie*. Meanwhile, George R.R. Martin only undertook his complex fantasy cycle late in his career when his skills had reached full maturity. Complex books like these should come with an FDA label: "WARNING! Trained professionals at work. Do not attempt this at home."

Struggling writers who wave off such warnings often pay

for their hubris by producing novels that simply don't work.

Telling a Story Effectively

Not only does the Potter series have a story to tell, it embodies a wide range of strengths that help it tell that story effectively. Unlike story, however, these other strengths are desirable but (as the bestseller list proves) none are essential. They are more in the nature of checkboxes.

A story is a powerful thing and can overshadow a number of other flaws. Still, if a writer leaves too many boxes unchecked, the cumulative vacuum can suck the life out of her work, and so it behooves her to pay careful attention to these "optional" qualities.

In the case of the Potter series, a lot of boxes got checked, usually with one of those really thick magic markers.

- The story feels original
- The story has a concrete, telegraphed structure
- Premise isn't mistaken for story
- The prose is strong without being florid
- Readers form an emotional attachment to main characters
- The story is tightly focused
- The story's use of POV is controlled and reliable
- The story contains a significant disturbance to the protagonist's world
- Settings are detailed and relevant, so that they become like characters within the story
- The story emphasizes showing, using telling in moderation and only as required
- Information is withheld until it is relevant
- Tense moments are stretched
- Almost every scene contains some form of conflict or suspense

It seems like a long list, and it is. Moreover, few bestsellers contain all these positive qualities. But these are all elements that contribute to the effective telling of a story, and the Potter series *does* embody all of these strengths.

Originality

Even if true originality is unachievable, a writer can still make her work *feel* original, and Ms. Rowling is masterful in this respect. Details are critical in creating a sense of originality in any story (more on this later), but the Potter series is original at a higher level as well.

First, the series ignored, and so redefined, the rules of both fantasy and young adult literature. It contains elements of horror, suspense, and mystery, and so resists easy categorization. In its physical construction, the series is also original, as it has a clear beginning, middle and end, while it avoids being either a media tie-in or fundamentally Tolkienesque (unlike the majority of fantasy novels published in the last umpteen years).

Second, the series makes use of archetypes in unfamiliar ways.

Archetypes

The Potter series contains a number of archetypes, but it uses them without seeming tired and overdone. Some of the archetypes are quite familiar (Harry as the normal person who discovers he isn't normal after all; Dumbledore as the wizened mentor) while some archetypes are less familiar (Hogwarts and Hagrid, for example).

Familiar archetypes are as easy to find as picking up a book by Joseph Campbell. But how does a writer go about locating, or else creating, unfamiliar archetypes? One approach is to merge two familiar archetypes, as the Potter series does with

Hogwarts, which melds the fairytale other-land and the gothic boarding school.

Hogwarts is a Never-Never Land, but one that is reachable by conventional means. Instead of falling down a rabbit hole, stepping through a magic closet, or being carted off by a tornado, Harry reaches Hogwarts by train (for the most part), adding a wonderful element of determinism to the magical situation. Also, while Harry is at Hogwarts, despite the immensity of the place, he isn't wandering aimlessly around in a planet-sized fairy land (something that can begin to feel like a slideshow of someone else's vacation). Rather, he is at a school, with classes to attend and sports to participate in.

Thus, the melding of two archetypes into one does more than make Hogwarts seem original, it also makes Hogwarts feel more deterministic and more accessible — important traits in a work of fantasy.

Hagrid, meanwhile, feels even less familiar as an archetype than Hogwarts does. Surely we could dig up a correlation between Hagrid and a character from some myth or legend. But for most of us, Hagrid is something we haven't seen before, and yet he has that feeling of being just right for his role in the story. Does he qualify as an archetype? Well, he at least fulfills the key requirement of being larger than life. In his case, literally.

By including unfamiliar archetypes like Hogwarts and Hagrid, the Potter series makes the more familiar ones feel fresh. Even after we spot the similarities, Harry doesn't seem like just another King Arthur.

Story Structure

By structure, we mean the way scenes are organized so as to provide a clear beginning, middle, and end to a story. For the Potter series, both individual books and the series as a whole demonstrate a mastery of story structure.

For one thing, the Potter stories are strongly sequential.

While we do get a few flashbacks here and there (via the Pensieve and Riddle's diary), we certainly don't get very many. None of the stories relies on a Prelude to show us events from the middle or near the end of a book. (While Preludes are a useful mechanism, beginning writers seem to use them excessively, perhaps hoping to make up for a weak first chapter.) Nor do the stories bounce us around within the timeline of the story. Even Book 3, *Prisoner of Azkaban*, uses its time travel device in a controlled manner, so that the linear, sequential feel of the storyline is never compromised.

The school calendar also provides a natural structure to each story. While this scaffolding becomes an obstruction in the later books, still we have to acknowledge that all of the books (but most especially the early ones) benefit from connecting key plot events to calendar events. Each book begins at or near Harry's birthday, during the transition from summer vacation to the start of the school year. Plot intensity ratchets up on key dates such as Halloween, allowing each book to reach a solid middle point during the winter holidays. From there, events move to their inexorable close at or about finals week.

Not every story can have something as congenial as a school calendar to leverage, but many novels seem not to have any sort of grounding schedule at all. As a result, readers begin to wonder, "Is this story *going* somewhere? Or will it just continue to flop around aimlessly?"

Another way of saying this is that the school calendar helps to telegraph the structure of the story, but without giving away any surprises. A telegraphed structure tells readers "This story is heading somewhere," without producing a sense of, "Oh, I know exactly where this is going." As such, the school calendar is a win-win solution, with but a single caveat: that it might get overused.

The Potter series as a whole also has a clear structure, one that readers are at least subliminally aware of. As we read, we have a sense that each book is right for its place in the series. In

Book 3, *Prisoner of Azkaban*, Voldemort's return becomes imminent. In Book 4, *Goblet of Fire*, his return is realized. In Book 5, *Order of the Phoenix*, he manipulates events from the shadows. In Book 6, *Half-Blood Prince*, he steps out into the open.

Thus, the Potter books aren't basically interchangeable. Books 1 and 2 form a clear beginning. Books 3 through 6 steadily escalate the conflict, and Book 7 brings the series to its climactic end.

For readers, this all feels right and correct, without feeling predictable. This is because the series manages to telegraph its structure without telegraphing the plot.

Finding the Beginning

Finding the beginning of a story is probably the most difficult task for a writer, as far as story structure is concerned. Consider Book 1, *Philosopher's Stone*, which starts shortly after the death of Harry's parents and the disembodiment of Lord Voldemort. Is this the true beginning of the story? It seems so.

Omitting the first chapter of Book 1 would leave readers in the dark as to Harry's true nature, so that the torments he suffers at the Dursley home wouldn't mean as much. Moreover, readers would be wondering not just "what is going to happen next," but "what is this all about?" Some readers are more patient than others, but by revealing Harry's true nature up front, along with his connection to the mysterious wizarding world, Book 1 caters to even those of us who have limited patience for coy, "try to guess what I'm thinking now" prose.

Similarly, Harry's experiences at the Dursley home are important to our understanding of him as a person. They let us become attached to him. Thus, to start Book 1 with Harry boarding the Hogwarts express wouldn't cut it. Yes, boarding the train is a powerful moment, and it marks the spot where the book really takes off. But the train scenes would lose much of their significance if we were strangers to Harry, having only just met him.

In sum, it seems unwise (or at least fruitless) to try and start Book 1 at a later time in the narrative.

Could it start earlier? In this case, not very easily. The opening of Book 1 could certainly be jazzed up, by exchanging its current focus on Vernon Dursley with something more Harry-specific, such as his being retrieved from Godric's Hollow by Dumbledore and Hagrid. But to start the book with Harry's parents still alive would be a mistake. Readers would be introduced to two people who immediately get killed. If Book 1 were meant to be primarily a horror story, such an approach might be appropriate, but even so, it would introduce a BEGIN ... END ... BEGIN quality to the very start of the book — and some readers might be put off, never getting past that second BEGIN.

Middle and End

With a beginning solidly in place, middle and end become a question of alertness. So long as the writer has a story to tell, and is telling that story, they need only ask themselves at regular intervals, "When was the last time the plot moved forward? When was the last time the intensity ratcheted up?"

In a long work such as a novel, the pace and intensity will naturally rise and fall, and subplots will occasionally take center stage. But so long as the writer remains alert, such things present no danger. Quidditch, romance, friendship, hobbies, and even day-to-day events can all play their part. Only when ancillary events derail the plot for long stretches, or subvert the plot entirely, do they become a problem.

Particularly in the early books, the Potter series demonstrates a mastery of interweaving subplot with plot. The first Quidditch game is more than an action sequence, as it introduces a threat to Harry's life. Chess games in front of the Gryffindor fireplace become significant later when the Big Three are trying to reach the chamber where the Philosopher's

Stone is hidden. In the second book, Harry's Parselmouth ability makes his life difficult in the near term, ratcheting up the conflict, while it becomes essential to the plot later on, as it allows him to open the Chamber of Secrets.

In sloppy commercial fiction, scenes too often fail to advance the story, making a novel feel like it is spinning its wheels, pointlessly padding the page count. By contrast, the Potter series is constantly moving forward, with readers convinced that the direction of movement makes perfect sense, no matter how surprising a development might be.

Because individual scenes clearly serve the story, readers are left eager for more.

Premise vs. Story

In some cases, broken novels don't tell a story, but merely work through a premise. This is an easy mistake to make, especially when the writer has a premise such as, "Living alongside us is an entire community of wizards and other supernatural creatures." A premise like that immediately grabs our attention, and readers eagerly snatch up their reading glasses.

The same is true of other premises inherent in the Potter series: "Imagine a boarding school full of witches and wizards." "A powerful evil wizard is out to take over the world." Each of these premises is a blockbuster, and the Potter series contains all of them, and more. But even such powerful premises would spell disaster if they were treated as story descriptions.

The Potter series is successful because Ms. Rowling knows the difference between a premise and story, and she keeps all of her premises (however powerful they might be) subservient to the story that she wants to tell.

Converting a premise into a story isn't as straightforward as it might seem. The premise can easily become an end in itself, or at least an excuse for why the writer hasn't included a clear protagonist, a meaningful crisis, or a powerful plotline. For many struggling writers, this is a stumbling block they never get past. As a result, no amount of otherwise sterling writing will save them.

Readers pay to be told a story, and this above all else is what the Potter series delivers.

Readability

At the level of the sentence and paragraph, the Potter series is eminently readable. It resides in a happy middle ground between florid prose on the one hand, and anorexic prose on the other. The style is direct without being simplistic. It gets out of the way so that readers can enjoy the story.

The strengths of Ms. Rowling's prose read like a summary of Strunk and White's *The Elements of Style*:

- Varied sentences, both in length and structure
- Use of the active voice
- Limited use of "to be" verbs and related constructs ("there were," "it was," "she was")
- Balanced use of rare verbs (slam, snatch, swagger) with more common ones (close, take, walk)
- A preference for concrete nouns that appeal to the five senses
- Carefully selected modifiers
- Use of more-specific transitional words and phrases (because, though, which) rather than relying entirely upon "and," "but," and "then"

The Potter prose isn't afraid to use adverbs (including adverbs in dialog tags), for which all writers should be grateful. The current backlash has all but removed adverbs from the language, and we need writers like Ms. Rowling to push back against this bigotry. Some writers might not be comfortable using adverbs as much as Ms. Rowling does, but that is one way writers create their own unique voice. It deserves to remain a matter of personal preference rather than editorial fiat.

The Potter prose also demonstrates courage by making positive statements. Graduate school timidity ("the toe on an ape is not unlike a thumb") has infected a lot of writers, but not Ms. Rowling. She doesn't tell us what something is not unlike; she tells us what it is like.

Reader Identification

The Potter series does an excellent job of getting readers to identify with Harry and the other key characters in the story. Consider the Big Three. They are all basically decent and admirable in a moral sense, valuing honesty, loyalty, friendship, and fairness. At the same time, they aren't saccharine, but are capable of stepping around arbitrary rules in order to achieve a lofty goal.

In addition, none of the Big Three are exactly perfect. They each have their flaws (Ron's insensitivity, Harry's laziness, Hermione's perfectionism), and these flaws make them more accessible, more believable as human beings. The Big Three are also capable of making mistakes, sometimes rather large ones. They solve the mystery of Book 1, for example, but do so erroneously, blaming Snape right up to the moment when Harry pulls the cards out of the little folder, and discovers it wasn't Mr. Mustard after all.

Antiheroes have their place, as do pure heroes like Superman, but the Potter series demonstrates the draw of heroic-but-flawed characters. We identify with the Big Three because being like them (spell casting aside) seems both possible and desirable.

Tight Focus

Each book in the Potter series stays focused on the issues relevant to that book. A few forward references appear now and then, but such ancillary bits are generally slipped in amid scenes that directly connect to the current story.

Most events, objects, and characters in Book 1, for example, tie directly back to the conundrum of the Philosopher's Stone. The mysterious object that Hagrid picks up during the trip to Gringotts Bank, Fluffy the three-headed dog, the troll encounter, Norbert the dragon, the Mirror of Erised: these all connect directly to Voldemort's presence at the school. Even Harry's flying ability and Ron's skill at chess become significant during the climactic buildup at the end of the book.

Ms. Rowling may have created working notes for every character in the story, all the way down to their favorite color, but she resisted the urge to belabor readers with nonessential details. Think about Dumbledore's backstory, which is left all but untouched until the last book of the series. Similarly, Voldemort's backstory receives major attention only in Book 6, *Half-Blood Prince*. Though Ms. Rowling had those backstories worked out much earlier, she resisted the urge to dump them on the reader until such time as they were germane to the flow of the story.

Consider also Durmstrang and Beauxbatons, two wizard schools that get no mention at all for the first three books of the Potter series. Even after their introduction, those two schools receive little attention except in Book 4, *Goblet of Fire*, where their presence is essential to the plot.

Throughout, the Potter series stays focused on Harry and the problems facing him. The last two books of the series, especially, could easily have gotten sidetracked into global political intrigue, but Ms. Rowling studiously avoids that trap. Azkaban, The Forbidden Forest, Hagrid's ambassadorial trip to the giants, the first war against Voldemort, Snape's running of

Hogwarts during Book 7, *Deathly Hallows*: these are all things that could easily have become sidetracks, but didn't.

The books of the Potter series set out to tell a story, and they remain focused on that goal, to the delight of readers.

POV

The number of point of view characters in a story affects the reader's opinion of how focused that story is. POV also influences the reader's emotional connection to characters in the story. Stories are about people, and the Potter series makes clear through its use of POV that it is about Harry. Other characters, settings, and events are important to the story only when they are important to him.

Some stories require multiple POVs, but commercial fiction often gets sloppy, switching POV unnecessarily. Consider the following synopsis, where one sentence represents a scene or chapter in a book, and the POV character is the subject of the sentence:

- Lisa discovers a dead body in the trunk of her car.
- Lt. Manning takes over the investigation into the mysterious corpse.
- George, Lisa's estranged husband, has an argument with Lisa about letting strangers place dead bodies in her automobile.
- A nameless individual sits in a dark room, planning a gruesome crime.
- Dr. Trace performs an autopsy on the previously-mentioned corpse.
- Chief of Police Henries gives Lt. Manning a dressing down over poorly prepared paperwork.
- Timmy, who works at Squeaky-Clean Car Detailing, experiences emotional trauma as he cleans out the trunk of Lisa's car.

- Alexander is jogging at night when he is attacked, kidnapped, tortured, and finally killed.

The synopsis above is make-believe, as well as incomplete, but it fairly represents the outline of many novels sitting in slush piles around the world. The switching POVs aren't the problem, but they are a *symptom* of the problem. The real problem is a failure to decide what story the novel wants to tell.

If asked to boil the above synopsis down to a single sentence, the best we could do would be, "It's a story about some murders that occur within a community." Unfortunately, that isn't a story summary, it's a premise. Stories are about people. The above synopsis describes a story that's about "everybody affected by the murders." Unfortunately, a story about "everybody" is most likely going to wind up feeling either scattered and unfocused, or else abstract and experimental.

Nothing's impossible, of course, and certainly writers like Stephen King have achieved success with novels that feature a large number of POV characters. For most beginning writers, though, trying to build a story around our synopsis would be disastrous. The result would lack focus, would wear readers out with all those POV changes, and would fail to make readers care about key characters. As the villain from *The Incredibles* says, "when everyone's special, no one will be."

Ms. Rowling wrote seven books using Harry's POV almost exclusively, and the few exceptions were a result of necessity. The opening of Book 1, *Philosopher's Stone*, can't be from Harry's POV because he's a year old. The opening of Book 4, *Goblet of Fire*, sets the stage for the rest of the book, and Frank Bryce's experiences in that first chapter directly affect Harry via his mental connection with Voldemort. The opening of Book 6, *Half-Blood Prince*, again sets the stage for the main plotline of that story. In every case, these instances of POV switching serve a real purpose.

Using a single, dedicated POV brings with it many

benefits, and it is certainly one of the strengths of the Potter series.

A Plot-Defining Disturbance

Each of the Potter books includes a major disturbance in Harry's world. These disturbances typically involve a threat to Harry's life, which is the sort of disturbance readers take seriously without needing additional motivation. Just as, in the last few books, we automatically take seriously the escalating situation, which threatens the entire wizard way of life — and perhaps the muggle way of life as well.

While the exact *nature* of these threats is sometimes hidden from the reader, the books reveal the *existence* of the threat early on. In Book 1, for example, Harry's scar flares during that first meal in the Great Hall, but he blames Snape, not realizing that Voldemort (hidden under Quirrell's turban) is the one responsible. A bit further on, Book 1 gives us a more overt clue that something is amiss when Harry is nearly thrown from his broom during a Quidditch match. Even then, though, the exact nature of the threat isn't revealed. In fact, the book goes out of its way to direct our attention to Snape and away from Quirrell.

All the Potter books have a major disturbance, one that readers can relate to. Those disturbances get introduced early, and they form the backbone of each book. Nearly every event in a Potter book either reveals new information about the disturbance, moves Harry closer to resolving the disturbance, or else exacerbates the disturbance. This is the *definition* of tight plotting, and the Potter series is a poster child for the cause.

Details and Immersion

Ms. Rowling's boxes of notes for the Potter universe are legendary. Those notes translated into highly detailed characters and settings that captivated readers. As much as the details themselves, Ms. Rowling's careful selection of *which* details to use — and which to exclude — illuminated the story world without derailing the flow of the story itself.

Generally, when a major character appears for the first time in the Potter series, they receive a sentence or two dedicated to their physical description — a description that often ties into that character's personality. These descriptions never degenerate into a bland list of details, nor are these mechanical head-to-toe descriptions. Instead, the story picks a select number of key features which, taken together, allow readers to form a mental picture of the person in question.

The first description of Harry, possibly the longest descriptive passage in the series, covers the color of his hair and eyes, the state of his glasses (held together with tape), his scar, and his scrawny build — accentuated by his hand-me-down clothes. Even though this is Harry we're talking about, his physical description doesn't appear the moment we meet him. Instead, we first see Harry waking up in his closet, dusting off a coating of spiders, getting dressed, and being ragged on by Aunt Petunia. Only then does the story pause to describe his appearance.

Also, the story uses this first bit of description to point out that Harry's life has been a difficult one. The tape on his glasses is there because Dudley picks on him. His scrawny build might have something to do with living in a cupboard. His hand-me-down clothes imply an impoverished childhood, one where Harry is a second-class citizen in the Dursley home.

Another key feature of Harry's appearance, his unruly hair, comes out not in the first bit of description, but several paragraphs later, in response to Uncle Vernon's telling Harry to comb his hair. Here again, a descriptive passage is made to do double duty, this time illustrating Harry's relationship to his uncle (the passage focuses not on the exact appearance of our hero's hair but on how his unruly hair makes his life difficult).

By weaving details in as part of ongoing action, the Potter

series keeps those details from being distracting. Instead, the descriptions become a natural part of the flow of events.

Settings receive a similar treatment. Minor settings, such as the Reptile House, are described in a few sentences — enough to ground the reader, but without belaboring a setting that will appear only once in the story. This understanding of proper emphasis is another sign of an author who knows what story she's telling, who recognizes what is central and what is ancillary, and who consciously places emphasis on key characters and settings, not letting minor figures distract the reader or delay the progress of the story.

As for a major setting like Hogwarts, details still aren't dropped on the reader in a single blob. Instead, they filter out as needed. We get hints about the school when Hagrid makes his appearance at the cottage on a rock. A few more tidbits come out during the trip to Diagon Alley, where Harry first hears about Quidditch and the four school houses. Then, when Harry first lays eyes on Hogwarts, the event is covered in a single sentence! This again shows that the goal is to keep the story moving forward, rather than reveal how much research the writer has done.

What we see in the Potter series is not only a depth of detail, but also a solid control over those details. Descriptions don't necessarily appear the moment a character or setting is encountered, and most descriptions are dribbled out over time rather than plopped down all at once. The result is that the Potter universe feels layered and immense, yet the reader never feels overwhelmed or bored. This is how it is supposed to be done!

Showing and Telling

The rule "show, don't tell" is an example of extremist thinking. "Prefer showing to telling" is much better as a writer's guideline. Telling and summary, like exposition and backstory, have their proper place in the writer's bag of tricks. Replacing an immersive scene with a brief summary can help to keep the pace of a story up, something the Potter series clearly understands.

Consider the opening of Book 2, *Chamber of Secrets*. The first paragraph of that book is actually telling, rather than showing. It summarizes events.

> Not for the first time, an argument had broken out over breakfast at number four, Privet Drive.

This grounds readers in the situation, rather than simply dropping us into the middle of a muddle.

If every scene opened with this sort of a summary, it would no doubt begin to feel like a mannerism. But as a way of leading into a book, as a way of transitioning between discontinuous events, or as a way of avoiding reader confusion during a complex, surreal, or unintuitive scene, summary and telling serve a useful purpose.

Still, one of the great strengths of the Potter series is its power to pull readers into this alternate universe. We are able to forget our mundane existence and live within the pages of the books as we read. What makes this possible is the immersive nature of scenes that *show* us events taking place.

Rather than tell us that Harry's summer has been an oppressive one, Book 2 shows us the exact nature of the oppression. His owl Hedwig has been locked in her cage, his school things locked in the cupboard. We see the Dursleys' irrational fear of Harry's magical ability when he says, "You've forgotten the magic word," and Mr. Dursley interprets this as a threat.

By experiencing a few exemplary moments of Harry's tortured existence, we understand and appreciate his situation better than if we'd been merely told about it — even if (and perhaps *especially* if) the book had gone on for several pages telling us about it.

Ms. Rowling also does a wonderful job showing us the emotions that characters are feeling. Rather than being satisfied with, "Harry was afraid," or with a cliche like, "Harry trembled with fear," she finds unfamiliar ways to convey the emotional state of characters. Fingers tingle and ears stop hearing the roaring crowd until — with golden egg in hand — the volume gets turned back up. As a result, readers are better able to empathize with the characters.

Showing and Telling in Dialog

At the beginning of Book 2, some information comes out via dialog. However, the story does this in a way that isn't distracting to the reader. Book 2 first tells us that Mr. Dursley was awakened by Hedwig's hooting. Then we get Harry saying, "She's bored.... If I could just let her out at night —" As a result, readers learn that Hedwig is kept locked in her cage.

Note that this mechanism could easily be misused. Consider a rewrite of the opening to Book 2:

> Harry walked to the kitchen table. "Mr. Dursley, I know you don't like me because I'm a wizard, and I'm sorry that my snowy-white owl, Hedwig, woke you up this morning with her hooting, but it isn't right that you make me keep her locked in her cage all the time."

This is an example of characters telling each other things they already know. The dialog feels artificial and mechanical because it *is* artificial and mechanical. A character has become an expository device, and the result is distracting.

As with many things in writing, the difference between appropriate and inappropriate use of dialog is subtle. The Potter books are wonderful examples of appropriate dialog. Characters say things that make sense based on their personality and their situation. Moreover, if a character reveals something via dialog, such as "If I could just let her out at night," then the prose leaves that bit of information alone. To do otherwise would be repetitive and might even feel insulting to the reader. Imagine, for example, that Harry's statement "If I could just let her out at night" were followed by a bit of prose that said, "Mr. Dursley made Harry keep his owl locked up all the time...."

Similarly, if a character has no cause to mention some bit of important information (such as that Harry has been a student at Hogwarts for exactly one year), then the story reveals that information either through exposition, summary, or flashback, rather than by forcing a character to include the information in dialog, monolog, or silent musing. While many successful novels include sequences of dialog where characters tell each other (or themselves) things they already know, those books would be more enjoyable if they didn't abuse their characters in that manner.

Appropriate use of dialog, along with appropriate use of showing and telling, accentuate the immersive quality of the Potter series.

Stretching the Tension

We've already seen that the Potter series is willing to delay descriptions of setting and character. This willingness to delay also applies to more substantial story elements such as the true motivations of characters, the exact nature of a threat, and the cause of mysterious events.

Consider again the opening to Book 2, where Dobby introduces tension into the narrative by explaining that "bad things" are going to happen at Hogwarts that year. His inability to say exactly what *sorts* of bad things makes Dobby the perfect spear carrier, as he's able to foreshadow without giving away anything of real substance. The resulting mystery becomes an additional reason for readers to stick around.

The Potter series also knows how to increase reader involvement by keeping a threat hovering over Harry's head as long as possible. For example, Voldemort returns from the wilderness in Book 4, *Goblet of Fire*, and he continues as a villain through the next three books.

At a lower level, consider how the three tasks of the Tri-Wizard Tournament are dealt with. For the first task, Harry has to struggle to learn a summoning charm, something he manages only on the eve of the task itself. For the second task, in typical Harry style, he puts off trying to figure out the golden egg clue through the entire holiday break and only begins to take the task seriously when time is running out.

Perhaps there are better ways to stretch the tension than to make Harry seem inept and lazy, but at a minimum, the Potter series understands the importance of stretching the tension. By keeping threats alive as long as possible, the series keeps readers worried about Harry's safety, which is to say, it keeps readers reading.

Conflict

Conflict, the engine that drives fiction, shows up at many levels in the Potter series, from the series-defining threat of Lord Voldemort, to book-defining threats like Sirius Black in Book 3, *Prisoner of Azkaban*, to daily annoyances such as Snape, Malfoy, and Colin Creevey.

One curious aspect of conflict is that it ratchets up the closer to home it gets. Given confrontations of equal violence, an argument with a stranger affects us less deeply than an argument at work, which in turn affects us less than an argument at home.

Harry doesn't have any problem getting into a fight with Malfoy, but confronting Hagrid about Norbert is another matter. Even more stressful for Harry is the temporary breakup between himself and Ron in Book 4, *Goblet of Fire*. Similarly, Harry's internal worries and uncertainties — about a Quidditch match, about his nascent relationship to Ginny, or about how he'll survive one of the Tri-Wizard Tasks — also serve as potent sources of tension within the books.

When conflict arises in a close relationship, the options of eliminate, dominate, and avoid aren't generally available. As a result, such conflict is stressful in a different way (and is *more* stressful for some people) than external conflict. One reason why an abusive spouse lashes out is that it ends the discussion. Such people can't handle the stress of interpersonal conflict, and they get rid of it in the quickest way possible.

Scenes without some form of conflict tend to be less interesting to readers, and the Potter series makes use of both external conflict (with Voldemort, Malfoy, Umbridge, and others) and internal conflict (with Ron, Hermione, and within Harry himself) to keep readers eagerly turning the pages.

Conclusion

By having a story to tell, and by telling that story in a way that suits her, rather than by fitting her story into a predefined category or genre, Ms. Rowling created a seven-book series that captivated readers worldwide. Her stories are dominated by characters, not premises or marvels, though the series overflows with both. Her prose is rich with details and specifics, but isn't overblown. Active scenes dominate the narrative, showing us events taking place, while exposition and summary are used to keep the story moving forward. By withholding select bits of information as long as possible, the series enflames the reader's curiosity. By stretching tension, the series heightens reader involvement.

The Potter series has earned its popularity and critical acclaim through its originality, the fertile imagination and artistic integrity of its author, and its dedication to quality, as evidenced in its many strengths.

But what really makes the Potter series work, what keeps readers coming back to it above all, is story. In the world of fiction, this is the bottom line, and this is ultimately why the Potter series achieved such phenomenal success.

Chapter 8:
Conclusions

A book-length critique of most commercial fiction on the shelves today would be a waste of time. First, the writers of such things are unlikely to care. They pump out stuff on schedule, cash their checks, and life is good. Second, most such works could be refined and polished indefinitely, and they would remain ultimately forgettable.

Despite its various flaws, the Potter series is worthy of a book-length critique exactly because of what has made it so popular: its captivating universe, its unique blend of genres, its inherent re-readability, and the positive, uplifting nature of its themes and characters. That the Potter series annoys religious extremists is merely a side benefit, though a very tasty one.

Though overwhelmingly critical, *Destiny Unfulfilled* wouldn't exist if the Potter series were some lesser work. Only because the series is clearly a masterpiece does it make sense to examine it in such depth.

Referring to the Beatles' *Sergeant Pepper's Lonely Hearts Club Band* album, John Lennon once said, "Most of the songs there had nothing whatsoever to do with this idea of Sergeant Pepper.... But it worked because we *said* it worked." Lennon, in one of his huffy moods at the time, was being a bit hard on the album in order to make a point, but his statement contains an important truth: anything the Beatles did would be given the benefit of the doubt. Audiences would assume that a song or album did what the Beatles claimed it did. These were the Beatles after all!

When people read the Potter series, they do so under the influence of Potter-mania. A first-time novelist who produced a book like Book 7, *Deathly Hallows*, would surely be savaged by readers and reviewers alike. A main character who is Hamlet without even a philosophical bent to recommend him? A central conflict that is resolved by having the villain effectively drop dead for no apparent reason? That might work as film noir. It might qualify as Dada fiction, where everything is chaos and nothing we do matters. But as mainstream fiction, it's hard to imagine a first-time book like that even getting published, never mind winning awards and selling millions of copies.

Sooner or later, Potter-mania will fade, at which point the Potter series will face closer, less generous scrutiny than it has so far. Of course the Potter series will still be around in a hundred years. The question is, how will it be regarded? Time will tell, but with Ms. Rowling alive and at the height of her powers, the Potter series needn't risk going into perpetuity as a flawed masterpiece. Via a revised edition, it could guarantee itself a place alongside the works of Shakespeare and Dickens as an *unqualified* masterpiece.

Part 2:
Book-by-Book Discussion

Note

Part 2 proposes a number of hypothetical changes to the Potter series. Astute readers will recognize that some of these suggested changes are mutually exclusive. The goal here is not to say, "This is how it should be done," but rather to answer the charge that, while we complain about various aspects of the current series, we fail to offer suitable alternatives — with the implication that, flawed or not, the current series remains an optimal solution to the problems it tackles.

In suggesting changes, we have several goals. (a) Place greater emphasis on characterization by avoiding out-of-character actions and by having key characters change in response to the events of the series. (b) Avoid cheating the reader with shaggy dog solutions. (c) Place greater emphasis on consistency.

Chapter 1:
Philosopher's Stone

The Opening

The first book of the Potter series starts off rather sedately, with Vernon Dursley going to work at his drill-bit manufacturing company, followed by lunch at a donut shop. While the story does a good job of adding suspense, alerting the reader that something unusual and exciting is afoot, still it asks the reader to endure half a chapter of mundane stuff right at the start of the opus.

Even the appearance of Dumbledore, McGonagall, and Hagrid in the second half of the chapter fails to significantly increase the level of intensity. The flying motorcycle provides a nice special effect, and McGonagall does at least question the wisdom of leaving Harry with the Dursleys, but she isn't about to vigorously challenge Dumbledore's decision, and so the scene is without any substantial conflict. It becomes a simple delivery, though with strange delivery people and an unusual package.

To be fair, some readers will prefer this sort of opening. It gradually builds tension in a way common to thriller and horror stories, while the mundane setting provides a nice contrast to the magical environment that will fill most of the book. However, we also have to admit that some readers will be put off by the uneventful nature of all this. The sedate opening may even be one reason Ms. Rowling had difficulty finding a publisher for this first book. "Grab the reader right away" is a good dictum, especially when that reader is a jaded editor at a publishing house.

The intensity of Book 1's first chapter could be increased by having someone not simply question but directly challenge Dumbledore about what he's up to. Professor McGonagall seems a poor choice for this, as does Hagrid. But if Professor Snape or perhaps Dumbledore's brother Aberforth also showed up and had a go at Dumbledore, it would provide some true conflict to the scene.

Another possibility for introducing conflict would be to use Dumbledore's point of view, rather than the current omniscient third person POV. Readers would then be party to Dumbledore's internal misgivings and perhaps see that he feels guilty over the death of Harry's parents (though we might not find out why).

Conflict aside, we have to recognize that Dumbledore's cavalier attitude regarding Harry's safety is out of character. Though Hagrid could still be the one to carry Harry, readers expect Dumbledore's attitude to be, "Harry cannot leave my presence until the magical contract is in place." The loss of the flying motorcycle is unfortunate, but that motorcycle — so long as it is a loaner from Sirius Black — is a serious non-sequitur. Dumbledore would "know" that Sirius is the traitor, so a friendly chat with Sirius resulting in the use of his motorcycle — well, it simply doesn't fly.

Similarly, while a child left on a doorstep is a classic archetypal image, it isn't Potter-specific, and it definitely isn't in character for Dumbledore. An orphaned child brought to the door by a long-bearded wizard who then rings the doorbell: that *is* Potter-specific, and fits with the idea of a magical contract that must be agreed to.

Would the reader benefit from witnessing Dumbledore and Aunt Petunia's subsequent conversation? That's hard to say. What isn't in question, though, is that readers want Dumbledore's actions to mesh with what we learn in later books regarding how dangerous the situation is, and the importance of the magical contract.

Something Completely Different

Now consider a radically different opening, one that shows Dumbledore retrieving Harry from the house in Godric's Hollow. This scene is already an inherent part of the story, but it happens off-stage. That seems most unfortunate. Let's imagine what such a scene might look like, if it were played out in front of us.

Perhaps Mad Eye Moody and/or Mr. Weasley are already at Godric's Hollow, studying a house that flickers in and out of sight, when Dumbledore arrives with Hagrid in tow. Dumbledore might have delayed his arrival, seeing the attack on the Potters as nothing but a ruse designed to draw his attention away from the Longbottoms. But now he has begun to suspect the truth.

The Fidelus charm hiding the Potter's house could be partially dissipated already, because the main beneficiaries of the charm are dead and the person they were being protected from is (mostly) dead also. This would make it possible for Dumbledore to erase the last bits of the charm, causing the house to come solidly into view.

The series tells us that the house was destroyed as a result of the backfiring Avada Kedavra. This seems an unnecessary effect, and we recommend having the house still be in one piece. Perhaps the image of Harry being pulled from a wrecked building is important for some reason, but we'll proceed under the assumption that the house is either not damaged or else that Dumbledore repairs it at this point.

With various members of the Order of the Phoenix standing guard outside, Dumbledore enters the house along with Hagrid. They find James dead downstairs. Upstairs they find Lily's body as well as Voldemort's.

Would Voldemort's wand be there? If the story can create a

believable wand trail from Voldemort's first body to his second, that would be a nice touch. One possibility is to have Dumbledore take Voldemort's wand and secure it inside Hogwarts. Another possibility is that Mad Eye Moody or another auror would take the wand and put it into the evidence locker at the Ministry of Magic. In either case, retrieving the wand would then become a task for the false Mad Eye during Book 4, *Goblet of Fire*.

Leaving the wand question behind, would Voldemort's spirit still be nearby? Would Dumbledore sense it and, in attempting to destroy it completely, drive it off?

While Dumbledore tries to make sense of the tableau, Hagrid wanders over to Harry's crib and discovers that Harry is still alive, his scar glowing. This bit of data helps Dumbledore put the puzzle together and reconstruct what happened.

Potentially, either Snape or Aberforth could put in an appearance at this point and take Dumbledore to task. "You used the Potters as bait, and look what happened!" Currently, the series presents Dumbledore as a plain vanilla good guy. Although worrisome tidbits do surface, such as Aberforth's opinion that Dumbledore is a glory seeker who uses people unconscionably, those insights come too little and too late in the series to really affect the reader's opinion. Allowing Aberforth to get his hooks in right here in Book 1 would set the stage for an edgier, more complex portrait of the headmaster.

The point of view for this scene could be an omniscient third, Dumbledore's, or possibly even Hagrid's. Being in Hagrid's POV might be rather a treat, but Dumbledore is the real mover here, and readers would benefit from seeing not only this scene, but certain scenes later in the series from Dumbledore's POV. As much as his actions, readers desperately need to understand Dumbledore's motivations in order to make sense of who Dumbledore really is.

The Potter series sticks very tightly to Harry's POV, departing it only briefly in a few places. Switching POV more often might offer significant benefits. Not only Dumbledore, but Voldemort could be a point of view character, even in situations where Harry isn't reading Voldemort's mind. Letting readers see what a villain is up to, and why, can make certain events more believable. Certainly, Ron and Hermione both seem like good candidates for POV scenes. Readers would enjoy having a closer connection to them, and the author would have a wider range of scenes to choose from, including more situations where Harry isn't present.

The question of point of view aside, the alternate opening proposed here has its own pros and cons. The pros are that it's more dramatic, it relates more closely to Harry and the main plotline of the series, it viscerally connects us to the death of Harry's parents, it can potentially give cameos to a number of characters who play key roles later in the series, and it sets up a long-range tension in the reader, as we wonder, "When will Harry find out about Dumbledore's role in all this?"

The cons of this opening are that it represents a significant change from the original, and it would introduce a rollercoaster effect for the reader, when the story moves from this other-worldly opening to Harry living a mundane existence with the Dursleys. Pace changes are a good thing, but this sort of dip might be more than is desirable. Moreover, with this approach, we lose the gradual buildup typical of a suspense story, where sinister hints suffice to keep us reading (or so the author hopes) until that first encounter with an actual tentacle. Or, in the case of Book 1, with that first step onto the Hogwarts Express.

Another potential objection to this opening is that it gives away too much information, but this seems a minor quibble. Yes, more information would be given, but nothing ruinous to the reader's suspense later in the series. We would no doubt learn about the Fidelus charm, but not necessarily about who the secret keeper was. We might learn about the Order of the Phoenix, might meet various members of that order, but we don't have to. Moreover, the original opening already introduces us to Dumbledore, tells us about Voldemort, and alerts us that Harry is a wizard. This alternate opening merely introduces that same information more dramatically, and it needn't give away any new information of significance.

The Torments of Vernon Dursley

Book 1 doesn't really take off, the adventure doesn't really begin, until Harry steps onto the Hogwarts Express. Unfortunately, readers must wait until page 80 (in the hardcover edition) for that happy moment, and many of those 80 pages are centered around Vernon Dursley rather than around Harry Potter. Even after Harry becomes the sole POV character, Vernon is too often the *focus* of the story, the one with a driving goal (keep Harry from going to Hogwarts), and the one suffering for his obsession.

While we all like the thought of Uncle Vernon being tormented, the problem is that readers are tormented right along with him. More importantly, this series is supposed to be the Adventures of Harry Potter.

One simple change would help enormously. When Harry's invitation to attend Hogwarts arrives, let it be a singular event, rather than the start of a flood of owls. Right now, Book 1 goes a bit overboard with its, "And the day after that, even more owls arrived." While the onslaught of owls might strike some readers as wonderfully silly, it is ultimately repetitive, fails to advance the plot, and gives us no new insights into Harry's personality.

As an alternative, when the first letter from Hogwarts arrives, let it contain a paragraph to the effect, "On July/August XX, a representative from the school will arrive at your home to show you how to acquire your books and other school supplies." This is a muggle family, after all, and sending a representative to help them out makes perfect sense.

Uncle Vernon's response to the letter would be, "Right. When their bloody representative shows up, we won't be here." Jump-cut to the Dursleys in a cabin on a rock in the Atlantic. The result is a much quicker pace, with the side-benefit of preventing the story from focusing overly much on Vernon Dursley.

If the author prefers a slower pace or wants to put greater emphasis on Harry's life prior to Hagrid's arrival at the cabin, coming up with more Harry-centric material seems the way to go. For example, readers could get some indication of how Harry's childhood has affected him. Does he have phobias? (If Harry shares a single trait with Ron, it might well be fear of spiders.) What neurotic tendencies has he picked up?

Similarly, we would like to think that Harry hasn't just passively accepted his morbid fate, but has found ways to either fight back or at least endure. Perhaps he has a secret comic book collection. Maybe he has an internal fantasy world that he retreats to in times of stress.

Expanding the opening by exploring Harry's fledgling state more deeply would be highly desirable for most readers. Stretching the opening with repetitive pages focused around Vernon Dursley, however, is a poor alternative, because astute readers recognize the material as ancillary, unrewarding of their efforts, and they skip over it.

Though Harry becomes the POV character after Book 1's opening chapter, he doesn't immediately become the protagonist. The textbook definition tells us that a protagonist needs a goal and needs to pursue that goal. Here, Harry is a passive observer of owls delivering letters. While he would like to know what is in the letters, he hatches no plot to accomplish this, has no part in calling down more owls, and is swept along by events outside his control, rather than being an active force.

Here at the beginning of the series, we're willing to accept passivity in Harry. It makes perfect sense as a result of his childhood experiences. But Book 1 hides these submissive tendencies behind a smoke screen of Vernon Dursley's frenetic actions, rather than exploring Harry's passivity, showing it as a result of his abusive upbringing.

Double Dipping

Hagrid's arrival at midnight on the day of Harry's eleventh birthday serves as a bright moment. However, it also misleads the reader, because we believe that the adventure has finally begun. When Harry is forced to return to the Dursley home for another full month after the trip to Diagon Alley, we feel teased, and not in a good way. August with the Dursleys, though covered quickly in the text, is yet another spot where repeat readers are likely to create their own jump-cut. It isn't as if we learn anything new about Harry or the Dursleys during that month. We've been inside the Dursley home, we know what it is like, and we certainly don't need or want to see any more of it.

We can think of several alternate approaches that would avoid teasing the reader. One would be for Hagrid to fetch Harry not on his birthday but on the day before the start of term. Harry could then spend the following evening at The Leaky Cauldron rather than return home.

Another option would be to retain the current timeline but use an authorial jump-cut from Diagon Alley to the train depot. The series seems to have a moral objection to scene breaks and jump-cutting. The result is that readers are occasionally bogged down with the equivalent of shoe tying, hair combing, and teeth brushing. As Hitchcock said, "Fiction is life with the dull parts removed."

In this case, the story could jump-cut from the shopping trip straight to platform nine and three-quarters one month later. Harry silently thanks the stars that the previous, horrible month is finally over, and then bumps into the Weasleys. It isn't intuitive, but readers will likely sympathize more with Harry if we haven't been asked to endure that horrible month right along with him.

Hagrid and the Cottage on a Rock

If the book decides to treat the Dursleys as real human beings rather than children's book villains, we have to wonder if the cottage on a rock in the Atlantic is a good idea. Aunt Petunia, especially, must realize that such a simple ploy isn't going to fool the wizarding world. Instead, what if Aunt Petunia coached Harry to reject the school's representative when whoever it is arrives?

"There are some dodgy people going about," she might say, "trying to convince children that they're wizards and then carting them off to be made into braunschweiger." This seems like both a more realistic and a more insidious approach, one that gives Harry a meaningful role, as readers wonder whether or not Harry will believe Aunt Petunia and turn down Hogwarts.

In a scenario like this, Hagrid seems a poor choice as the sole Hogwarts representative. While we enjoy watching Dudley grow a pig's tail, a more rational part of us also recognizes that such an action is counterproductive: Harry could be permanently evicted from the Dursley household or else exposed to even more severe abuse as a result.

As an alternative, suppose that Dumbledore himself arrives to inform Harry that he is a wizard. This would show how important Harry is, both to the wizarding world in general and more specifically to Dumbledore, and it would signal that Dumbledore intends to take a direct hand in Harry's education. Even if Dumbledore remains seemingly aloof during the first year or two, a few key interventions like this would set the stage for Dumbledore to become Harry's mentor and ultimately his father figure.

This approach would also create a stronger parallel to Dumbledore's first meeting with Tom Riddle, when Riddle was an eleven-year-old orphan, thus emphasizing both the similarities and differences between Harry and Voldemort. Here is Tom Riddle's response to meeting Dumbledore and learning that he is a wizard; and now here is Harry's response to that very same event.

Hagrid could still be the one to take Harry to Diagon Alley, but having Hagrid knocking down doors and cursing Dudley pales in comparison to how Dumbledore might respond when he discovers Harry's emotional and psychological state. Dumbledore's more potent threat, as well as his superior diplomatic skills, would not only guarantee that Harry goes off to school, but would also ensure that Harry receives better treatment when he stays with the Dursleys in future.

At the beginning of Book 6, *Half-Blood Prince*, Dumbledore puts in an appearance at the Dursley home and has a few harsh words for them. That visit and conversation, modified to fit the situation, might serve more purpose if moved here, to Book 1.

Would Dumbledore successfully convince the Dursleys to treat Harry better the following summer? Certainly. In fact, that change is not only desirable, but virtually required. First, it will help Book 2 avoid starting off with Harry in the exact same condition as at the start of Book 1: the pathetic, downtrodden orphan child.

Second, given the events at the end of Book 1, where Harry kills Professor Quirrell, returning Harry to an abusive environment would be a recipe for disaster. Readers expect that not only would Harry's situation have changed, so would *he*. In which case, having the Dursleys walk on eggshells around Harry would no longer strike the reader as silly. The Dursleys have every reason to tiptoe around this kid, because he could very easily lash out at them, something that finally happens at the beginning of Book 3, *Prisoner of Azkaban*.

Gringotts and the Philosopher's Stone

A few aspects of the trip to Gringotts don't quite add up. First, there isn't a clear reason for moving the Philosopher's Stone at this time, which makes the move look suspiciously convenient.

Perhaps an attempted theft of the Stone could occur earlier in the summer. Nicolas Flamel's home might be ransacked by former death eaters, or the attempt to rob Gringotts could simply be moved forward. In any event, it would be nice to have some motive for suddenly moving the Stone. After all, if Dumbledore fears that Voldemort might go after the Stone, why wait ten years before doing something about it?

Second, the piles of money in Harry's vault suggest that his parents were rich, but we get no indication as to where this money came from. Lily and James were a young married couple, caught up in the middle of a war, fighting for a lost cause, and on the run half the time.

If James comes from wealthy stock, fine, but this is a perfect time for Harry to pump Hagrid for that sort of information, either when Harry sees the piles of money or else sees the balance in his account. Such a conversation would do more than give backstory, it would show Harry actively trying to learn more about his parents, rather than passively waiting for information to be dribbled out to him. As he peppers Hagrid with questions, Harry would eventually be told that he needs to ask Dumbledore some of them, thus leading to another interaction between Harry and the headmaster during Harry's first year at Hogwarts.

A yearning to find out about his parents would be a perfect early goal for our hero. Currently, Harry is without any such goal but is merely a character pushed about by events outside his control.

Third, the goblins at Gringotts put each customer's money in separate vaults. While a minor point, this does reflect poorly on goblins, as banks make money by loaning it out at interest. Since we get to visit a storage vault for the Philosopher's Stone itself, we wouldn't lose anything if Harry withdrew money in a more rational way, such as by providing a thumb print, a drop of blood, or undergoing some sort of magical identity check. This would also remove the need for Hagrid to mysteriously have Harry's bank key in his possession, and for such a key to represent ownership of a vault.

Harry and Snape

In Part 1, we talked about how Snape's behavior doesn't mesh with what we learn of him later in the series. It seems that the change to Snape here in *Philosopher's Stone* would be relatively minor. It would be Harry's interpretation of Snape more than what Snape does or says, that makes Snape appear inherently hateful, mean, or out to get Harry.

While we can accept Snape leaning more on Harry than he does on other students, if his behavior crosses over from unsympathetic to abusive, Snape ceases to be a believable character. Snape's early reference to Harry as a celebrity is perfect in this sense, because it serves as a kind of reverse psychology. Here is Harry, already being treated oddly by students who see him as some kind of idol. That sort of thing can cause jealousy (as it does), but can also kill with kindness, making Harry seem unapproachable or an object of worship.

So when Snape refers to Harry as the resident celebrity, Snape can actually be trying to create sympathy for Harry in those students who tend toward jealousy, while giving others a reason for approaching Harry (to take his side against Snape's "abuse"). Snape's cutting Harry down also helps students see Harry as a person rather than as this mythic figure they've heard about.

Of course Harry won't see it that way, but that is perfectly understandable, especially given Harry's upbringing. This is a lesson he could learn, and his improved understanding of human nature (of Snape in particular) could then be part of Harry's character change as a result of the events of the book.

Quirrell

The central mystery of Book 1 revolves around Professor

Quirrell and his quest to obtain the Philosopher's Stone, with Professor Snape serving as the red herring. The Big Three investigate the mystery, gradually closing in on the truth, until finally we get the surprise revelation. This is a powerful and popular story structure, but while the Potter series does a good job of keeping the reader guessing, it accomplishes its goal by having key characters behaving irrationally, and by having events happen without sufficient justification. As a result, the final "aha" moment is diminished by the reader's recognition that the game was rigged.

Garlic notwithstanding, having Voldemort riding around on Quirrell's head puts the Dark Lord right under Dumbledore's nose for nine months. Even if Dumbledore is to be made less omniscient, which seems a wise move, this arrangement makes the headmaster (and the entire staff) seem rather dense.

Meanwhile, for Voldemort to expose himself simultaneously to both Dumbledore and Harry Potter, at a time when Voldemort is at his most vulnerable, is hard to comprehend. Because of the Chosen One prophecy and the events at Godric's Hollow, Voldemort must surely fear Harry as the agent of his ultimate destruction, even as he fears Dumbledore for various other reasons. (In fact, shouldn't *Harry* be "the only one he ever feared?" Giving this role to Dumbledore again robs Harry of his proper place as protagonist. Harry is the one with the power to destroy Voldemort, after all, and death is the thing that terrifies Voldemort above all else.)

One possible alternative would be for Quirrell to have an accomplice, another death eater, say, who plays host to Voldemort for most of the year while staying at the Hogs Head or some other off-campus location. The second death eater could be caught and sent to Azkaban near the end of the book or could die as a result of the long possession, and only then would Quirrell become host to Voldemort as a last-ditch effort to obtain the Stone.

Another possibility would be for Voldemort to spend most

of Book 1 as a disembodied spirit living in the Forbidden Forest, surviving off unicorn blood. Though lingering close to Hogwarts, Voldemort wouldn't actually be inside the castle itself: sitting down to dinner with Dumbledore, brushing shoulders with the suspected traitor Snape, and standing at the front of a class where Voldemort's nemesis, Harry Potter, is one of the students. Voldemort would again switch to riding Quirrell only at the very last moment, tired of waiting for Quirrell to go after the Stone on his own.

Whether Quirrell is possessed or not, his attempt to knock Harry off his broom at the first Quidditch game seems illogical. Surely the school is smart enough to have one teacher or another assigned as a safety net, ready to cast Arresto Momentum if someone gets knocked off their broom. Students falling to their deaths would surely get Quidditch banned, if wizarding parents have any concern for their children at all. But even without that, Quirrell's attack suggests that Voldemort is willing to risk discovery prior to obtaining the Stone, which is pretty hard to swallow.

What if this attack is an attempt by Quirrell to draw attention to himself? It could mean that Quirrell is battling the Imperius curse he's under, or if not under Imperius, that he now remembers what a pain Voldemort can be and suddenly isn't so keen on Voldemort coming back. Quirrell being a reluctant supporter of Voldemort has the advantage of making him no longer a purely evil character. Thus, when Harry kills Quirrell at the end of the book, that act takes on additional significance, an added weight of guilt for Harry to bear.

However, Quirrell's attack *still* has problems. First, it seems to call for Snape to cover for Quirrell, something that doesn't add up given Snape's role as Dumbledore's lieutenant. Second, it requires that Dumbledore ignore the attack. If someone attacked Harry in this fashion, it seems that Dumbledore would do everything in his power to track down the culprit. A reasonable first step would be to perform Prior Incantato on the wands of likely suspects to see which spells they had cast recently. Given that Quirrell is a new addition to the staff, he would be in line for just such a "probable cause" search.

If Quirrell's attack on Harry remains in the book, readers would at least like to have Dumbledore respond to that attack. Quirrell could escape detection by one means or another, but readers don't like to see Dumbledore twiddling his thumbs or looking the other way when Harry's life is threatened.

Troll in the Word Processor

One day during a classroom lesson, Hermione demonstrates the proper casting of a levitation spell, annoying Ron in the process. Ron later makes fun of Hermione, she overhears, and goes to one of the girls' bathrooms to cry. At supper that same day, Professor Quirrell runs into the great hall to announce that a troll is loose in the dungeon. Dumbledore orders all students to return to their dorms while the staff go and tackle the troll. In the ensuing confusion, Harry and Ron slip off to inform Hermione who, even though it seems hours have passed, is still in the bathroom crying. Coincidentally, the troll wanders into this very bathroom.

While the troll encounter is certainly an energetic moment in the book, it fails to convince. Given all the magical protections on Hogwarts, we have to wonder exactly how Quirrell managed to get a troll into the castle to start with. Meanwhile, that the troll would wander through the labyrinthine halls of Hogwarts into exactly Hermione's bathroom is a stretch in any universe. And finally, when the dust settles in the wrecked bathroom, why can't Dumbledore or Snape use Legilimens on the awakened beast (or speak Trollish to it), to find out who summoned it?

But even ignoring these caveats, with all the students sitting in the great hall, Dumbledore's best move is to have them continue dining while Snape and Hagrid (for instance) go handle the troll. Sending hundreds of students through the halls is bound to create confusion (as it does), and let us not forget that one fourth of those students, Slytherin House, have their common room *in* the dungeons. Thus, this action on Dumbledore's part makes him look incompetent.

If shouting "troll" is an attempt by Quirrell to draw attention to himself — a sign that he's fighting the Imperius curse or is otherwise disaffected with Voldemort — it raises a serious question: why *doesn't* Dumbledore become suspicious? We expect better from our headmaster, and his failure to put two and two together reflects poorly on him, especially when combined with Quirrell's eccentric behavior and the attack on Harry at the first Quidditch game.

While some readers will eagerly overlook these problems in order to keep the troll encounter, let us consider an approach that nevertheless avoids it. To do so, we must reproduce a number of important effects that the troll sets in motion.

(a) The troll allows Quirrell to sneak off to try and find the Stone. However, Quirrell's ham-handed ploy is ill-conceived and draws suspicion from Snape, if not from Dumbledore as well. Why can't Quirrell wait until he's the night hall monitor and slip into Fluffy's room when everyone else is asleep?

(b) Professor Snape, suspicious of Quirrell, gets bitten when he tracks Quirrell to the trap door that Fluffy is guarding. Since Snape's getting bitten happens off-screen, it can happen at any time. The Big Three could learn of Snape's injury when a substitute teacher takes over Snape's potions class one day — Snape is in the hospital having part of his leg re-grown.

(c) The troll encounter leads to the formation of the Big Three. While trial by troll is a wonderful mechanism for cementing friendships, in this case it requires a galaxy-sized coincidence and turns Dumbledore into an ultra-maroon (as Bugs Bunny would say).

What if, instead, Harry decides that he and Ron have to apologize to Hermione, thus demonstrating that he's a more empathic character than Ron? Getting Ron to apologize might require leaning on him a bit, but this would let us see Harry's latent leadership abilities and his courage in standing up not just to enemies but to friends.

While this path is more touchy-feely than the troll encounter, it makes Harry an active character, rather than merely a reactive one. This sequence would also allow deeper insight into Hermione's personality, as she could explain why a chance comment impacted her so much. (She might have had muggle friends who abandoned their friendship when Hermione started talking about being a witch, for example.) The result is a more believable sequence of events and a better understanding of the Big Three. Together, these benefits seem to justify the loss of one troll.

Showdown

Harry survives the final showdown with Quirrell by the miracle of Mother's Love. Readers can tolerate this so long as it doesn't signal a trend. We're in Book 1 after all, and Harry's lack of ability and magical skill here will serve as a good contrast to his final form.

However, having Harry rendered unconscious by the struggle doesn't seem like a good solution. If the author doesn't want Harry burdened with so much guilt, then consider letting Dumbledore erase Harry's memory of the event. This would make Dumbledore (rather than Ms. Rowling's word processor) responsible for Harry's fuzziness.

Dumbledore

In various places, people make comments to the effect that "Dumbledore knows everything that goes on around here," with the implication that he would surely step in if things really turned dangerous. To allow such loose talk robs climactic moments, such as those here at the end of Book 1, of their anxiety. The reader is left to wonder, "Is Harry really in danger or isn't he?" That question doesn't seem like something an author would want to encourage. Does this mean that

Dumbledore needs to be weakened? Most likely, yes.

Dumbledore's ability to get instantly from one place to another (which we see late in the series) conflicts with his rather lumbering speed in *Philosopher's Stone*. It would be nice if we had some explanation as to why it takes Dumbledore so long to return to Hogwarts when things are spinning out of control. One possibility is that when asked where Dumbledore is, McGonagall might not be entirely sure. Is he consulting with Fudge, attending a boondoggle for the International Confederation of Mugwumps, or off on some mysterious errand? So hard to tell with that man....

Character Change

It would be nice to see some sort of change in each of the main child characters in each book. Hermione's change came earlier in Book 1, when she learned to be not quite so bossy and prissy. It isn't clear what sort of change Ron might undergo here, though his chess victory, opening the way for Harry to reach the Philosopher's Stone, might help Ron overcome some of his insecurity.

For Harry, Book 1 offers the opportunity both for a transient change as well as a more lasting one. In his reaction to Quirrell's death, Harry's guilt might lead him to adopt a pacifist philosophy. "I don't ever want to kill anyone again." His destruction of the diary Horcrux in Book 2 might then make him question his resolution and/or his self-discipline. Then by the end of Book 3, Harry could decide that he's willing to kill to protect those he loves, perhaps even willing to kill to avenge those taken from him. Certainly, by that point in the series, we'd like to see Harry actively yearning for the chance to kill Voldemort once and for all.

As for a long-term change, Harry could gain insight into human nature. Harry's misjudgment of Quirrell and Snape, as well as the eye-opening monstrosity of Voldemort, would all play into this. Changing Harry's attitude toward Professor

Snape would be a wonderful way to signal that Harry has matured.

Book 1's final conversation between Dumbledore and Harry in the hospital wing is primarily expositional, aimed at tying up loose ends and making sense of what has happened. It goes on a bit long and misses an opportunity for Harry to demonstrate guilt over Quirrell.

One way to break up and enliven that scene would be to have Professor Snape show up, either with Dumbledore or alone. This would give Snape a chance to show that he doesn't hate Harry, while it would give Harry a chance to show that he now understands this. Instead of Dumbledore answering Quirrell's accusations — that Snape hates Harry because Snape hated James Potter — Snape would have a chance to answer the charges himself. And while Dumbledore might say things to cheer Harry up and get him over feeling guilty, what if Snape manages to get the message through most effectively? From Harry's point of view, Dumbledore is just being nice, but Snape wouldn't say something encouraging unless he actually meant it....

The Hidden Harry

Philosopher's Stone doesn't pay much attention to Harry's psychological makeup. While we don't want the book to become an introspective character analysis, the current approach seems too close to the opposite extreme. Harry lacks both inner drive and inner demons, is unaffected even by the most horrific events, and seems altogether unexceptional. Thus, it seems fair to say that Book 1 would benefit from paying more attention to Harry's personality.

Let's take a closer look at Harry as we find him in Book 1. He's spent nearly all his life with the Dursleys, where he's been neglected, forced to sleep in a small closet crawling with spiders, tormented by Dudley, treated as unwanted, and generally abused emotionally, if not physically.

After ten years of this, what kind of person is he? From what we see in Book 1, he's lackluster at school. He seems to be something of a loner used to living without friends. Perhaps he's had friends along the way, but if so, they were all driven away by one or another of the Dursleys.

Harry seems to have a dispassionate, objective view of the Dursleys, seeing them as nasty, petty people who he doesn't expect to change, but he shows no signs of acting out his rage toward them, nor does he make any effort to earn their affection. Has he made attempts in the past, all of which were laughed at or otherwise turned against him, and so he gave up trying? The series gives us no clues on this.

Harry doesn't appear to have any dreams of getting away from the Dursleys, never mind any concrete plans to in fact run away. Still, he isn't beat down. Rather, he's strangely unaffected by it all, as if he merely watched someone else experiencing ten years of emotional neglect and abuse.

What would psychologists call this? Lack of affect? Dissociation? Surely, any child raised in this environment is going to have psychological problems, most likely serious ones, and those problems aren't going to suddenly vanish once the proximate cause is removed. Harry would have a number of harmful beliefs: that he's worthless, that nothing he does is ever good enough so there's no point trying, that those in authority are not to be trusted, that trying to make friends just leads to painful disappointment, and so forth.

None of this is apparent in Harry. *Philosopher's Stone* falls prey to a mistake that plagues the entire series; it creates a situation and then trivializes it. The book invents an abusive environment for Harry, makes him live there through his most crucial formative years, and then has him walk away absolutely unaffected. Several times during the series, Dumbledore comments on how amazing this is. It isn't amazing, it's false, shallow, and a slap in the face to anyone who has lived through an abusive or neglectful childhood.

As with any human, we expect Harry's childhood to affect

his attitudes, beliefs, and behavior. Will he be stuck in place, forever burdened by misconceptions and the like? We hope not. But we suspect there would be chains on him, strange contact lenses on his eyes that distort what he sees. And getting rid of those chains, removing those lenses, would require real effort and involve real pain.

An abused orphan who moves in with a foster family doesn't jump up and down and say, "Gosh, this is great." They watch and wait. When the abuse doesn't start in a timely fashion, they grow uncomfortable. They fear they might start to like these people, which will only make it worse when something finally does happen. So they help the process along. A tantrum, say. Still nothing bad has happened? Hmm. What about those azaleas? The lady is always out there taking care of them. That was the first thing she pointed out upon our arrival. Ah, an axe. Chop, chop.

The misbehavior might result in a self-fulfilling prophecy or it might not. But however it turns out, the child's behavior reflects a particular worldview, a level of cynicism and distrust, a lack of confidence in people and, ultimately, in themselves.

This is all missing in Harry. When Hagrid shows up at the cottage, Harry is at first doubtful. This is both a reasonable and a stock response. It feels mild. There's no sense of real fear in Harry that his internal fantasy world is getting out of control. No sense of, "I am *not* going to let these jerks drive me totally insane."

As readers, we don't want Harry to be slow on the uptake or a doubting Thomas. While Harry's response to Hagrid's arrival might benefit from a bit more intensity, it is Harry's attitudes and behavior for the rest of the school year that we're most interesting in. Harry's approach to learning magic? He merely goes through the motions. His attitude toward Ron and Hermione? He accepts them as friends as if it were just another day.

During the trip to Diagon Alley with Hagrid, there is little in the way of conflict. It's a shopping trip, though admittedly in an unusual place. What if the story injected a bit of tension by having Harry work on Hagrid during that trip?

"Hagrid, what happens after I get all my school things?"

"You go back to the Dursleys for a month."

"Well, you know, Hagrid, after you gave Dudley a tail, I'm kind of afraid of what they might do to me. Can't I come stay with you for a month instead? I don't need much to eat. I could sleep on the floor. I can do all kinds of chores."

When Hagrid demurs, Harry wraps himself around one of Hagrid's legs and refuses to let go. Under the circumstances, wouldn't *you*? But currently, Harry demonstrates no cunning or manipulative tendencies toward Hagrid, and no insight such as, "The Leaky Cauldron is an inn, there are places to eat in Diagon Alley, and I have money. I don't have to go back to the Dursleys ever again."

Would Harry take right away to Ron and Hermione? Might he be something of an unreliable friend, so used to having friendships taken away from him for one reason or another that he's afraid to commit? Would he seem strangely aloof? Or possibly the reverse: clingy?

What if Harry psyched himself out so much that he was incapable of casting a spell for the first few months of school? We know from watching Tonks in Book 6, *Half-Blood Prince*, that emotional stress can affect your ability to cast spells. Talk about stress! Every day that goes by, Harry expects someone to tell him there's been a terrible mistake, they got him confused with someone else. Either that, or they'll decide he's a squib. Harry's insecurity keeps him from being able to cast spells, his inability to cast spells increases his insecurity, and Harry finds himself in a vicious cycle. With every passing day, the threat of falling in love with Hogwarts grows. In response to the mounting pressure, Harry starts to act out. He skips classes and becomes a disruptive student. Subconsciously he wants to get thrown out sooner rather than later. Get the pain *over* with.

At this point, suppose Harry gets called into Professor

McGonagall's office for a talking to. Unwittingly, McGonagall uses the threat of expelling Harry to try and wake him up, but this merely pushes Harry into some more extreme act, such as running off into the Forbidden Forest, determined that, even if he's to be expelled, he won't go back to the Dursleys. Maybe this is when Harry spots Voldemort drinking unicorn blood. After all, taking a group of first years into the Forbidden Forest as punishment is a bit out of character for Hogwarts, especially when something dangerous is on the prowl near the school grounds.

In any event, allowing Harry to be a real person, allowing his childhood to affect his attitudes and behavior, would make for a more purposeful first half of Book 1. Rather than simply walking us through various classes and injecting false tension into the story via Malfoy and Snape, there would be real tension, real conflict, all directly resulting from Harry's personality and situation, rather than from a canned, arbitrary sequence of events.

Back to the Dursleys

At the end of the school year, Dumbledore blithely sends Harry back to the Dursleys. This is unthinkable unless his goal is to destroy the kid. Harry will be safe there? Safe in what sense? Emotional and psychological scars take longer to heal than physical ones. Surely Dumbledore is smart enough to recognize as much.

Having Harry return home for the start of Books 2 and 3 would certainly reduce the extent of changes needed for those volumes. Therefore, we want a way to rationalize Dumbledore's insistence that Harry return to the Dursleys —.a better rationale than simply because of the magical contract.

One question to consider, in this light, is whether the Dursleys should be as sick as they are currently. The closet under the stairs, for example, is one bit of silliness that wouldn't seem silly to a child. Better if Harry slept in a bedroom, even if it's a small one.

More significantly, why not give Harry an emotional outlet with Aunt Petunia? For example, if Harry works hard and does all his chores, Aunt Petunia is pleased. Maybe she isn't exactly a cuddly mother figure, but Harry can at least get some approval from her, some glancing affection. Aunt Petunia would say, "That's the ticket. Hard work. No cheating! No being lazy! Here, have some cookies." When Aunt Petunia says, "No cheating," she really means, "No using magic." But of course, Harry wouldn't understand that until years later.

This change in Aunt Petunia would allow Harry to emerge from the Dursley home more or less intact. Most likely he would still be messed up, would still have issues, but at least he wouldn't be psycho-killer material. In addition, a less-abusive environment would make Dumbledore's sending Harry back to the Dursleys a more reasonable decision.

This change would also allow Aunt Petunia to become a deeper character, protecting Harry from the worst of Vernon and Dudley's abuse, though she's determined to sweat the magic out of him. As the origin of Harry's work ethic, Aunt Petunia could even play a part in his ultimate success — a nice counterintuitive twist.

These are all just possibilities, merely thinking out loud. But what we want to show is that there are veins of emotion in the Potter series that haven't been tapped. Book 1 takes shortcuts, leaving us with the shallow image of a generic helpless orphan rather than a deeper, truer portrait of that particular orphan, Harry Potter.

Who is Harry, really? This is a big question for the entire series, but how he starts off is the realm of Book 1. Giving Harry a real personality is dangerous, because he might just chop up some of the author's prized azaleas. But at least then we would all know that Harry is more than a fuzzy image in the author's mind, but a real, comprehensible human being, with his own goals and beliefs.

Tearing Harry Down

In Book 5, *Order of the Phoenix*, Harry displays classic passive-aggressive behavior. He's mad at Dumbledore for ignoring him, but he takes no action to address the problem. Rather than demonstrating initiative and backbone by confronting Dumbledore straightaway, Harry internalizes his anger. He stews over it, lets it fester. In effect, Harry lies in wait until something happens (in this case, the death of Sirius) that Harry can use as an excuse to explode in Dumbledore's face. The result isn't a positive confrontation, but a pathetic diatribe by Harry. "You ignored me and that made me mad." Harry finally reveals this to Dumbledore, but the revelation comes so late as to be useless as far as Dumbledore fixing anything.

For Harry to suddenly become passive-aggressive in Book 5 is an example of the series gradually tearing Harry down, making him regress rather than evolve. If there is a time for tearing Harry down — making him seem immature, passive-aggressive, lacking in understanding of human nature, and so forth — surely it's here in Book 1.

Imagine, for example, that Ron agrees to meet Harry following a Quidditch practice one day, but Ron forgets. He gets immersed in a chess game with Neville, say. Harry's response is to stew about this slight while acting distant and cold toward Ron. When Ron asks Harry what's wrong, Harry replies, "If you don't know, then I'm not going to tell you," a classic passive-aggressive response, an indication of an immature view of the world.

Ron finally wheedles Harry into revealing the cause of his displeasure. Ron responds with, "I'm a git. I'm a dolt. I'm sorry I forgot, okay? But don't give me the silent treatment. If I do something stupid, come and get in my face about it."

This kind of interaction between Ron and Harry would accomplish quite a few things. First, it shows that Harry doesn't quite know how to handle having friends. He doesn't know how to act, doesn't know how things are supposed to work. Second, it deepens Ron's character and connects him to his own upbringing. Ron comes from a large, closely-knit family. His mother's approach to dealing with misbehavior is to let the offending party have it. If Mrs. Weasley isn't shouting at you, then you aren't in trouble. It's a simple system that allows everyone to go about their business without feeling they have to walk on eggshells all the time, constantly trying to guess what the people around them want.

Taking this view, Ron's insensitivity becomes instead merely a thick skin. Ron grew up in a small house with a bunch of rambunctious siblings and an Irish mother. If you're upset with him, you have to let him know directly, otherwise he simply isn't going to notice.

In addition, Ron understands close relationships. It makes sense that, in terms of dealing with other people, Ron would be more mature and wiser than Harry. (He can be both knowledgeable and insensitive, after all.) If Harry's people-skills surpass Ron's later in the series, that would serve as a testament not to how Ron has shrunk, but to how Harry has grown. Some of Harry's growth would, in fact, come from his best friend: Ron chiding Harry when he misbehaves, patiently explaining to Harry how to act in certain social situations, and serving as an example of a basically well-adjusted kid from a loving home.

Similar interactions between Harry and Hermione would also make sense. Together Ron and Hermione might be the main cause of Harry overcoming his hypothetical mental block with regard to spell work. But in any case, these sorts of interactions would create deeper portraits of each of the Big Three.

Hermione

As we mentioned earlier, Hermione's emotional breakdown just prior to the troll scene is never fully explored by the book.

This seems triply unfortunate. Examining Hermione's emotional fragility would give us a better understanding of her, it would help us understand what it's like for a muggle (a more normal muggle than Harry, that is) to suddenly discover she's a witch, and it would create an important point of connection between Hermione and Harry.

While Hermione doesn't come across as a social butterfly, letting her have one close friend back in the muggle world would illuminate her emotional state. It seems strange that so many children adjust to boarding school without experiencing homesickness, feelings of abandonment, and so forth. In the case of someone like Hermione, the sudden discontinuity is an even larger one. Not only is she physically separated from her family, now she's separated from them by identity. Her parents' quiet acceptance that Hermione is a witch is admirable, but it might be well to contrast their open-mindedness with how Hermione's best friend (possibly her only muggle friend) has severed contact with her.

Imagine that Hermione's "welcome to Hogwarts" letter warns her to keep her magical identity secret. She violates this fundamental wizard rule, sure that her best friend will understand and will be as excited about the development as Hermione is. Perhaps Hermione's friend at first just thinks Hermione is playing a prank or has become caught up in some childish daydream, so Hermione teaches herself a simple spell and performs it for her friend, in order to prove she's in earnest. Unfortunately, not only does this turn her friend against her, but her friend's parents call the police, child services, or some such. In response, the Memory Reversal Squad has to come out to set things straight, and Hermione receives a reprimand for underage use of magic.

Whatever the exact sequence of events, Hermione's backstory seems worthy of further exploration as a means of deepening her character and also examining the difficulties of being a mudblood. Not only do pure-bloods look down on Hermione, much of muggle society would see her as a witch in the pejorative sense of the term: an agent of the devil. Ignorance and superstition are alive and well in the muggle world, as Ms. Rowling surely knows from personal experience. Here's an opportunity to fold that real-world quality into the story.

Hermione's muggle background also gives her a connection to Harry that most other students at Hogwarts, including Ron, don't share. Hermione and Harry both understand the shock of suddenly discovering they aren't normal. Harry can also empathize with Hermione's sense of loss. While Hermione's parents aren't dead, they are at least no longer available on a day-to-day basis, and it seems clear that Hermione is close to them. Meanwhile, Hermione's hypothetical best friend *is* permanently lost.

The movie adds a nice touch here, having Hermione find James Potter's Quidditch trophy and show it to Harry. If Harry is actively searching for information about his ancestry (setting up a similarity between Harry and Voldemort that Dumbledore might find worrisome), Hermione could help Harry via research in the library. She could locate pictures of his parents (and perhaps earlier generations) in old yearbooks, articles about them in old *Daily Prophet*s, and so forth. This would serve as yet another means of bringing Harry and Hermione together as friends.

Suspense, Plot, and Audience

How would all of these suggestions affect the structure of Book 1? Moving Voldemort off of Quirrell until late in the story would remove a source of suspense. Eliminating the troll attack would eliminate an energetic, exciting scene. Also, as a combined result of the suggested changes, Snape might seem a less-obvious villain to the reader, thus diminishing his value as a red herring.

However, these losses would be counter-balanced by the suspense that is gained as a result of Harry being a more believable, more complex character. The key question for Book 1 would become, "Will Harry adapt to this new environment, or will his phobias and neuroses, his insecurity and immaturity, cause him to self-destruct?"

The Philosopher's Stone and Voldemort's attack would then serve not as the core conflict of the book, but as a heightening of this other conflict. Just when Harry seems to be adjusting to being a wizard and having friends, he's nearly killed by Lord Voldemort. The reader then wonders, is this horrible event going to send Harry over the edge, make him lose it entirely? Rather than a discontinuous event, Harry's fight with Quirrell and Voldemort becomes part of the overarching concern: can Harry make it through Book 1 with his humanity and his sanity intact?

The mystery of *Philosopher's Stone*, even in the current version, really only impacts the last third or so of the book. As such, the introduction of this character-based conundrum actually increases the overall tension, and does so without requiring that both Lord Voldemort and Albus Dumbledore behave irrationally.

The contrived troll scene would be made up for — if not in special effects value, at least in intensity and reader involvement — by Harry's nearly being expelled and his running off into the Forbidden Forest alone, where he discovers that there is, indeed, some sort of monster loose there. A monster worse than is normal even for that place.

In this context, the game Dumbledore plays with the Mirror of Erised also takes on greater significance, as Dumbledore could be trying to get Harry straightened out, perhaps pull him back from the brink of self-destruction. (For Harry to be actively contemplating suicide at this point seems entirely reasonable. At a minimum, it could be something that Dumbledore fears.)

In addition to the Erised interlude, Dumbledore would surely have at least one major conversation with Harry regarding Harry's misbehavior and/or his inability to do any sort of magic. This would keep Dumbledore from seeming so aloof and distant, would demonstrate how important Harry is to Dumbledore, and would offer an opportunity for Dumbledore to share some of his own backstory. Not as a gratuitous information dump, but as Dumbledore's way of trying to connect with Harry, trying to pierce the layers of distrust and confusion that make Harry difficult to communicate with.

The result of these changes might be a book that no longer works for younger readers. It is hard to say. But the result would certainly be more honest and more sensitive to both the resilience and fragility of the human spirit. Existing themes such as the importance of friendship and the power of love would be intensified and made to resonate more vigorously. Overall, Book 1 would be elevated into the next sphere of greatness, regardless of who its target audience turns out to be.

Chapter 2:
Chamber of Secrets

We've already covered, in Part 1, the deus ex machina nature of the ending of *Chamber of Secrets*. To summarize, our recommendations were that the escape via automobile from the giant spiders be earned, probably by Ron making friends with the car and keeping it in repair during the preceding months; that the escape from Lockhart not be a lucky accident but the result of quick thinking or quick spell work on someone's part, probably Harry's; and that prior to going down into the Chamber, Harry would grab the Sorting Hat from Dumbledore's office and at least say something to Fawkes about what is happening.

Literary Purpose

The main plotline in Book 2 revolves around the mysterious attacks taking place at Hogwarts. While the Big Three do actively pursue the mystery, their main efforts (creating the polyjuice potion and going to see Aragog) come in the last third of the book. Hermione actively seeks out information about the Chamber of Secrets by trying to hunt down a copy of *Hogwarts: A History* and by asking Professor Binns about the Chamber. But other examples of active sleuthing are few and far between.

For starters, it would be nice if Hermione didn't give up so easily on finding *Hogwarts: A History*. She could, for example, ask the school librarian for the names of students who have the book checked out and then borrow the book from one of them just long enough to read the applicable section. Alternatively, she could loft an owl to her parents and ask them to send her copy along. This might give Hermione a chance at being the POV character, but would certainly demonstrate that at least one person around here has a goal and a willingness to pursue that goal, letting nothing get in her way.

Other clues to what is happening at Hogwarts do show up, but they're accidental. Harry is a parselmouth, able to speak to snakes, which explains why he can hear the strange voices in the walls. Unfortunately, Harry doesn't pursue either the voices or the parselmouth ability, not even so far as to obtain a pet snake so he can practice conversing with it. Here is another skill for Harry (and so far he doesn't have many), yet he ignores it. Given that so many wizards view parselmouth as an inherently evil talent, it seems doubly disappointing that this should become yet another of Harry's "now you see them, now you don't" abilities, obviously a convenience for the current volume with no lasting impact on Harry himself.

Harry also acquires Riddle's diary, writes in it, goes on a Pensieve-like journey into its pages, and gathers some interesting clues that point to Hagrid. Harry's active pursuit of the mystery begins here. However, his obtaining the diary is no more than a happy coincidence, and one that occurs rather late in *Chamber of Secrets*. A more active and more believable approach would be to have Hermione's research efforts uncover the connection between Hagrid and the first opening of the Chamber.

But the main thing missing in Book 2 is a goal that will drive Harry for the first half of the school year (and the first half to two-thirds of the book). Having Harry's goal in Book 2 be the destruction of Voldemort seems premature. Instead, what if Harry applied himself to perfecting his spell casting? He might have been blocked from doing this while at the Dursleys, but no more. Rather than lounging around the fireplace with

Ron, why not let Harry be just as driven to succeed as Hermione? She would continue as the bookworm and paper-writer extraordinaire, but when it comes to practical application, Harry would shine — not just in moments when the plot requires it, but as an extension of who he is.

Ron, meanwhile, might be preoccupied with finding and then fixing up his father's automobile. As with Hermione, letting Ron be the POV character for a few scenes would be a welcome treat for most readers. He needn't be merely a tagalong, but could develop into a character with goals of his own.

These changes not only help to deepen the Big Three, they inject additional literary purpose into the early part of Book 2.

Scene Analysis

Let's look at the general flow of scenes for the first half of *Chamber of Secrets*, and the purpose they serve:

Harry at the Dursleys

The Dursleys are mean, and Harry is a helpless victim.

This is a repetition of Book 1. No substantial changes are apparent in Harry or the Dursleys, and Harry is almost entirely a passive entity — poor, sad, and abused by the world, but also motiveless, goalless, and ineffectual. If the purpose here is to give readers deeper insight into Harry, it certainly isn't the Harry we were promised.

Harry at the Weasleys

We get insight into the characters of the various Weasleys, learn how to de-gnome a garden, find out that traveling by flue powder leaves something to be desired, observe various objects in Borgin and Burkes' shop (objects that are important to Book 6, *Half-Blood Prince*, but don't have much significance here), see how the diary made its way into Ginny's possession, and find out that Lockhart is a git.

While this is quite a lot, it also occupies two full chapters in the book, chapters where Harry is effectively a passive observer, a camera showing us what it is like to live with a wizarding family. Given that he's now in a house where magic is allowed, at least let him take advantage of the situation and practice his wand work — even if it gets him in trouble with Mrs. Weasley. What a nice touch, Harry risking (and earning) Mrs. Weasley's wrath in order to pursue his goal!

One tendency that shows up here is that readers are expected to dig clues out of long stretches of prose that serve little other purpose. Hiding clues as a reward for close reading seems fair enough. Creating passages just to hide a clue there-in? Not so much. In particular, the scene in Borgin and Burkes feels beside the point. Though we see the ruby necklace and the teleportation cabinet again in Book 6, that doesn't repay our efforts here.

For different reasons, the de-gnoming scene also seems of questionable value. If Harry used magic to accomplish the de-gnoming, especially if he got into trouble for it: that would make the scene something more than just a silly, but ultimately pointless, diversion. Similarly, flue powder is a clever gadget, but it leaves Harry as a passive observer in Borgin and Burkes, an observer of a scene that has little connection to the current story.

Similarly, the trip to Diagon Alley becomes a travelogue. Aside from the blow up at the book shop, there is a general lack of conflict in the trip.

Rather than (sigh) accidentally land in Nocturne Alley, what if Harry instead took a side-trip there on his own — even though Mrs. Weasley has explicitly forbidden any of the children from going there? To see Harry be uncooperative, to have him demonstrate willfulness: that would be a good thing, so long as it's an indication of who Harry is and where he is headed. On the other hand, if this side-trip is simply an excuse for Harry to witness an incident that is of little importance to the current story, then including such a scene seems like a bad idea.

Harry and Ron Take the Car

At platform nine and three quarters, as everyone else boards the Hogwarts Express, Ron and Harry are prevented from getting through the barrier. Subsequently, they decide to drive the Weasley car to Hogwarts. Unfortunately, their decision forces them out of character. They only need wait another thirty seconds before Mr. and Mrs. Weasley reappear. For Ron and Harry to reject the short wait and jump straight to driving the Weasley car all the way to Hogwarts (neither of them entirely sure where Hogwarts is, even) makes them seem more like Fred and George or, worse, like Crabbe and Goyle.

Providing additional motivation for Ron and Harry would make this sequence easier to swallow. For example, what if Fred and George have been taking the mickey out of Ron over the summer, calling him a good little boy who always follows the rules. As a result, Ron could suggest taking the car as an attempt to impress his older brothers, and Harry could decide, "This seems important to Ron, so I'll back him up on it." Providing additional motivation, whether via this means or some other, would make their decision to take the car easier to swallow.

To reiterate a point made earlier, it would also be nice if the car became something besides a bookend and took on long-term significance by showing us Ron's first steps in imitating his father.

Lockhart Releases Pixies

If we had any question about Lockhart being a git, our suspicions are confirmed when Lockhart releases pixies in his DADA class and then can't control them. However, since Book

2 shows us Lockhart being a git about a dozen times, any scene that does nothing but show Lockhart as a git seems like a good candidate for the cutting room floor. To give *this* scene a bit more purpose, perhaps Harry could use a de-gnoming spell to accomplish what Lockhart failed to, thus demonstrating Harry's growing skill as a wizard.

Though he goes about it differently than Snape and Malfoy, Lockhart is yet another nuisance character for Harry. Including Colin Creevey and Dobby, we now have five characters filling this space, and it's getting a bit crowded. (It would help enormously if Snape were portrayed as a legitimate teacher and a suitable lieutenant for Dumbledore.)

What these nuisance characters try to hide is that the first half of the book is sedate, with little real conflict or plot development. Giving the Big Three goals, especially goals that deepen them as characters and help them mature or evolve as individuals, would help immensely in this regard. Goals such as repairing cars out in the Forbidden Forest, say, or the endless practicing of spells.

Stuff

We have a Quidditch practice, see Malfoy being a jerk, get introduced to the term mudblood, visit Hagrid, see Lockhart being a git, hear murmurs in the walls, visit a death day party, and witness the first attack.

Things are happening and we finally get an inkling of the core plotline for the book, but we're still missing any sense of drive from the Big Three.

More Stuff

We have a Quidditch game, Lockhart being a git in repairing Harry's injured arm, Lockhart being a git in trying to teach people dueling, Harry learning he can talk to snakes, another attack, and finally the polyjuice potion.

With the potion, the Big Three begin to actively pursue the central mystery, but they seem far too cooperative with the author up until this point.

As You May Recall

Starting in *Chamber of Secrets*, each book spends time reminding the reader about characters and events from earlier books. While that sort of thing is common in multi-book series, it is also distracting for repeat readers. For the alternate version it would be nice to target the loyal fan. Which is to say, target readers who promise never to read Book 2 without having just finished Book 1 (or having Book 1 fairly memorized).

The Lord of the Rings is one example of a multi-volume work that dispensed with the "as you may recall, gentle reader" business entirely, and it has done well enough. The Potter series would benefit from a similar approach.

At the Dursleys Again

While the Dursleys display some fear of Harry's magical ability, the summer interlude here in Book 2 is all too similar to Book 1. Most significantly, we don't see any meaningful change in Harry. In the past year he has discovered that he is a wizard; learned the truth of how his parents died; met, fought, and driven off Lord Voldemort; and killed Professor Quirrell. Despite all this, it isn't clear that Harry has changed in the least. In effect, Book 1 might as well not have happened.

Harry quietly accepts the abuse he receives from the Dursleys, is passive-aggressive about not hearing from Hermione or Ron, and generally wastes the summer lounging around feeling sorry for himself. The one time he rebels and uses nonsense magic words to scare Dudley, it is a spontaneous outburst. Harry's response to the punishment he receives as a result (Aunt Petunia makes him do chores) is that work is the worst thing in the whole world, a stock children's book trope. What if, instead, Harry took great pleasure in having something concrete to do, something other than sitting around twiddling his thumbs or whatever it is he does?

Later in the series, passivity and laziness become debilitating illnesses for Harry. Better to nip it in the bud. If these tendencies are signs of depression, why doesn't the story address the problem rather than simply letting it fester? While Harry surely wouldn't be assigned a muggle therapist, he could at least receive antidepressant treatments from Madam Pomfrey, say, and regular counseling sessions with McGonagall and/or Dumbledore.

Let us step back, though, and ask ourselves, how *would* Harry behave this summer? To answer that question, what we need is a clear idea of how Harry managed to survive ten years of abuse in the first place. (Preferably, with the abuse not being as unrelenting as currently portrayed.) Let us suppose Harry survived his terrible childhood by retreating into a fantasy world of his own invention. Such an outlet is common for those in difficult situations, and what orphan doesn't have a fantasy (or a dozen of them) about someone showing up to take him away?

For Harry, that fantasy has come true. Now, when he attempts to make use of his old escape mechanism, he discovers it no longer works. His stock fantasies, while more idealistic and less painful, nevertheless pale in comparison to the reality of Hogwarts. Also, Harry now feels guilty, like he's wasting his life and giving in to weakness, whenever he descends into that inner world. Although Harry is stronger now, having matured and gained confidence over the last year, the result is that living with the Dursleys becomes even more difficult than ever.

These are just ideas. What we're trying to do is emphasize what has changed, how it has changed, and why it has changed, compared to Book 1.

Dobby's First Appearance

When Dobby shows up during the summer break, he tries to convince Harry not to return to Hogwarts. Following numerous failures to accomplish his goal, Dobby drops a pudding on the floor. The primary result of this is that Harry gets into big trouble with the Dursleys. But there is another result, which is that Harry comes off as dimwitted. He has plenty of opportunity to cotton on to Dobby's behavior, but he remains dense as a bludger, and the result is pudding all over the floor.

At times, Harry seems to be on the path of the classic hero, but his bravery, quick thinking, and cavalier treatment of the rules are all transient qualities that show up only when the series has need of them. Once the applicable moment has passed, Harry returns to being helpless, purposeless, even featureless.

Let us consider how our clever Harry might behave in the pudding scene. After several attempts to reason with Dobby, Harry clues in and simply lies. "Okay," Harry says, "if you give me the letters Ron and Hermione wrote me, I promise I won't go back to Hogwarts in the fall." This allows Harry to demonstrate that he isn't a git and that he's capable of being crafty when the situation calls for it.

This change would affect three linked events. (a) The pudding wouldn't be dropped. (b) The owl post, warning Harry not to cast spells out of school, wouldn't arrive. (c) Harry wouldn't be welded into his room.

Working backwards, having Harry welded into his room seems a bit over the top. If the Dursleys are to be portrayed as that abusive, fine, but the book treats their behavior as something of a joke. Putting someone in solitary confinement isn't a joke — maximum security prisons use solitary as an extreme punishment for a reason. Moreover, it seems unlikely that a large owl could survive months locked in a cage followed by days or weeks on a vegetable soup diet.

Humor is a desirable element in a series with this much

darkness in it, but turning serious events into silly comic relief tends to weaken the story as a whole. At a minimum, if Harry really does get locked up in this fashion, then we'd like the story to play fair and show Hedwig dying from a combination of confinement and starvation.

Better, however, if the bars on the windows are left off and the solitary confinement idea abandoned. It serves merely to reiterate the helpless orphan trope.

Next, what about the owl post, which reminds Harry that underage wizards aren't allowed to perform magic outside school? Such a letter could just as easily arrive earlier in the summer. Suppose that, shortly after his return to the Dursleys, Harry gets ahold of his wand and begins practicing magic, hoping to improve his skills. As a result, the warning letter arrives.

The benefit of this approach is that it shows Harry being something other than a passive little lamb. It gives him a goal (to improve his spell casting), has him act on that goal, and then puts an obstacle in his path. If Harry then looks for ways to overcome that obstacle, he becomes a classic protagonist, and the story suddenly has an integral plot, rather than merely a sequence of related but ultimately arbitrary events.

One side-issue that arises here is the Ministry of Magic's ability to detect the use of magic. This ability causes problems elsewhere in the series, such as at the start of Book 4, *Goblet of Fire*, when Voldemort kills Frank Bryce via Avada Kedavra. If the Ministry keeps a watch out for illegal spell work, surely the killing curse is at the top of their list and would be the equivalent of a five-alarm fire as far as the Auror Office is concerned. Similarly, for the Ministry to have such an ability raises major issues for the Big Three throughout Book 7, *Deathly Hallows*, as Voldemort controls the Ministry during that time. Consistency is the foundation for believability, and readers expect the series to establish what the rules are and then abide by them.

Another issue with the owl post is the Fidelus charm that

supposedly protects Harry while he is living with the Dursleys. If the spell keeps him hidden, then it should keep him hidden. If it doesn't, then his staying with his aunt and uncle doesn't make him especially safe.

One possible way of keeping the warning letter here in Book 2 would be to have it come from Dumbledore. Even so, it still feels like a stretch, but at least this would avoid giving the Ministry the power to detect spells being cast in arbitrary locations, and would respect the power of the Fidelus charm.

If we dispense with the solitary confinement idea entirely and move the owl post earlier in the summer, then the dumping of the pudding can be eliminated without further impact. The benefit is that Harry can earn our respect by demonstrating cleverness and quick thinking, rather than make us groan at his cluelessness.

As for Hedwig, it would be nice if Harry didn't take her being locked in a cage quietly. Might he demonstrate a bit of negotiating skill? "If I can't let her out at night, then let me send her to stay with my friend Ron for the rest of the summer so she doesn't die." Or alternately, might he willfully disregard Uncle Vernon's orders, as a further demonstration of Harry's disregard for the rules?

We aren't trying to make Harry's life at Privet Drive comfortable, nor are we trying to remove the various points of conflict. Rather, we're trying to differentiate Harry from his Book 1 form and turn him into a true protagonist, rather than have him continue on as merely a convenient POV character.

Finale

In addition to being weakened by shaggy dog cheats, as we pointed out in Part 1, it seems that the conclusion of Book 2 could do more with the forces it unleashes. For one thing, it would be nice if Harry not only saved Ginny, as he does, but also empathized with her and helped her deal with her guilt over her part in opening the Chamber of Secrets. Harry has had to live with his own guilt over the death of Quirrell, so he's well equipped to understand what Ginny is going through, and it would be a nice touch to have him just as concerned for her as he is for Dobby.

Another thing to point out here is that in destroying the diary Horcrux, Harry is destroying a part of Lord Voldemort's soul. Harry doesn't know about Horcruxes yet, but intuitively he understands that the ghostly Voldemort is tied up with the diary and that to destroy one requires destroying the other. This time with clear intent, Harry does just that. To what extent this would prey on his mind, who can say, but this is another reason why Harry's avoidance of Avada Kedavra in later books doesn't keep him pure and innocent. In Book 2, he has blood on his hands, not only of Voldemort, but also the basilisk, a magical creature with which Harry has at least some connection via his parselmouth ability.

Which leads to the question, might it be possible for Harry to use that ability to keep the basilisk from entering the fight? If Harry succeeded in such an attempt, the basilisk could then provide additional insight into the attacks at the school. Currently, it feels like a cheat that so many students escape death by one happy coincidence after another. What if we learned that this was intentional, not on the author's part, but the monster's — that the basilisk specifically chose moments when it could attack and give its victims at least a chance of surviving?

Having the creature available for questioning could also help clarify how Ginny and the basilisk managed to escape detection (even by paintings and ghosts) while trolling for victims and writing messages in blood on the walls of busy hallways. Voldemort-as-Ginny could easily have turned them both invisible during such forays, making the basilisk visible only long enough to accomplish an attack. Such an explanation would be more believable than the current suggestion that the basilisk is moving around inside water pipes. After all, the creature can't teleport in and out of the pipes for an attack, can it?

Moving on, at the end of Book 2 it seems likely that Harry would request to stay at Hogwarts — creating another nice parallel between Harry and Voldemort. He might start off propositioning Hagrid and Snape, but eventually the question would probably revolve around to Dumbledore.

"Why do you want to stay?" Dumbledore says.

"So I can practice magic. So I don't have to live with those gits."

Dumbledore would say it is impossible, and perhaps mention that Harry is safe when he's living at his aunt and uncle's house. "I have gone to great lengths to ensure your safety while there."

Reluctantly, Harry bows to the inevitable. This time. But by his asking, we see a character unwilling to meekly board the Hogwarts Express just because it is convenient. A real, flesh-and-blood Harry would resist returning to the Dursleys. Eventually, he would flatly refuse to do so. How much better for fans if the paper-and-ink Harry played his role as vigorously.

Chapter 3:
Prisoner of Azkaban

The Idyllic Summer

The blowup with (and of) Aunt Marge is a perfect way to end Harry's stay with the Dursleys. However, the weeks leading up to that climactic moment are simply more of what we've seen in the previous books.

If we imagine a flesh-and-blood Harry, it seems likely that during this particular summer vacation, he would be operating at the very limits of his patience and self-control. The sheer waste of three months' time would eat away at him. Combine that with the trauma of the Chamber of Secrets and Harry's suspicion that, even if he only killed a book, he would gladly kill Voldemort if he had the chance. Add to this that Harry is entering puberty. Stir it all around with a bit of neglect, boredom, and the unavailability of escape to the Weasleys as they're off in Egypt, and now we have a recipe for disaster.

Accordingly, we expect the opening of Book 3 to vibrate with tension long before Aunt Marge and Colonel Ripper put in an appearance. The current first scene — Harry calmly working on his summer essays — seems to trivialize the events of the previous books and makes us see Harry as a soulless cardboard cutout.

One possible break that the story might give Harry this summer is an appearance by Dobby, now out looking for employment. This would give Harry some relatively pleasant company for a few days, increase his attachment to Dobby, show Harry being empathic, and also provide the reader with a scenario less tiresome than Harry lying about, feeling sorry for himself.

Dobby's presence might also cause additional strain with the Dursleys, which could be quite good, especially if we sense that Harry is actively taunting the Dursleys — consciously or subconsciously hoping they'll give him an excuse to lash out. And when Dobby goes off to assume his position at Hogwarts, Harry is left feeling all the more lonely. His dark mood begins to creep in on him again, and then here comes Aunt Marge....

Rage

For Harry to have developed a violent temper by this point in the series seems perfectly reasonable. While he demonstrates certain tantrum-like qualities in Book 5, *Order of the Phoenix*, those are merely growing pains, a passing phase, and have nothing to do with the horrors that Harry has experienced. The temper we're most interested in would be the result of the events in his life and possibly a side-effect of the scar on his forehead.

Learning to control his temper could thus become a reasonable long-term goal for Harry. But first we need examples of him losing that temper. The interlude with Aunt Marge is fine but is presented as an accident and as something of a joke that gets waved off by those in power — again, a failure by the series to assign responsibility, trivializing what could have been an important event. Whatever happens to Aunt Marge, let Harry be the one to do it. Let it be a conscious act, even if it's done in a fit of rage and quickly regretted.

In Book 6, *Half-Blood Prince*, Harry (again accidentally) puts Malfoy into the hospital. Forget Book 6. What if Harry puts Malfoy into the hospital here in Book 3? It might begin as a duel, but having Harry get carried away would demonstrate not only his anger-management problem, but also his growing power as a wizard.

At times in the Potter series, Dumbledore's anger is described as a visceral force, radiating off him in waves. It seems, rather, that this description properly belongs to Harry. Let *him* be the force of nature, the one who is frightening — and even out of control — when his anger gets ahold of him. Near the end of Book 3, we see Harry's immense power revealed through his casting a huge Patronus. We see it again in the Riddle graveyard at the end of Book 4, *Goblet of Fire*, when Harry overpowers Voldemort. In the name of consistency, readers want that power to be Harry's 24/7, not just when the author decides to grant it to him. Having Harry's power radiate off him when he's in a rage would be a step in the right direction.

Consider a scene where Harry's anger is aroused. One possible spot occurs at the end of Book 2, *Chamber of Secrets*, when Mrs. Weasley chides Ginny about writing in her diary. "Never trust something if you can't see where it keeps its brain." Instead of watching silently as he does now, suppose Harry came to Ginny's defense. However, already stressed by events down in the Chamber of Secrets, having just learned that he must return to the Dursleys for the summer, perhaps miffed at Mrs. Weasley for interfering with his spell practice the summer before, and projecting the Dursleys onto Mrs. Weasley, Harry's defense of Ginny is done in a dark rage.

The addition of Snape to this scene would heighten the tension further. As Harry's anger fills the room, Snape straightens his back, draws his wand, and gives Dumbledore a worried look. "The Dark Lord is still here." Dumbledore shakes his head and quietly directs Snape's attention back to Harry.

The dark malevolence that Harry exudes when in a rage need be no more than a superficial quality, but it could still prove worrisome for Snape, Dumbledore, and others — up to and including the reader.

Ginny

Ginny is one of those characters that readers would like to see more of. An opportunity to increase her role occurs early in Book 3. On the Hogwarts Express, Harry wants to tell Ron and Hermione that Sirius Black is after him. Ginny is standing nearby and Ron tells her to get lost. This is a chance for Harry to demonstrate leadership, to demonstrate that he isn't Ron's twin when it comes to being an insensitive git, and to show sympathy for Ginny, who we assume must have had a difficult summer.

Unfortunately, Ginny's experiences in the previous book are treated as if they never happened. While Book 5, *Order of the Phoenix*, refers briefly to what she went through in Book 2, that's pretty much the extent of it. No lingering scars, no nightmares, no loss of self-trust, no sense that everyone around her is either treating her like delicate glasswork or else like a dangerous psycho. Here on the Hogwarts Express, having Harry invite Ginny to hear his secret would reflect well on Harry, but it would also give Ginny more screen time, and give readers a chance to see how she fared over the summer.

So many characters and relationships in the Potter series get pigeonholed immediately upon their first appearance. Ginny is one of the few characters in the series who changes, eventually overcoming her shyness around Harry. What if she now took on a larger role, perhaps even becoming part of the Big Three?

Adding Ginny to the inner circle implies that things are going to change and that nothing is sacred, with the result that readers wonder just how far the author is willing to go in upsetting the established order. Consequently, they pay even closer attention to the story.

Whether or not this is a direction of interest, it would be nice if Harry at least demonstrated empathy toward Ginny and leadership in overruling Ron.

Character Goals

While Book 3 introduces Sirius Black and the dementors early on, it still suffers from a lack of goals for the Big Three. Yes, Harry takes on the task of learning the Patronus charm, but Lupin doesn't begin to teach that spell to Harry until spring term. Similarly, the revelation that Black is Harry's godfather doesn't come until winter break, and even then Harry doesn't exactly drop out of school to hunt Black.

Ron's goal during the first half of the book is up for grabs, but Hermione at least has her perennial drive for academic excellence, and Harry could continue to focus on his spell work. By Book 3, it seems reasonable that his abilities would be reaching unmistakably high levels. Boosted by adolescence, the extent of his powers might garner him not only warnings (as with Aunt Marge), but also praise. While the praise might seem to wash off him, although he might still be held back by lingering uncertainties (perhaps now focused around fear of his own power and temper, rather than fear of inadequacy), the recognition Harry receives could ultimately play into his hypothetical breakout moment later in the book.

Thus, for the first half of Book 3, Harry's goals might include learning control. That would turn the interlude with Aunt Marge into something more than a passing tiff, by having it continue to affect his behavior and weigh upon his mind.

Snape

Snape's primary role in Book 3 comes toward the end, when he follows the Big Three into the Shrieking Shack, where they've come face-to-face with Sirius. For Snape to remain believable, we want his behavior here to make sense. The current portrayal has him motivated by schoolboy grudges and willfully unconcerned with justice, which again doesn't add up with his position as Dumbledore's trusted lieutenant.

In fact, this would be a perfect moment for one of Harry's rages to take hold, and *he* might be the one who won't listen and who seems insane with a desire for revenge. To twist things around even more, what if Snape is the one who keeps Harry from killing Black? Via his coach role, Snape convinces Harry to wait and see Pettigrew unmoused.

In the long run, we suspect that the job of getting through to Harry would be Ron's. Hermione (like McGonagall with Dumbledore) might be willing to raise an issue, but not willing to risk Harry's anger by forcing an argument. Ron, given how his mother is, *would* be up to facing Harry's anger, even when Harry is already in a full-blown rage. However, in this situation, Ron has a broken leg and is busy trying to keep Scabbers / Pettigrew from escaping, so it makes sense for Snape (rather than either Ron or, as is done now, Hermione's cat Crookshanks) to interpose himself between Harry and Sirius.

On a more minor note, currently it takes a bit too long for Harry and the others to clue in as to what is going on in the Shrieking Shack. Partly this is a result of Black and Lupin failing to make clear who they're referring to when they talk about "killing him." The result doesn't stretch the tension, as seems to be the goal. Instead, readers become frustrated because the characters are clearly being vague on purpose.

As for Snape's developing role in the series, what if we began to see a difference of opinion between him and Dumbledore? Suppose that for Dumbledore, Harry is the Chosen One, the fulfillment of the prophecy, the way to put an end to Voldemort once and for all. Snape, meanwhile, has his doubts. Harry is just a kid — a kid with some worrisome tendencies. It was one thing to put Lily and James Potter in danger. They were both adults, members of the Order of the Phoenix, and already being hunted by Voldemort. Using an underage boy, possibly a boy for whom Snape has developed a real fondness, for whom he feels a certain responsibility: that's another matter.

In any event, the believability of the series calls for Snape to remain a respectable character, not presented as he is here, shallow or even insane.

Stealing from the Movie

The third Potter movie did a few things more effectively than the book. For one, the movie's dialog was generally a testament to tight, natural-sounding conversation. For example, at one point the book has Hermione say, "I'm surprised Harry wasn't expelled." To which Harry responds, "So am I.... Forget expelled, I thought I was going to be arrested." In the movie, Harry's response is, "Lucky not to be arrested, actually." The movie's version feels crisper and more natural-sounding.

We also prefer the movie's approach to the scene where Harry learns that Black is his godfather. In the book, the Big Three are sitting at a table in the Three Broomsticks when Minister Fudge and several others enter. Hermione moves a Christmas tree over to hide the table she, Ron, and Harry are sitting at, and against all expectations, this bit of errant knavery works. The movie's approach, to have Harry put on his invisibility cloak and sneak into an upstairs room at the inn to overhear the conversation, is much easier to swallow.

Another insightful change occurs after Harry and Hermione have activated the time turner near the end of the book. In the book, Harry figures out that they are to rescue Buckbeak, while in the movie Hermione gets that part. Since Hermione is the brainy one, and Harry is still dazed by the time dilation effect, giving her this little tidbit seems a positive change.

Hermione blasting open the barred window of Black's cell was pretty jazzy as well, and might be justified in the book if Hermione said something like, "Let me do it, Harry. You're liable to knock down the whole building."

Run Forrest, Run!

Book 3 leads up naturally to a breakout moment for Harry. First, because of the dementors, Harry relives the death of his parents. Thus, the evil nature of Lord Voldemort becomes unmistakably clear to him, and it makes sense that Harry's desire for revenge would be aroused. While Harry focuses on Sirius at first, Voldemort is the true culprit and by the end of Book 3 Harry recognizes that.

Second, Harry overhears Professor Trelawney make a prediction that Voldemort is going to return — not in some hazy, distant future, but soon. Once Wormtail is exposed and runs off, "soon" begins to seem "immediately." This applies the pressure of time to an existing motivation.

Finally, we have Harry casting a huge Patronus at a critical moment, driving off a hundred dementors before they can kill himself and Sirius. True, Harry says, "I knew I could do it, because I'd already done it," which suggests that he needed the self-confidence that the time turner gave him. We'd prefer to have that bit of double-think discarded, and to have his earlier failure result from being under direct attack by the dementors. But either way, this is merely a second chance, a do-over. It's still Harry who casts the Patronus. Dumbledore isn't hiding in the bushes casting it for him. No one rushes down to hold Harry's hand or slip him an extra-powerful wand. Harry drives off a hundred dementors on his own, using an especially difficult spell that he worked hard to master.

This is what we have been waiting for! Finally, the protagonist solves the problem himself through a combination of talent and hard work.

Harry's casting of the Patronus seems the perfect time for his light bulb to go on. He could look down at his wand and think, "I can do this stuff." And then he could think to himself, "If I really wanted to, if I really worked hard, maybe I could stop Voldemort from coming back." Harry would then step onto the Hero's Path. From that moment on, Harry's single overriding goal would be to destroy Voldemort. Another benefit of adding a breakout moment here is that the dementors — who in a sense help push Harry onto the path of Chosen One — would be linked more directly to the Hero's Journey.

The first example of Harry's metamorphosis might then be his absolute refusal to return to the Dursleys. This would no doubt provoke a showdown with Dumbledore, and the headmaster — after failing to get through to Harry — would have several options.

(a) He could acknowledge that Harry is right. Part of the speech from the end of Book 5, *Order of the Phoenix*, might then move here. "I fell prey to an old man's mistakes.... I tried to protect you."

(b) Dumbledore could put a hand on Harry's shoulder and say, "Welcome to the program, Grasshopper. I have your course schedule all made up. You'll be staying here this summer, studying with me one-on-one."

(c) Dumbledore, worried at yet another parallel between Harry and Voldemort, might say, "If you stay here, it will cost you." "I don't care what it costs," Harry says, to which Dumbledore replies, "You should, because it means taking lessons from me during the summer break."

In any event, the coming summer would be very different from those we've seen before, even as Harry is now so very different.

Of course, this is all hypothetical, and it's possible that we've stepped outside the bounds of critique into the world of reinventing the series. In our defense, however, all of the key elements we point to exist in the series already: the dementors, Trelawney's prophecy, the big Patronus. The only difference is, in the current version, those elements fail to impact Harry and thus fail to interrupt the episodic cycle. Thus, we haven't really wandered so very far from the original text — though we have to admit, this alternate approach feels quite different even to us.... But different in a good way.

Chapter 4:
Goblet of Fire

Frank Bryce

Most of the first chapter of *Goblet of Fire* is told from the point of view of Frank Bryce, the caretaker of Riddle Manner and an eyewitness to Lord Voldemort's nascent return. Several minor, low-level issues tend to distract us as we read this opening chapter. As these same issues also appear elsewhere in the Potter series, it makes sense to whine about them just a bit.

First, *Goblet of Fire* begins by devoting nearly five pages to Frank Bryce's backstory. As with any long block of exposition, Bryce's history would probably receive more attention from readers if it appeared as and when needed, rather than being dumped on the reader all at once up front. Accepting this hypothetical change, the new first paragraph of Book 4 would become:

> It was Frank's bad leg that woke him; it was paining him worse than ever in his old age. He got up and limped downstairs into the kitchen with the idea of refilling his hot-water bottle to ease the stiffness in his knee. Standing at the sink, filling the kettle, he looked up at the Riddle House and saw lights glimmering in its upper windows. Frank knew at once what was going on. The boys had broken into the house again, and judging by the flickering quality of the light, they had started a fire. (p. 5)

One problem with this new opening paragraph is that it starts off rather slowly. The business about Frank's bad leg is important information, but it can easily come out in other ways. Moreover, if we start with Frank filling his *tea* kettle, we need no other explanation as to why he's looking out the kitchen window at this point. This allows us to remove not only the first two sentences of the quoted paragraph but also saves us from what follows: Frank trudging upstairs, changing clothes, and trudging back down again.

This revised opening avoids dulling the reader's senses with insignificant transportation details: get out of bed, go downstairs, fill the kettle, go back upstairs, change clothes, go back downstairs. The result is an improved focus on what is important in the scene, and also a much tighter sequence of events where Frank sees the light, grabs his cane, and is out the door heading for the Riddle house. In the space of a few sentences, readers get a sense of purpose and tension, without being distracted by actions that do nothing but move poor Frank around in a circle inside his home.

The opening of Book 4 also contains several level-of-detail distractions. First, Frank removed "a rusty old key from the hook by the door," then he "picked up his walking stick, which was propped against the wall," and upon reaching the back door to the Riddle house, "took out the old key, put it into the lock, and opened the door." These miscellaneous details neither add atmosphere nor visual substance to what is going on and are ultimately distracting because they interrupt the flow of the narrative.

Frank's hovel isn't an important setting, nor is it really germane where he keeps his key or his walking stick. These sorts of details, instead of bringing the image to life or adding a sense of verisimilitude, actually derail the reader, because we go from rushing out the door to focusing on petty nothings.

Taking out the key and putting it into the lock, meanwhile, seems like unnecessary detail. Most often, books on writing will use the telephone to illustrate this sort of thing. "The phone rang. George walked to where the phone sat. The phone rang again and then again before he was able to pick up the receiver and hold it, earpiece to his ear and mouthpiece to his mouth. 'Hello?' he said."

Such a level of detail fails to credit the reader with knowing how to answer a phone. This same principle applies to driving a car or unlocking a door. Unless a character has some unusual way of accomplishing such tasks, then these generic actions don't need to be covered in stepwise fashion.

Some of the extra details provided in this chapter wind up being misleading. During Frank's walk to the Riddle house, the story tells us that the "front door ... bore no sign of being forced, nor did any of the windows." This makes it sound as if Frank is walking around the house looking for how the kids got in. Perhaps he must go past the front door on his way to the back, but if so, why not just go in the front door and be done with it?

For Frank to make this sort of round-about trek is out of character. He fears the house might be burning down, after all. A real-life Frank would surely go directly to one door or another and let himself in.

Following his entry into the house, Frank spends one paragraph navigating the kitchen and another going up the stairs, turning left, and inching his way down the corridor. Here it seems the story is trying to stretch the tension, but unfortunately it does so by means of unimportant detail (the layout of the kitchen has nothing to do with the story) and forcing poor Frank out of character yet again (the house may still be burning down).

In this case, rather than cover Frank's every step, the story could stretch the tension by inserting some of the backstory that we suggested cutting earlier. That would provide not empty verbiage, not generic movement from point A to point B, but details that give us insight both into Frank as a person and also into how the Riddle house ties into the overall story.

Could someone with an average imagination turn Frank's

trip from his house to the Riddle mansion into 100 pages of stuff? Sure. (Check out James Joyce and some of those cats if you have any doubts on the matter.) Frank could encounter funny things, scary things, and horrific things as he turns left, right, goes up, and then back down. But however well written, however clever and imaginative, those 100 pages would still be without real purpose and worthy of a cut.

As the Wicked Witch of the West said, "These things must be done delicately, or you hurt the spell." True not only of acquiring ruby slippers from Kansas farm girls, but also of stretching the tension in a story.

Harry's Summer

Our recommendation is that Harry spend most of this particular summer at Hogwarts being tutored by Dumbledore and possibly Snape. Assuming that this course is the one taken, when Harry awakens from his dream of Frank Bryce and Lord Voldemort, he will find himself in his dormitory or some other reasonable location. As an indication of Harry's close relationship to Dumbledore (a real rather than an idealized relationship this time), as well as Harry's goal of destroying Voldemort, it seems reasonable that Harry would take news of his dream straight to Dumbledore.

The scenes that follow would show us what form the relationship between these two has taken. Readers might also be privy to a final examination of sorts, where Harry demonstrates what he's learned over the summer.

Which leads to a question, what *would* Harry have learned? Taking a cue from Book 6, *Half-Blood Prince*, it seems reasonable that Dumbledore would emphasize finesse and would spend some amount of time breaking Harry of his adolescent fixation on raw power. Subvocalization rather than shouting spells, the subtleties of magic, keeping one's power (and temper) under control, and subjects of that sort would make Harry a better wizard without loading him up with spells that might make him seem too powerful too soon. While we pass over the halfway mark of the series here in Book 4, it wouldn't do for Harry to reach his full potential just yet. Also, though the Potter series currently leaves Harry too weak, making him too powerful clearly wouldn't do either.

One useful bit of work that Harry and Dumbledore might undertake together (perhaps along with Sirius) is to prepare the Black mansion, making it a safe haven for Sirius and setting the stage for it to be a meeting place for the Order of the Phoenix in Book 5. This would serve a secondary purpose as well, by giving Harry a chance to get to know Sirius a bit better. As with Dumbledore, Sirius remains a distant figure that Harry never spends more than a few hours with. For Sirius' death to have real meaning for Harry at the end of Book 5, Harry and Sirius need to develop a real relationship.

Whatever we see of Harry's summer coursework, his relationship to Dumbledore seems like the key element. By the end of the summer, we suspect that Dumbledore would have taken over from Snape as the wizard that Harry admires most, and would perhaps now serve as Harry's adoptive father figure.

Similarly, prior to this summer, Dumbledore might have had real worries that Harry was going down the same path as Voldemort. By the summer's end, Dumbledore's full acceptance of Harry as all-around good guy would make for an interesting change of heart. Whatever problems Harry has with his temper, whatever superficial similarities he shares with the former Tom Riddle, Harry isn't a Dark Lord in the making, and after three months with Harry, now Dumbledore knows as much for sure.

Just so things don't get too cozy, the Quidditch World Cup could serve as a point of conflict between Dumbledore and Harry. Harry would prefer to spend those extra days at Hogwarts with Dumbledore, while the headmaster is convinced that Harry needs to take a break. When Harry has his dream of Frank Bryce, he could use it as an excuse to raise the World Cup subject once again and try to beg out of that sidetrack.

This would offer a chance for Dumbledore to speak some words of wisdom about the dangers of single-mindedness, the importance of having friends, or something else appropriate.

Getting Ready for Swimsuit Season

Book 4 really takes off when Harry's name comes out of the Goblet of Fire, which happens (in the hardcover edition) around page 270. The problem with page 270 is that many of the preceding pages are flab. My house elf tells me that fully 200 of those pages could be cut without losing any plot development, character development, or insight into the wizarding world. Cutting that much, in other words, wouldn't leave behind an anorexic with ribs showing through, but a curvaceous hottie.

We all want the Potter series to pull us into the wizarding world, and readers are willing to accept scenes that do nothing but deepen their understanding of that alternate universe. However, there isn't much of that going on in the first 270 pages of Book 4. Rather, those pages are home to a lot of repetition. The most common example of this is "Gosh aren't wizards weird (and not too bright, either)," which dominates the first chapter of the Quidditch World Cup coverage.

One or two examples of any such message would be enough, especially as this particular subject is silly comic relief. If we muggles can learn terms like Expelliarmus and Quidditch, why can't wizards learn terms like electricity? We're quite comfortable with concepts like flying broomsticks and apparition, so why does the internal combustion engine or the telephone so stump these people? At times, Book 4 is like a drunk who — having gotten a laugh with a joke — repeats the joke without letup for the next several hours. Yes, let the book keep some of this, but let it also recognize when enough is enough. And in this case, one or two examples per book is plenty.

In addition to "aren't wizards weird," the early part of

Book 4 packs the weight on in numerous ways. The writing seems to eschew scene breaks, with the result that readers are treated to quite a few mind-numbing passages that contain little more than transportation details. We get up early in the morning, get dressed, have breakfast, go out the door, walk down the street, go up the hill, hunt around for an old boot. At the site of the Quidditch Cup, we walk around, go get water, make a fire, put up a tent, go buggy-eyed that the inside of this magical tent is larger than one would expect (making Harry look like he wasn't paying attention in Book 2, *Chamber of Secrets*, when Mr. Weasley's car worked the same way), walk to the stadium, up the stairs, and so forth.

Similarly, the exposition on portkeys feels gratuitous. Reader's don't really need the history of these magical objects, not when we see one of the things in operation. "Here's a boot. Grab ahold, count to three, and we're off."

To summarize, in suggesting that the early part of Book 4 go on a diet, our goal isn't to have a story devoid of details or one that misses opportunities to pull us deeper into this alternate reality. Just the opposite. What we want is a story that allows us to fully appreciate the important elements, rather than wear us out with page after page of pointless blubber, so that the important facets are overshadowed and hard to find.

Harry's Schedule

Harry's hypothetical goal at this point is preparing to face Voldemort. Accepting that hypothesis, one indication that Harry is pursuing his goal would be that he quits the Gryffindor Quidditch team. This might not be an easy decision for him, and most likely it would be accompanied by shrieking from Professor McGonagall in particular. She might even enlist Professor Snape to talk sense to Harry, which Snape could do. This would again show that Snape isn't a shallow git (he fully expects Harry to wallop the Slytherin team yet again), and it might also signal a growing difference of opinion between

Snape and Dumbledore as to how best to handle Harry.

While Snape might try to talk Harry back onto the Quidditch team, Dumbledore could approve of the change. Harry might even continue his lessons with Dumbledore during the year via after-school or weekend sessions.

In addition to dropping Quidditch, it makes sense for our goal-oriented Harry to also drop Divination. His goal requires that he make the most of his time at school, and sitting in Trelawney's class isn't the way to do that. Something like Ancient Runes would surely serve his needs much better. As for Care of Magical Creatures or Wizard History, Harry might drop one or the other in favor of a heavier subject like Arithmancy. If Harry continues in Wizard History, he might at least start skipping the class in favor of more time in the library or elsewhere, sure he can pick the material up more readily on his own and via Hermione's notes, rather than listening to Professor Binns.

Whatever the exact details, readers want to see Harry actively pursuing his goal of preparing to defeat Voldemort. If this interferes with the plot outline, great. If it throws a wrench into the established order of things, even better.

Harry and the Tri-Wizard Tournament

When his name comes out of the Goblet, Harry's response is one of dismay, where he all but says, "Gosh, I'm just a little kid. I can't do that stuff." Once again, the story goes fishing for reader sympathy by casting Harry as a hapless boy threatened by forces too powerful for him to handle. That sort of manipulation became tiresome two books ago, and is physically painful to endure here.

In fact, after hypothetically spending the summer with Dumbledore, it seems reasonable that Harry's biggest problem in Book 4 would be egotism. After his name comes out of the Goblet and his surprise passes, why not let Harry wave the tournament off and say, "Not interested," without bothering to get up from the dinner table. When told he doesn't have a choice, he huffs into the side room with the other contestants, worried not about any lack of ability, but only that the tournament will cut into his busy training schedule.

When Fleur Delacour refers to him as "that little kid," Harry could momentarily consider going through with the tournament just to show her a thing or two. Far from scuffing the floor with his shoes, shoulders hunched, Harry could be some combination of defiant, disinterested, and perhaps big-headed. Rather than standing silently while the adults argue over the strange development, Harry could jump into the fray with something like, "Don't worry. I just won't show up to any of the events." The tournament doesn't scare him, it's just a distraction he can't afford.

Dumbledore's response to this might be different as well. Please don't let him behave out of character as he does in the fourth movie, shoving Harry around and making the Hollywood mistake of equating violence with intensity. Rather, suppose that the headmaster takes Harry aside and asks him, "Did you put your name in that Goblet?" After Harry says he didn't, Dumbledore says, "Are you sure? Because of all the students here, you're the only one who could have erased my age line, fooled the Goblet, and then put the line back."

This would be much preferable to Dumbledore's current behavior, which effectively says, "Yeah, right. Harry put his name in the Goblet? What a joke! The kid can barely tie his own shoelaces." Book 4 tears Harry down numerous times, and this is one example of that. By this point in the series, we expect Harry's abilities to be a source of amazement. Of course he would remain immature and flawed, but even so, readers are ready to be impressed, and at times even alarmed, at Harry's power, and we long for characters in the story to behave accordingly.

Tri-Wizard Tasks

We've talked already about Harry earning Moaning Myrtle's help on task two, and also his earning the gillyweed information by reaching out to Neville. Dobby could still play his part with that hypothetical approach; by virtue of Harry's continuing relationship with Dobby, it makes sense that if Harry asked, Dobby would be willing to snatch the gillyweed for him. But this would then be a result of Harry actively seeking out help, rather than having success handed to him free of charge.

As for the dragon task, the main source of tension currently involves a summoning charm that Harry is made to struggle over. Seeing Harry still struggling with junior high school stuff is irksome. Suppose instead that Harry is blasting through everything they teach in the classroom. Whence commeth the tension then? What if Harry's hubris displays itself, and he tries some other solution first? Maybe he tries stunning the dragon, counting on his raw power to get past the dragon's thick hide. Only when that fails does he fall back on the broom idea. On the other hand, even if Harry goes straight to summoning his broom, his flying maneuvers are rather dramatic enough to carry the first task, without forcing Harry to struggle with a simple spell.

As for the idea to summon his broom, Harry could still get that from the fake Mad Eye Moody. In that conversation, though, Harry's "I don't have any talents. Well, flying," feels rather too self-effacing. How much better if Harry said, "I'll just knock it out. Thick skin on a dragon? Bah, that doesn't mean anything to me." But Mad Eye would talk up the flying approach, and might convince Harry by mentioning that broken eggs will count off Harry's score, and a stunning spell will surely lead to such.

In any event, casting Harry as a shuddering, helpless waif is no longer an appropriate way to increase reader anxiety or sympathy. If we have a concern for this teenager, let it be due to his disregard for his own mortality. Let us connect to him through understanding how so much power could easily go to anyone's head.

Tri-Wizard Ball

For the mid-winter dance, Harry and Ron are portrayed not only as asexual, but as nearly identical in their response to the event. They don't act fourteen going on fifteen, but more like eleven going on twelve. For both of them to still view girls with indifference, rather than as objects to be pawed and drooled over, suggests that the book has regressed to year one mode.

What exactly are the personalities of these two main characters? It seems that someone raised under a staircase might approach a party with great excitement, might not mind so much getting dressed up and having a good time. On the other hand, Harry could easily view this event as merely another distraction, his impatience keeping him from appreciating the experience. As for Ron, why not let him show interest in the dance, even if only as a chance to perhaps cop a feel?

Harry and Ron are often indistinguishable. Here is a chance to give them both a bit of personality.

The Portkey Problem

One unexplained detail in Book 4 is why Barty Crouch Jr. (the fake Mad Eye Moody) waits until the end of the school year to transport Harry to the Riddle graveyard.

While having Crouch pass himself off as Dumbledore's old friend Moody for an entire year, right under Dumbledore's nose, is stretching things a bit, most readers can swallow it without too much trouble. Unlike Quirrell in Book 1, Moody isn't carrying Voldemort around on his back, so the level of inattention required on Dumbledore's part isn't as great, nor is

Voldemort asked to expose himself to automatic destruction as part of the ruse. If Crouch is discovered before the plan unfolds, that will be very bad from Voldemort's point of view, but not irrevocably fatal — as discovery likely would have been in Book 1.

Moreover, Dumbledore could honestly suspect Harry of entering the Tournament on his own behalf. Having Dumbledore project his own youthful lust for glory onto Harry not only explains Dumbledore's failure to search vigorously for some other culprit, it illuminates his personality in the bargain. While this certainly constitutes a mistake on Dumbledore's part, it is an understandable mistake, reinforcing what we know of the headmaster rather than making him seem doltish, inattentive, or otherwise unrecognizable.

Even so, the long delay before Crouch hands Harry a portkey remains a sizeable problem. Why not just call Harry into the office for a talk and a portkeyed cuppa?

Alternatives to having Crouch about the entire year all seem to heavily impact the rest of the book, so what we need is an approach that keeps him in place but makes the long delay seem reasonable.

Several factors might produce just such a delay. First, as a result of Harry's dream at the start of the year, followed by an obituary of Frank Bryce appearing in a muggle newspaper, Dumbledore might make a trip to the Riddle house, or ask the auror office to do so. If the aurors determine that Bryce was killed by Avada Kedavra, Dumbledore would likely conclude that Voldemort was at the Riddle house, just as Harry's "dream" suggested.

Though Voldemort isn't there anymore, Dumbledore still might ask the auror office and/or various members of the Order to put a watch on the Riddle house, under the theory that Voldemort showing up there was no accident. This serves as a brilliant deduction on Dumbledore's part, as Voldemort does in fact need something from the Riddle grounds in order to complete his restoration: he needs a bone from his father's grave. Learning that the Riddle house is under surveillance, Voldemort might be forced to rework his plans, and might only then decide that he needs the Tri-Wizard Tournament as a way of getting ahold of Harry. Dumbledore has won the first round.

Next, if we move the final task of the Tournament off the grounds of Hogwarts, then we can have portkeys be inert *within* the grounds. This change would be in keeping with the various magical defenses of Hogwarts (portkeys seem a fairly dodgy exception anyway), and would explain why the third task is so important to Voldemort. Not only will the third task take Harry away from Hogwarts (perhaps to the very same location as the Quidditch World Cup, in order to support a larger audience), the third task will also very likely pull surveillance from the Riddle house — as Dumbledore will want all aurors and Order members to act as security at the event.

In this case, *Voldemort* guesses correctly. Dumbledore, suspecting that some attempt will be made on Harry's life, does in fact order all available forces to the third task, unwittingly opening a window of opportunity for Voldemort to return to the Riddle house and graveyard. Dumbledore's concern for Harry's safety backfires — a wonderful reversal. With Crouch Jr. posing as Moody, a fox is already in the henhouse, and the extra security at the third task goes for naught. Voldemort wins round two.

One other factor could come into play as far as the long delay is concerned: the recovery of Voldemort's wand. If that wand is being held either by Dumbledore at Hogwarts or else by the aurors' office at the Ministry, then recovering it would fall to Moody. It makes sense that Voldemort would want his wand present when he resumes human form, and so might put off the restoration ceremony until that task is completed.

In the current version of Book 4, Crouch Jr. questions Harry following Harry's return from the Riddle graveyard. That could still happen with our hypothetical approach, although the questioning clearly wouldn't take place inside the

Hogwarts castle. Suppose, instead, that Crouch side-along apparates Harry with him to Crouch Sr.'s home, now vacant. This would made sense, as Crouch wouldn't want to risk leading any possible pursuit to Voldemort, nor would he want to risk having to share the glory of Harry's death with anyone.

At this point, we get Crouch's exposition of what has been going on. Dumbledore either shows up, having traced the path of apparition, or else Harry overpowers Crouch on his own and sends a Patronus to let Dumbledore know where he is.

While this might seem like a lot of changes, the actual impact on the novel's flow of events is minimal, and the benefit is that both Crouch Jr. and Voldemort play their parts more believably, no longer simply sitting around twiddling their thumbs until the author gives them the green light. (The muggle green light, that is, rather than the Avada Kedavra one.)

House Elves

Hermione's goal of freeing the house elves is quite wonderful. However, while Ron's shrugging her organization off feels right, for Harry to do so as well is troublesome. This is another opportunity to show that Ron and Harry are distinct characters with distinct personalities.

Harry does at least buy Dobby socks and the like for Christmas, but it would be nice if he approached his relationship to Dobby with a bit more excitement. This is a kid who grew up as a muggle, and now he has a friend who's a powerfully magical elf. For Harry to be bored by this feels bogus. Ron? Yes, let Ron be bored and find Dobby's weird behavior annoying. But why would Harry be so jaded both by the magical world and by having made a few friends along the way? Given Harry's upbringing, it seems more likely that being friends with Dobby would be a real treat, a laugh, something that Harry truly values. Given Dobby's powers, Harry's maintaining ties with the elf would also show Harry taking after Dumbledore.

Meanwhile, Harry's treatment of the bereft Winky is terribly insensitive. Once again, Harry takes on Ron's defining characteristic. Not only does Harry grill Winky in her misery, he makes absolutely no attempt to help her, which feels like a missed opportunity. Why not give Harry a side goal of figuring out how to get through to Winky. Harry could enlist Hermione to help him, getting her to look through various books on how to treat with house elves, etc.

When Harry puts off working on the egg clue until the last minute, let it be a result of his working on things like helping Winky rather than because he is lazy. Children being lazy and carefree, stuffing themselves with food at every opportunity, is a standard trope of children's literature. While we can all relate to that sort of behavior, it doesn't fit with Harry's role or his life experiences. It is hard to be carefree when every time you turn around, someone is trying to kill you.

Harry might eventually figure out how to get through to Winky, possibly by performing some ritual that binds her to him as his personal house elf — a solution that outrages Hermione and perhaps even creates a temporary rift with Dobby. But it was either that or let Winky drink herself to death....

End of the Big Three

We recommended adding Ginny to the Big Three in our discussion of *Prisoner of Azkaban*. Now it is time to get serious. When Harry's name comes out of the Goblet, Ron temporarily abandons their friendship. This is a perfect opportunity for Harry to begin helping Neville achieve his potential. The result might be the formation a Big Five, or perhaps of a growing circle of knights that evolves into the D.A. of the next book.

At any rate, upon Ron's return to the fold, Harry could begin to help his best friend just as he has hypothetically begun helping Neville. Ron's poor performance in school is a result of insecurity, not lack of ability. In short, Book 4 gives Harry a chance to demonstrate his leadership skills and his teaching ability with Ron and Neville. His doing so would be another lead-in to the next book.

The Rift

When Ron breaks off his relationship with Harry, isn't this an example of passive-aggressive behavior? The short answer is, no. Ron doesn't sit and stew, he confronts Harry. They have an argument, one which ends unhappily. Ron's subsequent distance and coolness isn't a sign that he wants Harry to read his mind and take some action to repair the rift; both the distance and coolness indicate a real change in their relationship.

As for Ron and Harry getting back together, this too makes sense. Enough time has gone by for Ron to think through his position and to wonder if he was wrong to doubt Harry. More importantly, the first task serves as the perfect impetus for Ron to step forward and repair the rift. Ron's statement, "I reckon someone *is* trying to kill you," is all the explanation a reader needs to understand Ron's actions here. (Harry's current response is, "Cottoning on finally?" Given our hypothetical new Harry, a better response would be, "They're gonna need a lot bigger dragon, if that's what they want." And Ron could complete their rapprochement with, "You ass" or something along those lines.)

This rift can also result in lasting changes — changes above and beyond altering the Big Three dynamic. If Harry has, in fact, been acting a little big headed lately, and if he knew about the Tri-Wizard Tournament ahead of time but kept that information from Ron and Hermione, those actions could play their part in the rift and subsequent recovery.

During their big argument, suppose Ron takes Harry to task for his egotism. During the subsequent weeks, Harry ponders his own behavior and decides that Ron has a point. Following the rift, maybe Harry puts greater effort into seeing that Ron and Hermione get their share of the spotlight and their share of the credit for various accomplishments. Or, maybe it is Ron's comment that leads Harry to reach out to Neville.

As for Harry knowing about the Tournament ahead of time, that could play out several ways. One approach would be to have Harry lie. While at the Quidditch World Cup, Ron asks Harry if he knows what is going to happen at school that year. From Ron's point of view, it makes sense that Harry might know, since Harry spent the summer with Dumbledore. Harry says, "He wouldn't tell me."

When the Tournament is announced at school, Harry then lets out that he knew about it all along. He might brag about this to Fred and George, say, with Ron nearby. This sparks an argument with Ron, who doesn't appreciate being lied to, and sets the stage for Ron to distrust Harry later, when Harry claims he didn't put his own name into the Goblet.

When Ron and Harry get back together, Harry will have learned that he should never lie to Ron and his inner circle. If Harry has a secret that they can't be privy to, Harry will say as much. "I can't tell you that just yet." This prepares Harry for handling a situation that will likely arise again in the future: the need to withhold information that is for his eyes only.

Another approach to handling the rift would be to have Harry say, "I can't tell you" straightaway at the Quidditch World Cup. In this case, Ron would take offense, not willing to accept that — despite their friendship — Harry doesn't trust Ron with certain bits of information. Then, when Ron returns to the fold, he would have come to understand that, because of who Harry is, Harry will in fact have secrets that he can't share, not even with Ron.

This would indicate that Ron is beginning to accept Harry's role as Chosen One. At certain times, Harry will be Ron's best friend and will need Ron to behave as such. At other times, Harry will be King and will need Ron to respond accordingly.

If either of these paths is taken, it could also highlight

Dumbledore's wisdom and insight. The Tri-Wizard Tournament, after all, is hardly a state secret. But Dumbledore could have pressed Harry to treat it as one, suspecting that just this sort of painful learning experience would arise.

Rather than being merely a transient source of conflict, the rift between Harry and Ron would then serve several literary purposes at once. Most importantly, it would contribute to the protagonist's progress toward his ultimate goal.

Avada Kedavra

When the false Mad Eye Moody teaches Avada Kedavra to his class, it presents Harry with a bit of a dilemma. Though Harry is hypothetically on the path of destroying Voldemort, and Avada Kedavra seems the most likely method, this is how Harry's parents were killed. Though it seems plausible that Harry might struggle with this, readers would also understand if Harry ultimately placed responsibility with the murderer, not on the instrument used.

Would Harry go to Mad Eye Moody and, as he did with Remus Lupin the previous year, ask for additional instruction? It seems reasonable, if not certain. Recognizing that the killing curse is illegal, Harry might determine to practice it in secret, sneaking out into the forest at night to test it on helpless forest creatures, say.

Harry's use of Avada Kedavra could merely be one worrisome sign among many. For Hermione, Harry's growing circle of followers could look like Voldemort's death eaters. Harry's capacity to enter a killing rage (which Book 3, *Prisoner of Azkaban*, showed with Aunt Marge and with Sirius in the Shrieking Shack); his dark dreams of what Voldemort is up to; his arrogance, which characters fear may be more than a passing phase: all these signs would worry those around Harry. They probably would worry Harry himself.

These sorts of changes would give readers a deeper, more complex portrait, one where Harry as a sympathetic character isn't a given. Soft, cuddly, and innocuous would no longer be the main adjectives people associate with Harry Potter.

Snape

Snape's attitude toward Voldemort is understandably complex. While he has rejected the Dark Lord's methods, Snape was once a follower and remains awed by and fearful of Voldemort's power even now. Snape could have, thirteen years before, been wobbling as to which side to support, even after taking the position of potion's master at Hogwarts.

In Book 4, we get hints of Snape's distress at the return of the dark mark. Might more be made of it? Voldemort coming back must be a catastrophe for Snape, something he has prayed would never happen, at least not in his lifetime. Seeing some of this from his POV or else via a conversation with Dumbledore, might give us deeper insight into Snape, and a better appreciation of what it means for him to head off and become once again the double agent, as he does at the very end of Book 4.

Climax and Resolution

We've already talked about how inappropriate Expelliarmus is in the duel between Harry and Voldemort. To maintain their respect for Harry, readers need him to cast Avada Kedavra instead. It seems reasonable that Harry would also use the killing curse when fleeing the graveyard. In ordering Cedric Diggory killed, Voldemort has demonstrated that the situation is serious. Now let Harry return the favor. Firing blindly over his shoulder or not, one of his spells could very well connect.

This suggestion is certainly arbitrary, but it could provide a linkage into the next book. Rather than threatened with being expelled from school for casting Patronus, Harry would be charged with murder via the use of an illegal curse. If not a death eater, Harry could be charged with the murder of Barty Crouch, Jr., say.

Though Voldemort is restored to his body here at the end of Book 4, he remains fairly inactive until Book 7. This slow ramp-up is currently explained away as a result of Voldemort's fear of Dumbledore, his desire to learn the complete prophecy, and his need to rebuild his forces. All these explanations are fine, but another one deserves to be added: Voldemort's fear of Harry.

Chapter 5:
Order of the Phoenix

Defining Elements

In analyzing Book 5, we find that two key elements control the structure of the story. One element is Trelawney's Chosen One prophecy — specifically, the copy of that prophecy stored in the Department of Magical Mysteries. The other element is Dolores Umbridge. Our first question then is, are these the right two elements for Book 5?

The Prophecy

It certainly makes sense for Voldemort to want to know the entire prophecy. After all, he was nearly destroyed the first time he tried to kill Harry and has failed three more times to defeat the boy. On the last occasion, Voldemort's failure occurred in front of his death eaters, something that must be raising questions and doubts in their minds. Some of them would seemingly prefer that Voldemort had never returned. The previous war happened fifteen years ago, long enough for the fires of youth to have burned down and for a love of comfort, if not some common sense, to have grown.

Voldemort will realize this and will no doubt be tormented with paranoia and distrust toward his own followers. Getting rid of Harry thus becomes a high priority for Voldemort, and learning the complete prophecy first seems a prudent move. For all Voldemort knows, the secret to destroying Harry might be contained there-in. So readers can easily accept that one of Voldemort's primary goals is to get the prophecy, though that serves merely as a stepping stone to eliminating the Potter boy himself.

Consequently, Dumbledore's goal to keep the full prophecy out of Voldemort's hands (and to keep Harry safe until he is ready to take on the Dark Lord) also makes sense. The question is, though, why does Dumbledore choose to protect rather than just destroy the copy of the prophecy at the Ministry? Given how easy it is to destroy the glass vial, this seems the most logical solution. Dumbledore's failure to do so smacks of plot necessity.

The story suggests that Voldemort doesn't retrieve the prophecy himself for fear of being revealed to the Ministry, but that explanation fails to satisfy. Voldemort could easily sneak in, snatch the prophecy, and be gone before anyone was the wiser. Given that Harry and half-a-dozen Hogwarts students did as much, clearly the Ministry hasn't invested in burglar alarms.

What if we have Dumbledore destroy the physical copy of the prophecy? Can we come up with something else for Voldemort to go after?

The prophecy gives us the following results. (a) Harry saves Mr. Weasley's life. Mr. Weasley is on duty, protecting the door that leads into the prophecy room when he's attacked by Voldemort's snake Nagini. Harry observes the attack via his mental connection to Voldemort and is able to raise the alarm in time to keep Mr. Weasley from dying. As this is perhaps the most dramatic moment in the book, we're loath to lose it.

Suppose that Dumbledore has in fact destroyed the bottled prophecy. Most likely, he would have destroyed it fifteen years earlier during WW1 when it was first recorded, to prevent Voldemort from going after it even then.

Could Mr. Weasley be guarding something *else* at the Department of Mysteries? We know that they keep a supply of time turners on hand, for example, and it is feasible Voldemort might use one of those to kill Harry's parents before he is even born or something. However, given Voldemort's magical ability, he could just as easily create his own time turner if it came to that. Thus, it seems best to put a limit on the things — they can take you back no more than twelve hours, say — and be done with it.

So, back to the prophecy. With the one physical copy long destroyed, suppose Voldemort went after the next most likely source: Professor Trelawney. Previously too impatient for this approach, Voldemort would now begin a game of chess with Dumbledore for ownership of Trelawney.

First, Voldemort orders Snape to retrieve this particular copy of the prophecy by using Legilimency on Trelawney. Snape, walking a razor's edge, merely goes through the motions and tells Voldemort that Trelawney doesn't recall ever giving the prophecy. This is quite a reasonable answer, since Trelawney seems to black out during her trances. Voldemort, however, might decide that *he* can get at the memory, even if miserable Snape can't.

Going onto Hogwarts grounds to retrieve the prophecy doesn't seem like a viable option, so suppose Voldemort has his agent, Dolores Umbridge, evict Trelawney from the school. This approach has the merit of fitting well with the existing storyline. Dumbledore negates Voldemort's victory here by allowing Trelawney to continue living at the school, even though she's no longer a teacher there. Move and countermove.

Voldemort then arranges for one of Trelawney's relatives to die. While Trelawney is away from Hogwarts for the funeral, the Order of the Phoenix keeps her under guard. Voldemort, accompanied by Nagini, arrives at her hotel room during Mr. Weasley's watch.

The problem we face here is that with Mr. Weasley mortally wounded by Nagini, nothing would stop Voldemort from questioning and/or kidnapping Trelawney. That would be acceptable, so long as she really *doesn't* have any memory of the prophecy.

Voldemort needn't kill Trelawney, he could just erase her memory of his visit. But with Mr. Weasley expected to die, this spot of delicacy on Voldemort's part is questionable, and Trelawney doesn't seem like much of a loss, really.

(b) The second outcome the prophecy gives us is that Harry is lured to the Department of Mysteries for the book's climactic scenes. During the battle that ensues, Sirius is killed and Voldemort's return is revealed undeniably to the Ministry.

It doesn't seem essential, however, that the climactic battle take place in the Department of Mysteries. Some of the gadgets revealed there are neat, but they also tend to distract us from the battle. All the story needs is for Harry to leave school grounds in the company of various members of the D.A. The Hogs Head tavern, the Riddle house/graveyard, or any number of other places could serve as well for the climactic fight. Similarly, Harry can still be lured away via a false dream, or he could venture forth as part of his own plot to draw Voldemort out into the open.

In summary, it seems not only possible but more believable to eliminate the Ministry's copy of the prophecy and use an alternate approach to achieve the same effects.

Dolores Umbridge

As currently portrayed, Umbridge isn't an especially convincing character. She doesn't seem to be working for

Voldemort, either consciously or under the Imperius curse, but is merely a representative of Minister Fudge's office. As such, her hunger for power is reasonable, as is her goal to discredit and oust Dumbledore. However, her overt sadism and her disrespect toward other teachers are at odds with these goals. While most parents won't care one way or another who the headmaster is at Hogwarts, they certainly *will* care if they feel students are being abused, if the quality of education is declining, or if the very existence of the school is in danger.

Meanwhile, that Harry can't keep his mouth shut around Umbridge paints him as a nitwit. After ten years with the Dursleys, after four years of being taunted by Malfoy and badgered by Snape, Harry's response to Umbridge would likely be either to laugh her off or else blast her through a wall. The childish business he gets into with her is Book 1 material. For crying out loud, Umbridge has Harry writing lines! This is grade school stuff, designed once again to paint Harry as the poor, helpless, abused waif. Umbridge doesn't up the ante, doesn't move the series inexorably toward its climax, she returns us to square one.

What we need, first of all, is clarity. If Umbridge is really out to take over the school, then let her do so with a bit of intelligence. Let her suck up to the other teachers, ingratiate herself. Let her spy quietly, waiting for some misstep on Dumbledore's part that she can exploit. Even if Umbridge is Voldemort's pawn, her extreme behavior would too easily get her replaced before she can complete her mission. Fudge wants Dumbledore gone as quickly and quietly as possible. Hundreds of irate parents sending him owls doesn't fit that description.

Whether working for Voldemort or not, let us assume that Umbridge proceeds more cleverly. Her non-violent, theory-based approach to teaching Defense Against the Dark Arts is perfect and is bound to have a lot of people cheering her on. Her goading Harry seems reasonable enough, so long as he doesn't fall prey to the obvious trap. Moreover, as soon as Harry discovers Umbridge's class is going to be a waste of time, we would like to see him drop it, or at least *attempt* to drop it. If someone is going to mouth off at Umbridge, let it be Ron or Colin Creevey. By this time, readers expect Harry to be smarter, wiser, and more mature than that.

One way that Umbridge might really get under Harry's skin is to make it difficult, perhaps impossible, for Harry to continue his private lessons with Dumbledore. Before Dumbledore can safely begin talking to Harry about Horcruxes, etc., he has to make sure Harry can keep Voldemort out of his head, but now Umbridge makes it impossible for Dumbledore to teach Harry Occlumency. Given that Snape can give Harry those lessons, Umbridge's interference still hasn't become fatal, but it would certainly move her onto Harry's enemy list.

If Harry then decides to fight back, we'd like him to do so in a more clever and devious way than shooting his mouth off. Currently, various pranks are played on Umbridge, but are done in a rather ad hoc fashion. What if Harry *arranged* for those pranks? What if they were done systematically? The D.A. is taking shape, and annoying Umbridge would be good training for them, a kind of practical application to help prepare them for the coming war.

While these suggestions are drifting off into the weeds a bit, what we're asking for is that Book 5 make Harry an active participant in the storyline. Not just the helpless innocent, not just an observer of Umbridge's increasingly dangerous attacks against the school, but a player in the game. This would allow for Umbridge to be more believable as well. Rather than being a motiveless psycho, her behavior could be a response to the ever-escalating attack-and-retaliate between her and Harry. While Book 5 has the flavor of this already, Harry's moves are unplanned outbursts, and the actions of the Weasley twins are done without Harry's knowledge, never mind his prodding.

One key point here is that Umbridge would matter to our Harry-as-protagonist only because she blocks him from pursuing his primary goal: destroying Voldemort. So long as she remains merely a nuisance, however hateful, we expect Harry to ignore her, even if doing so requires a lot of tongue biting. When she interferes with the hero's quest, *then* she becomes a true hindrance, and readers can accept Harry turning his full attention on her. Would Harry be willing to kill her? Willing to put her under the Imperius charm? Those might be real fears for Umbridge and might help explain her forming the Inquisitorial Squad.

Even the reader might wonder just how far Harry will go to rid himself of this impediment.

Goals

By giving Harry a goal, and then by turning Umbridge into an obstacle to that goal, the story would turn Harry into a true protagonist while simultaneously making Umbridge an integral part of the story, rather than merely an annoying character.

One nice aspect of Book 5 is that many of the other characters already have goals. As we've seen, Voldemort has one, as is essential for a villain. Dumbledore has his goal of thwarting Voldemort. Hagrid has a goal of socializing his brother Grawp. Hermione continues to pursue House Elf rights (awesome: a goal that extends beyond a single book!), while she also actively supports Harry by helping to set up the D.A. and arranging the interview with Rita Skeeter.

The only person who continues to miss out is Ron.

The Opening

If Harry doesn't go to the Dursleys this summer, then the dementor attack on Harry probably wouldn't happen. This seems an improvement at least as far as Umbridge's character is concerned. For her to order a dementor attack changes her from misguided politician into a criminal, someone worthy of spending the rest of her life in Azkaban.

If we dispense with the dementors, we need another reason for Harry to be in front of a disciplinary hearing. One possibility is that Harry killed a death eater and/or Barty Crouch, Jr. at the end of the previous book. As a result, Harry wouldn't be threatened with expulsion, but charged with murder. A number of angles have to be looked at here.

(a) Would the Ministry of Magic want to stir up this much dirt? Quite possibly they wouldn't. Performing character assassination on Harry is one thing. Going for actual assassination, or life imprisonment, is another. One potential explanation is that the trial starts off as a mere threat. If Dumbledore steps down as the headmaster of Hogwarts, the charges against Harry will be dropped. Only, Dumbledore and Harry decide to call the bluff.

(b) Would Voldemort be interested in seeing this sort of trial take place? Possibly. With the Ministry treating Harry as a nutcase, the next step seems natural. In his delusions of grandeur, Harry decided so-and-so was a death eater and killed the poor son-of-a-bludger. Given that we have a dead body and Harry's wand has Avada Kedavra in its Prior Incantato list, the case against Harry is pretty strong, especially with half a dozen witnesses like Lucius Malfoy ready to testify on behalf of the prosecution.

It is a dicey proposition, with a chance of backfiring by convincing people that Voldemort really has returned, but the payoff seems worth the risk. If Harry is found guilty, the Ministry would do Voldemort's dirty work for him.

Fudge might be horrified to find his justice department vigorously pursuing this case, but he might also be powerless to stop the process once it starts. Thus, he could easily find himself outmaneuvered, his mud-slinging playing right into Voldemort's hands.

(c) Would a charge of murder represent a shaggy dog threat to Harry? After all, we expect this case to dissipate of its own at the end of Book 5 when Voldemort's return becomes an accepted fact. This is a serious problem, but perhaps not fatal.

Pursuing the case does makes sense for Voldemort. Meanwhile, the charges can have a real impact on Harry. Suppose, for instance, that Harry is allowed to return to Hogwarts for the school year, but is neither allowed to take his wand (naturally it has been bagged as evidence) nor is he allowed to possess or even use a wand so long as the charges are pending.

This would limit Harry's ability to do magic for most of the book, but the result needn't be entirely negative. The wand is merely a tool, though a critical one. Harry blew up Aunt Marge without a wand, after all. Thus, Harry's training this year, in addition to Occlumency, might focus on getting him past his psychological dependence on his wand. In which case, a negative turns into a positive by means of Harry's powerful work ethic, his raw power, his (sometimes overdone) self-confidence, and his positive mental attitude. As a result of spending a year without his wand, Harry emerges stronger than ever. This sort of reversal of expectation is always nice to have, and makes the murder trial gambit look rather appealing.

The Cost of Surprise

Though we recommend skipping the Dursleys entirely here in Book 5, it seems worthwhile to examine one sequence of events that occurs at the Dursley home in the current version. Following the dementor attack, as Uncle Vernon is about to kick Harry out into the street, a howler arrives and delivers its shouted message, "Remember my last, Petunia." Petunia instantly recognizes Dumbledore's voice in the howler, while Harry is left to wonder, "Who was that?"

Though this might seem a minor point, it isn't the only place in the Potter series where characters are forced to act out of character in order to (apparently) perpetrate a surprise on the reader. In this case, why should Aunt Petunia recognize Dumbledore's voice in a howler? When was the last time she heard a howler? When was the last time she spoke with Dumbledore? Harry, meanwhile, is quite familiar with both howlers and Dumbledore's voice. The role-reversal here is made all the worse by its pointlessness. The scene could just as easily have played out with Harry saying, "Why is Professor Dumbledore sending you a howler?" Aunt Petunia gasps, "Dumbledore!," collapses into her chair, and then tells Uncle Vernon that Harry must stay.

Not only this scene, but the entire rest of the book remains unchanged right up to the very end, with Harry in Dumbledore's office. Harry could say, "What's up with you and my Aunt Petunia?" instead of his current (spoken in a Gregory Goyle voice), "Duh, it — was — you — who — sent — the — howler."

In order to perpetrate a surprise on the reader, the story is willing to make Harry a nitwit not once but twice. Only, the surprise here is a mirage. Harry already knows that Dumbledore had Mrs. Figg watching over him all along. Readers know it was Dumbledore who left Harry with Aunt Petunia, even if Harry doesn't. So where's the surprise? There isn't one, and all that's left is a horrible testament to the story's lack of concern for characterization, even as it applies to the title character.

For many people, surprise is a highly valuable commodity. However, some kinds of surprise can destroy the audience's enjoyment of a story. In the movie *Unbreakable*, the last scene is a surprise on both the audience and the hero when Mr. Glass reveals himself as a villain. Unfortunately, the movie values the surprise so highly it allows Glass to stand there, chuckling at his subterfuge, while effectively holding out his hands and saying, "Please call the police and have me arrested, because I'm a really bad man."

Okay, Glass might be a villain, but in no way is he a very plausible or scary one.

Meanwhile, for many of us, surprise is the least valuable effect from any work of art. Surprise works the first time around, and for those of us in search of enduring stories with lots of replay value, even minor inconsistencies can reveal a surprise as nothing but an artificiality perpetrated by the author, and can leave us feeling cheated.

Number Twelve Grimmauld Place

Much of what goes on at the Black Mansion would benefit from cutting. Harry's shouting fit is one example. While people do have such low moments, Harry's behavior is part of a passing phase that doesn't lead anywhere and paints Harry as passive-aggressive.

Meanwhile, housework at number twelve fills our attention for a painfully long time. The purpose seems to be that the name Regulus Black is mentioned and a Horcrux locket is spotted. Thus, we have quite a bit of prose that doesn't seem to accomplish very much.

Finally, transportation details fill quite a few pages of the opening. Scene cuts are again eschewed, and we are forced to sit through a long broom flight, a trip to the Ministry of Magic, riding up in an elevator, walking to Mr. Weasley's desk, riding back down again, and following yet more hallways.

The Invincible Headmaster

At one point, a mole reveals the D.A.'s existence to Umbridge. This leads to a meeting in Dumbledore's office, where Dumbledore decides to take the rap. This means not just that he is dismissed as headmaster, but now the two aurors in attendance want to take him to Azkaban.

Unfortunately, at this point Dumbledore becomes invincible, treating Azkaban like a joke and ultimately knocking out Fudge and the two aurors without breaking a sweat, all of this while Harry is relegated to being a mere observer of the scene, pulled out of the line of fire by McGonagall. This is most unfortunate and smacks of, "Let's make Harry smaller in order to make Dumbledore larger."

While Harry is, according to our hypothesis, without his

wand at this point, we would still like him to have a role in this scene. He might grab Fudge's wrist to keep him from drawing his own wand, or could even just duck out of the line of fire on his own — demonstrating that he is at least smart enough and mature enough to do that much when the situation calls for it. Meanwhile, if Dumbledore keeps his remark that Azkaban is for sissies, the story could avoid turning him into a demigod if he eventually shrugged that comment off. "A bit of bravado never hurts when you're in a pinch," or words to that effect.

In addition, it might be nice if this scene happened after our proposed big rift (coming soon!) between Dumbledore and Harry. It would show that Harry can keep his priorities straight even when he is miffed at someone.

Communication

Harry and Cho Chang

Harry's relationship with Ms. Chang never gets off the ground, primarily because of Harry's lack of empathy toward her. As at the Tri-Wizard Ball, Harry is portrayed as being indistinguishable from Ron, viewing Cho as a "human hosepipe" and so forth.

While readers don't really care if this relationship gets very far, it seems that Harry would at least recognize and respond to Cho's distress. Even if he doesn't fully understand the specific cause of her pain, Harry at least understands pain itself. Let him demonstrate as much here. If he soon decides the situation is too complicated for them to pursue a romantic relationship, or if he simply can't spare time from his training to have a girlfriend, so be it. But we'd like to see Harry have spine enough to tell Cho as much straight up, and empathy enough to do so tactfully.

Harry and Dumbledore

With Dumbledore worried about the mental connection between Harry and Voldemort, it makes sense that Dumbledore would hold off telling Harry certain things. However, a benevolent Dumbledore wouldn't leave Harry swinging in the breeze. He would communicate to Harry the reason for the secrecy. To do otherwise isn't an old man's mistake, it is simply stupid. Dumbledore's failure to communicate with Harry appears to be another example of the story trying to perpetrate a surprise, even when the result doesn't add up.

As for Harry, by now we expect him to be mature enough to understand the gravity of the situation. However much he hates being left out of the loop, the mature Harry's hate would be directed at Voldemort not at Dumbledore.

Harry and Voldemort

Nevertheless, a rift could still open between Harry and Dumbledore — a rift fostered by Voldemort. Once Voldemort discovers the connection between himself and Harry, as a good villain he would use it to his maximum benefit. What might he do?

(a) He could channel his anger and hate into Harry, hoping to drive Harry insane or else make Harry lash out at someone. Harry might initially respond in kind, channeling his hate right back, only to discover that this makes things worse rather than better, and that his best bet is to suck up the pain and get on with business. Though Harry might at times come very close to lashing out — particularly at someone like Umbridge — we expect that Harry would survive Voldemort's mental attack by means of his inner strength and goodness, the support of his friends, and the things he learned about self-control while studying with Dumbledore.

(b) Voldemort could reveal to Harry that Snape knew the first part of the prophecy, and that Snape told that part to

Voldemort fifteen years earlier, with the result being the death of Harry's parents.

But wait, isn't Snape one of Voldemort's guys? Sure, but Voldemort wouldn't care about putting Snape at risk, not compared with the possibility that Harry would wind up questioning Dumbledore's judgment and maybe even attacking Snape. That last item would be exactly what the doctor ordered. From Voldemort's point of view, it would give Snape an opening to kill Harry in self-defense. Even if Snape fails and is killed himself, Harry's actions would certainly cause him to be expelled and would play directly into the murder trial gambit.

(c) The next logical step would be for Voldemort to tell Harry, "Dumbledore sent Snape back to me, hoping to lure me out. Dumbledore thought he could kill me and win glory for himself. The old man served your parents up as bait."

As a result of all this, Voldemort would be playing his part more vigorously, breeding distrust right at the core of the grand alliance.

Ultimately, it might be best if the connection between Harry and Voldemort didn't extend to mind reading, as that will make it difficult if not impossible for Harry to be at the center of the planning against Voldemort. One possibility is to give this mental connection two aspects. One aspect is when one of them sees and hears what the other is seeing and hearing. This aspect of the connection could be blocked via Occlumency. However, Occlumency might *not* be able to stop the active sending of thoughts and emotions — something quite different from reading or pulling information.

In any event, what we have here is an inescapable dark voice inside Harry's head. It endlessly chips away at his self-control, his grip on reality, and his belief in those he wants to trust the most. By comparison, Dolores Umbridge is nothing but a minor distraction. She might inadvertently step into the line of fire, she might unknowingly feed the flames, but she is far from the central point of conflict. Lord Voldemort is back, and from now on that center position rightfully belongs to him.

Sirius

At one point, Sirius gives Harry a mirror that will let them communicate with each other. This mirror gets set aside and used only after Sirius is dead, as a means of confirming that Sirius has in fact moved past the veil. Unfortunately, the effect of this mirror is to make Harry look like a dunce. Harry needn't be perfect, but since he already takes a beating over Sirius' death, adding the mirror on top of that pushes his punishment into the realm of child abuse.

If the climactic battle is moved out of the Department of Mysteries, then Sirius will have to be killed by some other means, most likely Avada Kedavra. In which case, any question of Sirius being somehow reachable goes away, and the mirror becomes unnecessary.

The Climactic Battle

During the final battle, Dumbledore shoves Harry aside. This paints Harry as untrustworthy and impotent even as it turns Dumbledore into a hotdog glory seeker. If Harry isn't up to participating in the fight, readers at least expect him to be smart enough to stay out of the way. Similarly, we expect Dumbledore to respect Harry enough to let Harry participate in the fight if Harry chooses to do so. Possibly, given our new, improved Harry, the mere appearance of Dumbledore alongside Harry might be enough make Voldemort switch to possessing Harry straight-away.

In the current version, this possession bit is an attempt to get Dumbledore to kill Harry. While that is one possible answer, it might work better if it is, rather, an attempt to get Harry to kill Dumbledore. (Again switching Harry from helpless lamb to active force.) From Voldemort's point of view, he's driven Harry to the point of hating Dumbledore.

Now he thinks he can force Harry to lash out. If Harry kills Dumbledore, the murder case would then include Dumbledore as a victim, and almost certainly Harry will be taken out of the picture by the Ministry.

Only Voldemort has misjudged, and Harry instead demonstrates forgiveness and loyalty, refuses to attack Dumbledore, and forces Voldemort out of his head.

The denouement would then play out. Dumbledore, now with a better understanding of how the mental connection works between Harry and Voldemort, feels comfortable filling Harry in on the Plan, etc. For his part, Harry emerges with his ego somewhat chastened, with a deeper understanding of how insidious Voldemort is, and with a better appreciation of how difficult some decisions can be. It isn't just Harry's own life on the line, but the lives of those he cares for and who trust him.

Confrontation

Thinking along these lines, the big blow-up between Harry and Dumbledore might therefore occur, not at the very end as it does now, but earlier in the book. Having been fed truths and half-truths by Voldemort, Harry confronts Dumbledore, who acknowledges that the gist of what Voldemort has revealed is true.

"Why didn't you tell me?" Harry says.

"I knew I would have to," Dumbledore says, "but I wanted to wait —"

"Until when?"

"Until you could understand why I would take such a risk."

"You didn't take a risk! My parents took it, and Neville's. But for you it was all just the hope for glory."

Harry could then go fume somewhere, wondering how much of what he feels is him and how much is Lord Voldemort.

This blow-up would then stand in contrast to the final conversation between Harry and Dumbledore, following the death of Sirius. Harry tells Dumbledore, "You *did* take a risk."

Harry would end Book 5 understanding the frightening responsibility that comes with power and authority. He has felt the full weight of the crown upon his head for the first time.

Chapter 6:
Half-Blood Prince

As we move deeper into the series, when we offer alternate approaches, we increasingly look as if we're trying to recreate the series in our own image and to our own liking. To some extent, that is in fact what we are doing. Certainly, we don't expect to escape such criticism, nor should we. It is impossible not to have opinions, and there is no point in trying to hide our own.

Still, our goal in offering these alternate approaches isn't to say, "Here's how it should be done," but rather, "Look at the many available paths. Don't some of these paths seem more exciting, more in keeping with what we were promised, than what we were given?" Which path is best? That isn't our place to say, but at least let us advance various options and discuss them as objectively as we can.

Opening Chapters

Neither of the first two chapters of Book 6 are from Harry's point of view, a rarity in the series. It seems likely that the first chapter of Book 6 is included primarily to make the second chapter stand out less. Chapter One does little but establish that Voldemort is now operating in the open, using giants, dementors, and death eaters to attack both muggles and wizards. If, in the revised version of the series, Ron, Hermione, and Dumbledore are all POV characters, then the first chapter of Book 6 can be eliminated. If we aren't going to witness these attacks happening first hand, but are merely going to hear about them, they can easily be boiled down to a few sentences.

They certainly don't seem to warrant an entire chapter.

The second chapter shows us Snape making an Unbreakable Vow with Draco Malfoy's mother, so that if Draco fails in his assigned task (which we later learn is to kill Dumbledore), Snape will complete the mission himself in order to save Draco from Lord Voldemort's wrath. This seems a worthwhile chapter. By having it from the point of view of Draco's mother, we avoid seeing Snape's true motivations, which helps maintain the ambiguity of his character. But we still get to see Snape playing double agent, see him treading the razor's edge, and see how he has managed to fool Voldemort. (Or else, how he managed to fool Dumbledore.)

The Ring

Book 6 has Dumbledore locate and destroy the ring Horcrux on his own. This is something the benevolent Dumbledore wouldn't do. As Book 7, *Deathly Hallows*, makes painfully obvious, Harry needs to be involved in this task as a learning experience, if nothing else. Given this hypothetical change, would the ring be destroyed during the summer vacation (as it is now) or would it rather be destroyed more toward the middle of the year, after quite a bit of investigating, searching, and researching? Both approaches have their merit.

(a) Destroying the ring later in the school year allows more space for investigative work. Instead of being handed key bits of information for free via the Pensieve, Harry would help track them down, playing detective alongside Dumbledore. This approach feels more logical, since it seems a tad strange to research Horcruxes after having already tracked down and destroyed one of them. Not an insurmountable problem, surely, but something to at least consider.

(b) Destroying the ring during the summer means that Dumbledore will learn of Snape's Unbreakable Vow *after* Dumbledore is (we suspect) mortally wounded by the ring's curse. This will make Snape's revelation more dramatic, as the clock is ticking on Dumbledore's life. While his death can be delayed by various means, it can't be delayed indefinitely. To lose both Dumbledore and Snape would rob Harry of his two greatest assets. Thus, Dumbledore would likely be furious with Snape, but eventually would accept the situation and devise a plan: he will sacrifice himself for the cause. Not to save Draco (or even Snape, per se), but to give Harry a chance to succeed in his task. Harry will absolutely need Snape working on the inside of Voldemort's team once Dumbledore is gone.

The Horcrux Curse

Currently Dumbledore's hand is injured by his putting on the ring Horcrux. This doesn't quite add up. It seems, rather, that a Horcrux would gradually possess and/or drain the wearer (as the diary does with Ginny, and as the locket tries to do with Harry in Book 7). Thus, what if Dumbledore's injury came from his *destroying* the Horcrux, rather than merely wearing it?

If so, why wasn't Harry the victim of such a curse when he destroyed the diary Horcrux? One possible answer is that the diary was Voldemort's first Horcrux, and Voldemort hadn't yet hit on the idea of protecting his Horcruxes with a killing curse.

But a seemingly better answer is that, by virtue of his connection to Voldemort, Harry has yet another power: he is able to destroy Voldemort's Horcruxes with impunity. Taking this approach, the retribution of a destroyed Horcrux, rather than being an additional spell, could be inherent to the Horcrux enchantment itself. Only the one whose soul is encased there-in can safely destroy the beastie. (The Horcrux texts, having never encountered a scar like Harry's, remain silent as to the loophole it grants him.)

This second approach seems to offer the most dramatic potential. Harry and Dumbledore locate the ring Horcrux together. Wanting to emphasize the vague nature of the Chosen One prophecy, Dumbledore asks for the privilege of destroying this Horcrux. Not only has Harry already had his turn when he destroyed the diary, this will also show that Harry is merely the catalyst for Voldemort's downfall. That is, Harry doesn't have to personally destroy every single part of Voldemort's soul in order to fulfill the prophecy.

Dumbledore destroys the ring with Gryffindor's sword and is immediately struck by the curse. Harry manages to hold the curse at bay, restricting it to Dumbledore's hand. (Rather than Snape doing this by virtue of his insight into dark magic, we recommend that Harry alone have the ability via his tie to Voldemort.) However, naturally even he can't fully eradicate the curse. Finding a way to do so then becomes a likely goal for Harry during the following weeks and months.

By this time, suppose that readers are used to a Harry who is obsessed with destroying Voldemort. We see him bypass Cho Chang as a possible distraction. We see him quit the Quidditch team for that same reason. We see him rearrange his course schedule, work late into the night, and so forth. Thus, readers would understand that nothing can distract Harry from his pursuit of Voldemort. When this threat to Dumbledore's life *does* distract Harry, it emphasizes Dumbledore's importance to our hero, and serves as a powerful commentary on the strength of Harry's affection for his mentor.

As a result, the investigation into the nature of Horcruxes, and Voldemort's use of them, would take on additional significance. A way to save Dumbledore's life may rest in some long-lost book or scroll, or in the mind of someone like the wand-maker Ollivander.

Suppose Harry tracks down a rare tome on Horcruxes, and Hermione and McGonagall (or whoever the Ancient Runes teacher is) translate it. The news isn't good, and suggests that not only should Dumbledore already be dead, but so should Harry for his destruction of the diary. This clarifies that Harry's special connection to Voldemort has protected him.

As a result of the new insight, Hermione might come up with the idea of blood transfusions. Harry's blood does in fact push back the curse. But with each transfusion, the effect diminishes. Dumbledore's life expectancy is now measured in months, if not weeks.

Although it seems we've drifted off into the weeds a bit here, what we're asking for is that Harry be an active participant in the destruction of the ring Horcrux, and that Horcruxes behave consistently. In addition, Dumbledore's sacrifice at the end of the book will seem more reasonable if readers know that he's going to kick off pretty soon anyway. (Maybe that is the case in the current version, too, but if so, the reader is never told as much.) Also, searching for a cure to save Dumbledore gives Harry a much-needed goal to occupy him during Book 6.

Snape's Vow

We get hints in Book 6 that Snape isn't happy with his role in the war effort. His accepting the Unbreakable Vow certainly indicates as much. At one point in Book 6, Snape is overheard telling Dumbledore, "You're asking too much of me." From this, it appears that Snape would prefer to let the Unbreakable Vow kill him, rather than save himself by killing Dumbledore.

It makes sense that Snape would be tired of being an object of hate and suspicion on both sides of the fight. He could also fear that he is once again falling under Voldemort's influence, and that without Dumbledore to help him remain balanced, Snape will find himself drifting off into the madness that Voldemort instills in his followers? Or, with Dumbledore gone, Voldemort will no longer skimp on Snape's obedience sessions?

In any event, Dumbledore convinces Snape that the only viable solution is for Snape to fulfill his vow. If Voldemort becomes impatient, unwilling to wait for the curse to finish Dumbledore off on its own, then Snape will likely have to kill Dumbledore.

Does Dumbledore tell Harry this part of the plan? Keeping the plan secret enhances surprise value, while revealing the plan not only shows Dumbledore's trust in Harry, but also introduces a different kind of suspense. Rather than "What is going on?", readers wonder, "What will Harry do in the end?" Harry could reject the plan initially, but over the course of the book, as all efforts to push back the Horcrux curse fail, Harry accepts the inevitable. His final choice could be made as he silently watches Snape kill Dumbledore at the top of the Astronomy Tower. Not Harry pinned helplessly and passively in place, but Harry — able to intervene if he chooses — actively deciding to do the hard thing that the situation demands: nothing.

As a result, though not a surprise, the climactic scene would remain a moment of high drama even for repeat readers.

The Locket

The trip to retrieve the locket Horcrux raises a number of questions. First, why is it necessary to swim out to the cave where the thing is kept? Perhaps there are magic spells preventing apparating directly. If so, the reader longs to be apprised of this. Without such an explanation, Dumbledore and Harry jumping into the ocean for a swim seems pretty loony. Second, even if apparating directly is nixed, why not bring a broom along? Or even levitate oneself over there? Either solution seems preferable to swimming.

Hypothetically speaking, given our modified Horcrux curse, Dumbledore by this time would be too sick to make this trip. Thus, rather than Harry being an ineffectual tag-along for Dumbledore, it seems likely that he would either come to the cave alone or else with a small number of others. Ron, Hermione, Ginny, and Neville all seem viable candidates for watching Harry's back — though Ginny might be watching a different part of it than the others.

In any event, when they finally reach the inner sanctum of the cave, Harry and Dumbledore discover that the locket has been taken and a replacement left behind. For this reason, the tedious and not-especially convincing potion-drinking business could be done away with without harm. After all, having gotten rid of the potion and taken the real Horcrux, would Regulus Black have bothered, or even known how, to restore the original enchantment? It seems unlikely the spell would automatically restore itself. Voldemort would want some clear sign that his Horcrux had been tampered with, after all.

Whether Harry comes alone or brings along one or two people is perhaps significant, in terms of his personality. But the potion business feels like a distraction. With Dumbledore already sick, we don't need the potion to explain his debility on the Astronomy Tower.

Our goal in suggesting these various, seemingly minor changes is to eliminate inexplicable details that leave many readers scratching their heads. The combination of swimming in the ocean, rowing a boat across a pond, drinking ten glasses full of stuff out of a little font that hides a necklace: these seemingly arbitrary actions give the cave sequence an "it came to me in a dream" quality, and not in a good way. While these details could all no doubt be explained, it seems more reasonable to switch to an intuitive set of events and be done with it.

Moving on, suppose Harry takes Ron with him to the cave. Upon their return to Hogwarts, when they come upon the scene of Dumbledore's impending death, it seems reasonable that it would be Ron who gets pinned to the wall (by Harry) so that Ron can't interfere in something he doesn't fully understand. As a side-effect, this might cause Ron (or whoever) to question which side Harry is really on. Is Harry out to destroy Voldemort in the cause of goodness and light, or merely so Harry can take the Dark Lord's throne for himself?

The Luck of Slughorn

A new professor is needed to fill in for the departed Dolores Umbridge, and Horace Slughorn seems a reasonable choice.

Harry's lucky acquisition of Snape's old potions book, however, followed by his acquisition of a bottle of luck, are events that undercut the seriousness of the situation in Book 6.

First, we expect that Harry's grades in potions would be high enough to allow him into Professor Snape's NEWT-level course. Thus, he would bring the required potions book with him and have no need of luckily being handed Snape's old one. While it could be that Ron or someone else *is* in need of a book, why bother? Snape's old book becomes a distraction. The world is now at war and people are dropping left and right. To be concerned with "I wonder who the half-blood Prince is" trivializes the situation. That's the sort of information we prefer to see in the *Potter Encyclopedia* or as a minor aside here, rather than as a major conundrum that spans the entirety of Book 6.

Second, readers recognize that luck is simply a way for the story to force events to turn out the way it wants, even when it doesn't make sense. Luck favors the prepared. Let that be enough for the characters in the Potter series, just as it is for the rest of us.

As for obtaining the crucial Horcrux memory from Slughorn, we'd like for Harry's understanding of human nature to have evolved enough for him to accomplish this task without needing divine intervention. He might accomplish it via the same sequence of events, even, except that he would work from a plan that he devises himself, rather than by following a trail of bread crumbs laid out for him.

The Department of Magical Transportation (DMT)

In Book 6, Dumbledore moves about via various magical means. He takes Harry to visit Slughorn and the Horcrux cave via apparition, for example. Yet we also know that the new Minister of Magic, Scrimgeour, is curious as to Dumbledore's movements. Why can't Scrimgeour track Dumbledore via the DMT?

When a squad of people come to pick Harry up at the start of Book 7, *Deathly Hallows*, we're told that the DMT can track every sort of magical movement. When the story wants to add tension to certain events in Book 5, regarding Sirius and the flue network, the Ministry are again given that power. However, when such ulterior motives are missing, the story forgets about the DMT, as happens here in Book 6 and also for most of Book 7, where the Big Three constantly apparate without being detected.

Though minor, this inconsistency still undercuts the believability of the series.

Roles

Hermione

By the time we get to Book 6, we expect each of the Big Three (or Big Five, if it has come to that) to have identifiable roles within Harry's organization. Hermione is perhaps the easiest to keep busy, by having her undertake tasks that befit her intelligence. What might Harry ask her to help him with? (a) Find a way to detect if someone is Imperiused. This seems like a major gap in the current wizarding repertoire. It shouldn't be necessary to guess whether Fudge or anyone else is operating under compulsion. (b) Look for a way to undo the Imperius curse. No doubt there are ways to do so already, just that they leave the person insane or something. Hermione could be tasked with eliminating the unwanted side effects.

Once Dumbledore is stricken with the Horcrux curse, Hermione would surely join the search for ways to undo the curse. She could learn the name of a rare book she needs and then hand the task of recovering it to Harry. If the ring is destroyed early in the book, then Hermione's research into things like the Imperius curse might not even start until Book

7, as her time in Book 6 will be devoted to Horcruxes. But the idea remains the same. By undertaking these sorts of tasks, Hermione's talents become more than arbitrary character traits, they apply directly to problems that Harry is trying to solve.

Ron, Neville, etc.

If we allow Hermione to evolve toward Mad Scientist, what will Ron's role be? Is he the ever-loyal sidekick? Or, via taking after his father, the Inventor? One benefit of making Ron the Inventor is that it would require Ron and Hermione to pool their talents in order to fulfill the Mad Scientist role. Their collaboration would give them a much-needed point of commonality and a reason to work together as a pair.

Because Dumbledore cashes out of the game and Snape moves out of reach at the end of Book 6, we need someone who can rein Harry in, get through his thick skull, etc. Hermione generally plays that role currently, but Ron seems a better choice. Rather than being a yes-man, Ron could be the one capable of questioning Harry's decisions. Even if many of the concerns that Ron raises originate with Hermione, it seems reasonable that Ron would be the one willing to risk Harry's anger in forcing an issue. His bravery in doing so would serve as something Hermione admires in Ron, helping explain her attraction to him.

If Neville evolves into more than a shadow presence, then he seems perfect as the absolutely faithful knight (given what happened to his parents), and one of great prowess as well (both his parents were aurors, after all). If we suppose that Ron is frequently Harry's companion on various outings, and Hermione is tied up with various forms of research, then Neville could take over running the D.A. on a day-to-day basis, serving as an operational lieutenant. That seems close to his current role in Book 7, though Book 7 has Neville operating on his own, without any guidance from Harry, which is unfortunate. On the other hand, if Ron becomes the Inventor, then it could be Neville who most often has Harry's back on dangerous forays.

The Romantic Ron

Starting toward the end of Book 6 and carrying over into Book 7, Ron's attraction to Hermione gets stuck in first gear and ultimately makes him seem passive-aggressive. If Ron has some question about Harry's interest in Hermione, it seems he would be the sort to bring the subject up directly. Similarly, even if he isn't the most romantic or tactful fellow, we still expect Ron to let Hermione know how he feels ("Baby, are you hot! What do you say?"), rather than silently moon about in the shadows.

A romantic relationship simmering on the back burner does keep us paying attention, but this is another case where at least some readers will opt out if the ploy is carried on too long. We expect that an attractive bookworm like Hermione will have several choices available to her, and most likely will be beating them off with a broomstick. But even if this isn't the case, we would still like to see Ron follow the standard male dictates of, "If you snooze, you lose" and, "Get in there fast before someone else beats you to it." Basically, for Ron to silently carry a torch seems out of character given his seemingly brusque personality.

Ginny

Although Ginny becomes Harry's main squeeze, she's allowed no more than a token role. While it makes sense for Harry to want their relationship kept a secret, it would be nice if putting the relationship on ice were either impossible for him or rejected violently by Ginny.

Harry is a kid of sixteen who is not only the Chosen One, destined to bring Voldemort down (or die trying), but (according to our hypothetical flow of events) is already having to take over the mantle of warlord from the failing Dumbledore. Everyone is looking at Harry like "What's our next move, boss?" Or else, "This is the Chosen One? We're all gonna die." Couldn't we cut Harry this much slack, and give him a Ginny to fall back on?

Voldemort

Voldemort waits for Draco to fix a magic cabinet so that a large group of death eaters can storm into the castle. Then, having waited a full school year for this happy moment, the death eaters flee the scene immediately after Dumbledore's death.

This doesn't add up. In attacking Hogwarts in force, Voldemort has just alienated every former student of the school and every parent who has a child there. Why do this and then simply abandon the castle? If the goal was to take it over and use the students as hostages, then do so. By now the magic luck potion is wearing off, and even if Voldemort's death eaters are so wimpy and incompetent as to be held at bay by Expelliarmus and Bat Bogey Hex, Dumbledore is now gone and there is nothing to prevent Voldemort himself from joining the fight.

On the other hand, if Voldemort's goal is simply to have Dumbledore killed, then why send in all these death eaters? Voldemort is clearly willing to cashier Snape and Draco both in order to get Dumbledore. As a teacher, Snape in particular can move about Hogwarts as he pleases at any hour of the day or night, no matter how many aurors and Order of the Phoenix are guarding the corridors. Thus, either Snape or Draco could lure Dumbledore out to the Astronomy Tower on a ruse, kill him while his guard is down, set up the dark mark, then flee before anyone is the wiser.

In fact, it might not even be necessary for Snape or Draco to flee Hogwarts. So long as no one sees the murder take place, it becomes a whodunit, with the possibility that Harry himself could be framed for it.

One thing that would make sense of The [First] Battle for Hogwarts is for Voldemort to want both Harry and Dumbledore killed. Given that Voldemort still doesn't know the complete prophecy, it seems reasonable that he would want no part of Harry personally. "Something is protecting this kid from me," Voldemort would think, "but maybe it won't protect him so well against some of my death eaters."

It also makes sense (if we stretch just a bit), that Voldemort would want Dumbledore killed before any attempt is made on Harry, under the assumption that Dumbledore has been protecting Harry all along via some arcane equivalent of the Mother's Love spell. With Dumbledore gone, any such protection should vanish, which means Harry will have to stand on his own, and can therefore be cut down just like anyone else.

Following this logic, we expect the death eaters to flee only when it becomes apparent that Harry is more than they can handle. Not because Harry is protected by the lingering effect of Mother's Love. Not because he downed a bottle of luck. But because Harry *is* the Chosen One, ready, willing, and able to at least capture, if not kill, every death eater he gets his hands on.

As it stands in the current version, the flight of the death eaters is inexplicable, while the duel between Harry and Snape outside the Hogwarts gates shows us a Harry who is something of a joke, a child screaming and swinging wildly, while Snape calmly puts a hand on top of Harry's head and holds the impotent kid at arm's length. It is the end of Book 6, and look what has become of our hero.

Distraction and Opportunity

Assuming that most of our suggested changes are implemented, by the time we reach Book 6, the series has a lot of irons in the fire. In addition to preparing himself for the final showdown, Harry has to learn about Horcruxes, direct the D.A., and look for a way to save Dumbledore from the Horcrux curse. He has relationships to maintain with Dobby and Winky, Moaning Myrtle, and Hagrid, not to mention Ron and Hermione. He's inherited the Black mansion, which makes Kreacher his personal House Elf — and Kreacher is an elf who needs special attention. Harry might also be learning how to treat with giants, merfolk, centaurs, goblins, and various other races.

Meanwhile, Dumbledore, Snape, Voldemort, and the Ministry of Magic all have agendas that have to be taken into account. We'd like Ron and Hermione to both have clear roles to play in the grand alliance, and would love to see Ginny and Neville added to that list.

Thus, Book 6 has its work cut out for it. The large number of subplots and secondary characters could easily swamp the main plot, so care has to be taken to keep ancillary events from growing out of proportion. Which brings us to the subject of Quidditch.

Quidditch

It seems reasonable that by Book 6, Harry's Quidditch days are over. However, what about Ron, Ginny, and whoever else plays on the team? Might Harry try to keep all the D.A. from participating in the sport? Perhaps. He might succeed, earning himself quite a bit of disgruntlement from Ron and various others. Or he might be talked out of such rash action by Dumbledore. If so, Harry could then attend one match or another as a spectator, letting go some of his stress if only for an hour or two. In any event, given the rising body count in the outside world, for Book 6 to contain so much Quidditch coverage makes it seem a bit lopsided.

Draco Malfoy

Harry's obsession in book 6 is, "What is Draco up to?" This doesn't feel right. While Neville or someone like that might spot Draco's strange behavior and bring it to Harry's attention, by this time we expect that Harry would have little time to spare for small potatoes like Draco. (a) Harry might totally ignore Draco and later regret his underestimating the kid. (b) He might assign the D.A., Dobby, and/or Kreacher the task of figuring out what Draco is up to. (c) Harry might try to have a meaningful talk with Draco. Naturally, such an attempt would (at least initially) be for naught, but Harry certainly has some insights into Voldemort that he can share with Draco, and this would let Harry demonstrate that he is past schoolboy bickering.

In any event, it seems unlikely that Draco would be more than a momentary distraction for Harry. What Draco is up to might prey on Harry's mind a bit, but in our opinion Harry's plate is too full, and Draco too small a fish, for Harry to personally devote time to following him around.

Politics

Harry's handling of the new Minister of Magic seems misguided. We appreciate that Harry is eager to demonstrate loyalty to Dumbledore, but Harry's conversations with Scrimgeour turn into Dumbledore pep rallies. Given Dumbledore's emphasis on "we must all work together" and "Voldemort's greatest strength is in dividing us," shouldn't Harry be willing to cooperate with the Ministry? Are there hard feelings over Dolores Umbridge, the disruption at Hogwarts, the media attacks? Sure. Should Harry be willing to forgive, forget, and move on in the name of unity and kicking Voldemort's butt? It seems so.

In the lead-up to that other WW2, Winston Churchill didn't go straight from back bencher to Prime Minister. Rather, he joined Neville Chamberlain's cabinet as First Sea Lord. Was there bad blood? Yes. Was Chamberlain handling things absolutely the way Churchill wanted? No. But Churchill still took the position when it was offered.

Should Scrimgeour be willing to let Stan Shunpike out of Azkaban in order to get Harry on as mascot? Hard to say, but if Scrimgeour is even a half-baked politician, he understands the importance of compromise. Should Harry ask for something more substantial than just one person's release from prison? Should he ask for some official title for himself and/or Dumbledore? A promotion for Mr. Weasley? All of the above and more?

Like it or not, Harry is a celebrity. Not a media celebrity but more of a Field Marshal Montgomery type. Let Harry throw his weight around, call press conferences, show that he understands that war isn't always about who has the biggest guns, but who has the most industrial capacity, the best propaganda, etc.

Our analogy has already sprained an ankle, but the point is, Harry's flat dismissal of Scrimgeour is naive and fails to make use of a tool ready at hand. We expect Harry to be capable of better. If his doing better requires first a brisk talking to from Dumbledore, fine. But either way, *Dumbledore* certainly understands how the game is played, and we assume that he would waste no time in making sure that Harry understands as well.

The New Godfather

Since the analogies are flowing hot and heavy, let us pull in another. Vito Corleone isn't going to last much longer, and he needs someone to take over the family business. Rather than wait until it is too late, Vito proactively turns control over to his son Michael, telling his various lieutenants, "Do you trust me? Then be a friend to Michael and do what he tells you."

We reach a similar situation here in Book 6. Dumbledore may have planned to hand the reins of power to Harry eventually, but now his timing is thrown off. Events are moving way too fast. Harry isn't even legally an adult yet. What to do?

This is a tough question. Is Harry the best choice to fill in as head of the Order of the Phoenix? Why not Remus Lupin, Mad Eye Moody, or Mr. Weasley? They are adults, all with experience from WW1 to draw upon.

In searching our feelings, it doesn't seem to matter if Dumbledore hands the reins to Harry or to someone else. Harry has enough on his plate already, and one of these other choices might be better for various reasons. But for Dumbledore to simply ignore the question of succession, especially once the Horcrux curse has him in its grip, is inexcusable. That is a mistake the wise Dumbledore wouldn't make.

Chapter 7:
Deathly Hallows

Hornswoggled

For six books, the Potter series has gotten away with cheating the reader. In Book 7, the former pastime becomes an addiction. It is a tame chapter that goes by without some sort of double-think, happy coincidence, or outright miracle.

1. During the motorcycle flight to safety, Harry's wand acts of its own accord to save him from Voldemort.

2. At that point, Voldemort conveniently gives up the chase.

3. Apparently Hagrid's skin is thick enough to resist both gravity and the Dark Lord's spells, since our giant friend survives the flight and subsequent crash with no more than a few inconveniences.

4. When death eaters attack the wedding, we learn that all they care about is kidnapping Harry. Given that the death eaters had Harry in their grasp at the end of Book 6 and failed to nab him, this new approach fails to convince.

5. Two death eaters are let go by the Big Three, but the price of that action is left vague and, most importantly, never brings any of the Three to feel guilt or a sense of inadequacy, to the extent of, "If we weren't such wimps, maybe Lupin and Tonks would still be alive."

6. Several Hogwarts students wander past the very campsite where the Big Three are staying, so as to provide us with news of current events. It is a small world indeed.

7. The location of Gryffindor's sword is revealed to Harry by a friendly Patronus of unknown origin.

8. Harry gallantly lets Ron destroy the locket Horcrux, though surely he must believe that doing so will kill Ron. Instead, the locket Horcrux makes a not-to-be-repeated attempt to mess with Ron's mind. Ron destroys it and suffers no ill effects. Later on in Book 7, we learn that it isn't destroying a Horcrux but rather wearing one that is dangerous. Except that Harry and the others have been taking it in turns to wear the locket which (much as we would expect) behaves more like the diary, and attempts merely to possess rather than kill the wearer. As a magical device, Horcruxes need to behave consistently. Their failure to do so undermines the reader's confidence in the universe of the story.

9. Held hostage in a dungeon, Harry grabs a snitch and yells for help. Incredibly, this approach works and help does in fact arrive. Shades of Book 2.

10. Ron opens the Chamber of Secrets on his own. Apparently he has remembered and can replicate the required parselmouth phrase from five years earlier.

11. A magical cabinet, source of the invasion of Hogwarts in Book 6, a clear violation of the security of the campus, has neither been disabled, destroyed, nor removed, but merely left in the Room of Requirement for an entire year.

12. Crabbe unwittingly destroys the diadem Horcrux by means of fiendfyre. Hermione bonks herself on the noggin at this. "Oh yeah. Well, the book did talk about that, but fiendfyre's kind of hard to control, so I never mentioned it until now." That would explain several hundred pages of "how do we destroy one, gosh I don't know." The fiendfyre is left burning by the Big Three, but apparently some happy aspect of the Room of Requirement keeps the entire school from being consumed. Apparently, nobody knows how to stop the wretched thing once it starts.

13. The tide of the final battle is shifted in favor of the good guys by the appearance of reinforcements which, the book admits, pretty much come out of nowhere.

14. Despite Harry's total failure to counter Voldemort or his death eaters, by the end of Book 7 the death toll of good guys we know by name is limited to Hedwig, Mad Eye Moody, Dobby, Fred Weasley, Snape, Lupin, Tonks, and Collin Creevey.

While we would have a hard time finding any fan of the series who longed for the death of Hagrid, Ginny, or any other friendly character, still, readers need a convincing reason why so few people die, and neither Voldemort's preoccupation with Harry (a non-threat if ever there was one) nor with the Elder Wand (learn to delegate, my man) fit that bill.

Voldemort

One thing that doesn't quite add up with Voldemort is, why would someone like Lucius Malfoy crawl around on the ground and grovel for this guy? Voldemort is totally lacking in charisma and doesn't seem to bring much to the table.

While it might seem that bigotry was Hitler's primary hook into pre-WW2 Germany, it wasn't that simple. The country was economically devastated, and voting results show that Hitler did best when the social situation was at its worst. If inflation slowed and the economy improved, the Nazis lost seats. Desperation resulting from chronic food shortages, unemployment, and a generally bleak outlook created the environment where Hitler could not take, but be *handed* the reins of power on a silver platter.

What the Potter series lacks is a similar situation or threat that would make people like Lucius Malfoy turn to Voldemort as a leader. Simple prejudice against non-pure-blood wizards isn't especially convincing in this regard.

Another distraction crops up here as well. Prior to Hitler becoming Chancellor, the Nazis were involved in attacks on Jews, but few people imagined that things could go so far as they eventually did, with death camps and killing squads. In

Voldemort's case, while people might have missed that he was a raving nutcase prior to WW1, they have no such excuse when he returns fourteen years later and wants to pick up where he left off. Voldemort's return in Book 4 is the equivalent of Hitler showing up not-quite-dead today. While he might be able to gather a following amongst skinheads and the like, human nature being such as it is, a return to power on his part is hard to imagine.

Moreover, while Hitler did fly into rages, made disastrous decisions, and spent more time watching movies and lounging around than he did running the country, he was also charismatic and good at delegating power. His speeches over the radio and to large crowds are legendary, and even late in the war, with things totally going against the Third Reich, Hitler was able to restore drive and excitement in despairing underlings by the force of his personality.

What we see in Voldemort is a psycho with no redeeming qualities and nothing to offer other than a fanatical desire for genocide, the price of which was made pretty clear during WW1. Except for Greyback and various other sociopaths, even Voldemort's death eaters don't seem especially happy that he's returned, and who can blame them? If they really care about the purity of the wizarding race, surely another war is the last thing they want. How many pure-blood families will remain once WW2 is over?

In addition, Voldemort makes no attempt to win popular support, but seems content to go after the entire world (muggles included) with, say, 100 each of death eaters, giants, dementors, and an indeterminate number of undead. (By comparison, in the muggle WW2, Germany fielded more than 100 divisions, with a division containing as many as 25,000 soldiers.) Far from threatening the safety of modern society, Voldemort's approach looks suicidal. Even laughable. What sort of person would support such lunacy?

In short, Voldemort as a character doesn't add up. One possibility for making Voldemort more believable would be to make him more charismatic. A charismatic Voldemort, no matter what he really looks like, would surely transfigure himself to look like the handsome Tom Riddle, for example. He would also understand how to create loyal followers and how to tell people what they want to hear. Voldemort's charisma could be magically enhanced, even, as a way to explain the fanatical loyalty he inspires in a wide range of people.

Another thing that might help make the situation believable is some sort of threat to the wizarding world, a threat that Voldemort is willing to address directly and vigorously. One likely candidate for this sort of threat is the encroachment of muggle society upon the magical world.

The Muggle Threat

Spy satellites are now so sophisticated, they can tell whether a snitch-in-flight has been autographed or not, and a Hogwarts-sized gap in Google Earth wouldn't go unnoticed for long. Add to this advances in medicine and forensics, and sooner or later someone is going to notice something.

Fifteen years after WW1, the threat of the wizarding world being revealed is greater than ever. And being revealed is no small thing. Muggle society has moved past burning witches at the stake. If they can't already, soon they'll be able to build biological weapons that target only those with a particular genetic sequence. Wizards, for example.

The threat isn't just to wizards, either. It applies to giants, goblins, werewolves, vampires, unicorns, dragons, merfolk, centaurs, and so forth. People like Dumbledore might talk about getting along with the muggles, but what about muggles getting along with wizards? All muggles have ever done is reproduce at prodigious rates, pollute the planet, chop down all the best hiding places, and kill any magical creature they come across.

The muggle threat, then, could very well be something that

most wizards fear.

Suppose that Voldemort's main political platform is to reduce (or eliminate) the muggle threat. If he can get various muggle politicians under the Imperius charm, then Voldemort might be able to arrange a few nuclear missile strikes as a way of getting the muggles to wipe themselves out. Or he might make use of biological weapons, spreading diseases that wizards can cure themselves of with no difficulty but that will kill 95% of all muggles. (*This* is where AIDS came from!)

What Book 6 describes (giants on the rampage, dementors wandering around London, and so forth) sounds like the opposite of what this sort of Voldemort would really want. Though the muggles write off even the giant attacks as freak storms, such a response offends the reader's credulity. Instantaneous communication and television coverage make the risk of exposure for Voldemort's forces virtually a guarantee. As Arthur C. Clarke said, sufficiently advanced technology is indistinguishable from magic. And some of what the muggles have these days is very advanced indeed.

On the other hand, if the Dark Lord is simply a hateful lunatic, fine. But in that case, it seems his following would be different. Rather than having widespread support, we'd expect Voldemort to be surrounded by a small circle of psychopaths. Greyback is a good example. Lucius Malfoy, not so much.

What if the Dark Mark that Voldemort brands into his death eaters had certain qualities of the Unbreakable Vow associated with it, so that once a wizard becomes a death eater, he is unable to change allegiance without dire consequences? If so, how to explain Snape's double-agent role and Regulus Black's attempt to destroy the locket Horcrux?

Ultimately, what we see here is that making Voldemort a believable, consistent villain is a real challenge. For example, if Voldemort is charismatic enough to be elected Minister of Magic during WW1, that turns Dumbledore and the Order of the Phoenix into counter-revolutionaries, and it is hard to imagine Dumbledore retaining his position at Hogwarts during

WW1 under those circumstances.

As it stands, the series does a very good job of staying focused, not letting itself get lured off into a swamp of global political intrigue. In that sense, the Muggle Threat approach seems unwise, as it could easily open a whole barrel of gargoyles.

Wizard Protocol

Given that dueling seems an accepted practice in wizard society, what if we take things one step further, and have wizards adhere to a kind of chivalric code? If wizard A can defeat wizard B in a duel, that makes wizard A right. In addition, if wizard B is sufficiently highly regarded, defeating him in a duel might also raise the prestige of wizard A such that wizards who are lower in the pecking order naturally accept wizard A as their superior and show him deference.

This sort of an approach seems to offer several benefits. For one, it helps to explain how Dumbledore could wield so much authority regarding Harry's upbringing. Surely the wizarding world must have some equivalent of a Child Services Department. At a minimum, with someone as famous as Harry, it seems likely that quite a few people would want the honor (and the attendant benefits) of raising him themselves. For Dumbledore to unilaterally leave Harry with his aunt and uncle, for Dumbledore to not be even challenged much less overruled by one committee or another, does seem a bit convenient.

Although the series shows us that Dumbledore is highly respected, it might be nice if that respect had a bit more oomph behind it.

Another benefit of the "might makes right" approach is that it seems to fit well with Voldemort having a wide following during WW1, perhaps even having a majority of the votes in the wizard congress, despite his lack of charisma and his lunatic approach to things.

Dumbledore, meanwhile, could retain his post as headmaster during WW1 even if he is actively running a counter-revolutionary operation. The rationale would be that Dumbledore has issued a challenge to Voldemort, but Voldemort — afraid of Dumbledore, and perhaps having rejected the chivalric code — has failed to respond to that challenge.

Thus, as a way of explaining the current flow of events in the Potter series, a medieval mindset seems quite useful. Giving wizards this sort of unfamiliar philosophy would make them seem strange and alien. As such, a chivalric code could be the serious cousin to "gee aren't wizards weird."

Tasks for the Main Actors

Harry

Book 7 already has the Big Three accomplishing all the tasks that are absolutely required for Voldemort to be killed. Namely, they hunt down the remaining Horcruxes and destroy them, then kill Voldemort himself. The manner in which these tasks are accomplished is, however, not especially satisfying. In particular, readers expect Harry to know what the Azkaban he's doing.

Aside from hunting Horcruxes, there are a number of additional tasks that Harry might conceivably undertake. (a) He could fill Dumbledore's role as counterweight to Voldemort. That is, he would force Voldemort to move cautiously and to work through his death eaters rather than become personally involved in any fights, for fear of Harry.

If Harry isn't strong enough to fill this role, then we feel the series should end with a larger number of dead bodies. What we have now is a wimpy Harry and a happy ending. As pointed out in Part 1, that particular cheat is offensive, to say the least.

(b) Harry could take over Dumbledore's political role.

While point (a) faces outwards toward Voldemort, this one faces inward toward the government and the Order of the Phoenix. In this role, Harry could serve as a rallying flag for the resistance movement and any government-in-exile that might form. Associated with this role are tasks such as treating with giants, goblins, and the various other magical races.

(c) Harry could assign tasks to Hermione, Ron, and other members of the D.A. This is similar in nature to the previous point, but focuses on Harry's inner circle.

For Hermione, there are a number of potential Mad Scientist tasks: figure out how to destroy (not just drive off) dementors; develop a way to recognize the Imperius curse and safely free people from it; and so forth.

Readers can accept that some of these tasks will fail for one reason or another. But what we want is to see our beloved characters thinking, maximizing their abilities, and generally working their butts off, rather than blithely sitting around a campfire like delicious, hot schmoes.

Voldemort

In Book 7, we see special care taken to protect the Dursleys. We also learn that the Weasley house is under heavy protective spells and that Hermione's parents have gone into safe hiding. It feels a bit late for all this. Voldemort has been back two full years now. He would have had no difficulty finding out that Ron and Hermione are Harry's only real friends, and for Voldemort to go after Hermione and/or her parents would have been an obvious move on his part. Thus, providing special protection for these folks seems like a task for Dumbledore to undertake as far back as the end of Book 4, *Goblet of Fire*.

As for taking over the Ministry of Magic, it makes little sense for Voldemort to delay this action as long as he does. The Voldemort we have been told about would also go after everyone who represents a threat to him. As such, Scrimgeour wouldn't be the only target. Every member of the Order of the

Phoenix would be on the hit list. People like Professor McGonagall would get the zap just as soon as Voldemort has Hogwarts under his control (via Snape as headmaster).

No matter what Voldemort's psych profile looks like, no matter how illogical and irrational he might be, if he has trump cards, readers will accuse him of collusion with the author if he fails to play them. If Voldemort holds back his hand for fear of Harry, awesome, so long as Harry represents a real, not an imagined, threat.

Showdowns

We list no showdown with Dumbledore here. If Dumbledore is going to die, we suggest he remain dead, accessible via his portrait in the headmaster's office but not elsewhere. As we've already counseled, we feel that Dumbledore's back story should appear before his death, so that any woodshedding can be done face to face.

Harry and Malfoy

The last meeting between the Big Three and the even bigger three of Malfoy, Crabbe, and Goyle results in a battle over control of the diadem Horcrux, and thus connects to the main plotline. Harry takes an action and, at some risk to himself, pulls Malfoy to safety as the fiendfyre advances across the Room of Requirement.

All of this sounds pretty good, and yet this final confrontation feels a bit empty. Yes, Crabbe does die, but it is his own fault for starting the fiendfyre, and there isn't any real chance for someone to save him. The result is that the Big Three are again able to emerge from battle with their hands clean. Worse, this isn't a true showdown. There is no tense moment where Harry tries to talk sense to Draco. No attempt by Draco to come over to the other side (though we have clear indications he would like to). There is just a brawl that ends with everyone going their separate ways (Crabbe's path being a bit more separate than the others), no lessons learned.

In the Epilogue of Book 7, we see that nobody has learned nothing. Draco remains an antagonist, his children destined to butt heads with those of the Big Three. Same stuff, different day.

As a result, the climactic fight with Malfoy becomes indistinguishable from the various altercations of the preceding books. The emotional substance is still of schoolboys incapable of overcoming their petty differences, incapable of recognizing the seriousness of the situation. Malfoy never admits his mistake in taking up with the Dark Lord, and yet Harry is never forced to kill Malfoy in the name of the greater good. It feels like another cheat, another hedge, another diminishment of the seriousness of the situation.

Harry and Snape

We've discussed elsewhere the problem with having Snape simply die while Harry serves as an impotent observer of the event. Given that Snape killed Dumbledore, it seems only fair that he have a chance to demonstrate which side he is on, and demonstrate it in a dramatic way — preferably with his chance actively granted by Harry.

Harry and Voldemort

The current chaotic battle inside Hogwarts winds up being distracting. While it ranks high in terms of special effects value, in terms of emotional intensity it falls short. The complexity of the final scenes numbs the reader, and seems intentionally designed to hide the Expelliarmus cheat.

Rather than have a running battle going on inside the great hall, we recommend letting the centaurs serve as a covering force. Which is to say, the centaurs would ensure the rank-and-file death eaters, giants, and so forth, stay out of the fight, so that Harry and Voldemort can throw down mano a mano.

The goal here is to shine a spotlight on this critical confrontation, rather than obscure it with smoke and noise.

Let us imagine how such a showdown might work. First, we suggest that the "I'm not *quite* dead" business be skipped, along with the weird interlude out in the Forbidden Forest and the expositional visit with Dumbledore.

When Harry enters the Hogwarts great hall where Voldemort waits, students, teachers, and death eaters line the walls, possibly forced out of the way by the centaurs, or simply in deference to orders from Harry and Voldemort to not become involved. (Here is another place where a chivalric code might factor into the situation.)

Rather than running around wearing an invisibility cloak for endless pages, Harry immediately starts in on Voldemort. They go back and forth, more or less as they do now, though preferably with a sharper edge.

"Before we get started," Harry might say, "I think it only fair to tell you two things." Too weak to stand, Harry draws up a comfy chair and sits down. "First, if you die here, you die for real, because all your little Horcrux thingies have gone bye-bye." A faint smile. "Except for Nagini of course, but not to worry. I'll take care of her."

Then Harry starts in on the prophecy. "Snape knows the whole thing. But since he hasn't told you, let me do it. Just so you know what you're getting yourself into." Harry recounts the prophecy, then muses on how vague prophecies can be, how open to interpretation. "The most interesting part," Harry says, "is that I don't have to kill every part of you. Dumbledore destroyed the ring Horcrux. Regulus Black, if you remember him, destroyed the locket."

As an aside, it might be nice if Regulus had in fact destroyed the locket, rather than merely retrieved it. Assuming that all Horcruxes are cursed, Regulus would have died as a result of this, but his success would reinforce the idea that Harry doesn't have to destroy the piece of soul inside

Voldemort's body in order to fulfill the prophecy.

"No," Harry would say, "I just have to *arrange* for you to die. The killing of your body, why, anybody can do that. Professor Snape, for example."

And then Harry turns his back on Voldemort and zaps Nagini. Voldemort has a choice. He can kill Harry, turn on Snape, or perhaps attempt to flee. Which choice he makes, or if Harry's psychological warfare will cause Voldemort to hesitate just long enough at this critical moment — well, that is where the mustard gets cut.

Horcrux Harry

While Harry being a walking Horcrux has a nice feel to it, clearly it raises problems. For one thing, if Harry decides to let Voldemort kill him as a way of eliminating himself as a Horcrux, fine, but bringing Harry back to life after that via the Deathly Hallows feels like a cheat.

On top of which, if Avada Kedavra can be used to destroy a Horcrux, why can't that spell be used on the diadem, and so forth? Because those things are inanimate objects? Well, Harry's body would be an inanimate object too, once he was dead.... In other words, Harry dying from Avada Kedavra shouldn't affect the Horcrux enchantment that has been embedded in his body. Which would make Harry lying down for Voldemort totally pointless. At a minimum, wouldn't Harry at least have doubts about such an approach? Doubts strong enough to eliminate such an approach as a viable option? To suggest that Dumbledore knows for sure that such an approach would work again makes the old man omniscient, knowing more about Horcruxes than even the ancient texts.

As an alternative, Hermione might come up with a means of eliminating Harry's Horcrux, one that involves "killing" him with Gryffindor's sword, then having Madam Pomfrey heal and resuscitate him before brain damage kicks in. However, since the Horcrux curse might be too powerful to be fooled in such a way, it could be that to get out from under Voldemort's Horcrux and live to tell the tale, Harry will have to create a Horcrux of his own, so that he can be truly killed, have his body destroyed by fiendfyre, and then resurrect himself via the same ritual that Voldemort used in the Riddle graveyard.

What these alternatives do is make Harry and his inner circle the active forces in overcoming the rogue Horcrux, rather than leaving that task to the author (wearing a very unconvincing Dumbledore mask). It assigns a real cost to getting rid of the Horcrux, in that Harry will either have to die for real or else take a big step down the path that Voldemort followed, probably with serious implications for him, one way or another.

Naturally, eliminating the Horcrux idea entirely would also work. The magical scar carried the day for six books without any problem, and would continue to do so through the seventh.

As for the Deathly Hallows, while they may strike some readers as a wonderful invention, full of surprise, other readers see the sudden introduction of three godlike magical artifacts in the last book as the equivalent of a big red button appearing on the wall with a sign under it that says, "Push this for a happy ending."

Reader Expectation and Surprise

When we call for Snape and Harry to play more significant roles in the climactic battle, some readers may counter that our approach is formulaic, stock, and all too predictable. Meanwhile, the current approach carves out new ground by avoiding the familiar and tired paths of modern commercial fiction.

Certainly, what we have suggested will fit more closely to what readers expect to see. However, in this case, that expectation is based on promises made to the reader along the way.

To have a seven book series where a character like Snape

plays little or no part in the ultimate downfall of the villain is perhaps surprising, but it is also disappointing. More than disappointing, it makes us wonder why so much time was spent on Snape.

One of a writer's jobs is to pick the people and situations that best evoke a story. When readers are bombarded with randomly-selected information, the story begins to feel like a graduate student exercise in nihilism or surrealism, rather than something explicitly designed to entertain us. Nothing wrong with that, except that in this case it violates our trust.

Similarly, for the protagonist of the Potter series to be overshadowed in the last book by three magical artifacts that we have never seen before is definitely a surprise, but it again fails to repay our efforts and leaves us feeling cheated. (Yes, we saw the invisibility cloak as early as Book 1, but as far as we knew, it was just an invisibility cloak.)

In the end, some expectations seem like formulas because violating those expectations also violates the reader's trust. Having said that, also note that one of our suggested alternatives has Snape, not Harry, killing the corporeal Voldemort. While perhaps not a surprise, that at least wouldn't be stock and formulaic. Can you think of a single revenge flick where the hero doesn't kill the bad guy — usually by beating him to a lifeless pulp, since just shooting the guy doesn't quite work out all the angst? For this reason, though we acknowledge that readers will anticipate both Harry and Snape playing roles in the final confrontation, we think that events can be orchestrated to avoid being too predictable.

But in any case, avoiding the predictable at the expense of making Dumbledore seem omnipotent, Harry seem unnecessary, and Snape seem pointless — well, that strikes us as too high a price to pay.

Change

The muggle's WW1 was a nearly pointless war, and some

historians have suggested that WW1 and WW2 will eventually be viewed as a single conflict separated by a brief interlude. Even so, WW1 brought changes to the world. Dada art, American isolationism, and the pursuit of blitzkrieg warfare by the Germans, to name a few. The changes following WW2 were perhaps more impressive, as the war introduced nuclear weapons to the world, pushed half of Europe behind the Iron Curtain, restored democracy to West Germany, and introduced true democracy to Japan.

After seven books, what has changed in the world of Harry Potter? From the looks of the Epilogue, not much. The old animosities remain, suggesting that we only need a new Voldemort to start the ball rolling all over again.

Prejudices don't die easily, and wars seldom leave people truly enlightened. Still, it would be nice to see that some sort of change has come about as a result of what happened in these seven volumes. Emancipation for house elves, wand rights for goblins, a protected zone for giants. Something, anything, to let us feel that these dead have not died in vain.

Wrap Up

Putting it Together

This seems a good place to reiterate and summarize the issues we have raised in *Destiny Unfulfilled*.

(a) We would like to see Harry become an empathic character. When Ron tells Ginny to get lost near the start of Book 3, *Prisoner of Azkaban*, let Harry invite her to stay. Let Harry reach out to Neville, Winky, and Kreacher. Let him be sympathetic to the pain Cho Chang is in after Cedric Diggory's death. Let him treasure his friendship with Dobby and actively pursue friendships with Moaning Myrtle and others.

(b) We would like to see Dumbledore play the wizened mentor role more aggressively, actively taking Harry under his wing, tutoring him in magic, keeping him at Hogwarts over at least one summer, and so forth. We also hope that he will remain human. Hints that he is omniscient, along with the suggestion that nothing bad will happen so long as he is around, should go away.

(c) We would like Voldemort to be a more believable character (a chivalric code for wizards seems useful in this regard) and a more consistent villain, one who lives up to his billing and plays his hand aggressively.

(d) We would like to see fewer caricatures. Gilderoy Lockhart and Rita Skeeter can remain silly straw figures without damaging the integrity of the series. But to extend such an approach to the main players strains the reader's credulity. The Dursleys provide the environment where Harry's personality and character form, and as such they deserve to be taken seriously. Neville Longbottom and Ginny are two characters we would like to see more of. And we would like to have Snape's personality be consistent with his role as Dumbledore's lieutenant.

(e) We hope the series will dig a bit deeper. Currently, Harry grows up in a difficult environment (true even if the Dursleys are made less fairytale evil), he kills Professor Quirrell at the end of Book 1, destroys part of Voldemort's soul at the end of Book 2, and yet he is unaffected by any of it. The result isn't a Harry who seems especially strong and resilient, but a Harry who seems inhuman. The issues of the Potter series are weighty, and as such the series has an opportunity to leave deeper footprints behind it than if it were typical children's book fare.

(f) We would like for characters to behave consistently, and for the laws governing this alternate universe to remain the same throughout the series. If a Horcrux kills you when you put it on, then it always does. If the Weasley car runs out of juice and is miffed at Ron and Harry, then it remains so unless efforts are made to redress the situation. If Voldemort is afraid of Dumbledore, then Voldemort won't go riding around on Quirrell's noggin for an entire school year.

(g) We would like more trains smashed together. Several head-on collisions are currently set up and then turned into sideswipes: Harry and Voldemort, Harry and Dumbledore, Harry and Snape, Harry and Malfoy.

(h) We would like to participate in key events, rather than have them take place off stage. Currently, the reader is left in the dark as to Dumbledore's motivations and his insecurities. We never see how the Plan was decided upon, never truly know how the headmaster feels about Harry. The result isn't surprise or suspense, but a sense that the series is hedging its bets, is being vague and cagey on purpose so it can more easily change its mind back and forth as required without being called to task for it.

By enacting key events on stage (such as digging Harry out of the wreckage at the beginning of Book 1, or Dumbledore leaning on Snape to fulfill the Unbreakable Vow in Book 6), the series would prove to us that things make sense and would convince us that characters are driving the story. The result would be a more involving, more trustworthy epic. Spreading out the POV duties would also allow the author more freedom of movement, and would likely give readers a deeper connection to characters like Ron and Hermione.

(i) We would like the series to fulfill its implicit promises. Letting Harry become the Chosen One, the true hero of the series, means allowing him to grow up and take on personal goals which may at times conflict with the plot outline. It means that, after Book 1, he can no longer be a talentless, cute, cuddly, downtrodden orphan. Instead, the Potter series will have to do the hard work of making him sympathetic in other, less manipulative ways.

As a result, the episodic nature of the series would be diminished. Harry simply can't achieve his destiny if he is constantly "kept safe" and wastes his summers at the Dursleys. Similarly, characters like Ron and Malfoy would benefit from being allowed to grow and evolve.

This Could Really Happen!

Will Ms. Rowling undertake a revised version? Only Trelawney knows the answer to that one. But we have to admit, from Ms. Rowling's point of view, there are a lot of negatives to overcome.

(a) After writing seven books, going through seven movies, and enduring all the attendant mania, whenever the Harry Potter business comes up, Ms. Rowling probably jumps out of her chair, claws at her flesh, and yells, "Get it *off* me!"

(b) Burnout aside, undertaking a complete revision implies another seven years, say, of Ms. Rowling's professional life devoted to nothing but Harry Potter. For a writer with such a fertile imagination, that's the equivalent of a long sentence inside Azkaban.

(c) Should she undertake the revision, Ms. Rowling will no doubt come under attack for profiteering, devil worship, sexual misconduct with underage nifflers, and god knows what else.

On the other hand, anyone with common sense will realize that Ms. Rowling doesn't need more money. Adding a couple billion pounds to her bank balance isn't going to change her lifestyle, after all. So, what would her motivation be?

Ms. Rowling should begin by asking herself exactly how many masterpieces she expects to come up with. As Fleetwood Mac says, "Lightning strikes once, maybe twice." In the case of an opus like the Potter series, lightning strikes once or twice a *century*. When you have conceived a masterpiece, you owe it to yourself to make the most of it. Not in a monetary sense, but in an artistic one. While the Potter series has a lot going for it, it also has room for improvement.

Moreover, it seems entirely possible that, subconsciously, Ms. Rowling is aware that something went wrong somewhere along the line. As the series progresses, it increasingly calls attention to its own weaknesses. Harry points out in Book 4, *Goblet of Fire*, that he only has one skill, flying. In Book 5, *Order of the Phoenix*, Dumbledore says that it was a mistake to hide the prophecy from Harry for so long, and that the cause of Dumbledore's mistake was his affection for Harry, which he allowed to take precedence over what was needed to bring the Plan to fruition.

In Book 7, *Deathly Hallows*, the author's subconscious seems especially active, rising up time and again to point out major problems: Harry's inadequacy, Dumbledore's failure to provide Harry with the information Harry needed, Dumbledore's failure to hash out with Harry certain darker secrets from Dumbledore's past. Each of these issues is explicitly addressed by the characters themselves, in thought, word, and action. As a result, we remain hopeful that at least some of the issues raised in *Destiny Unfulfilled* will resonate with worries and a sense of dissatisfaction that Ms. Rowling herself may have felt as she was completing the series, but which she couldn't put her finger on because she was too close to the problem.

Naturally, it's possible that Ms. Rowling will either ignore us entirely or else will reject our arguments through some process of rationalization or another. If we became strident on occasion, it was only to avoid such an unhappy outcome.

Since it' is possible our stridency will get Ms. Rowling's back up, let us emphasize that our goal has never been to attack either the author or the series, but rather to provide the sort of tough love that Snape (and Ms. Rowling's editor) *should* have been dishing out. Maybe we have come across as a shallow, vindictive, unstable git, just as Snape did. But it nis a risk we're willing to take, given the potential payoff: a revised seven books. Books that would allow us to once again immerse ourselves in the Harry Potter universe.

Bibliography

Plot & Structure. James Scott Bell.

Self-Editing for Fiction Writers. Reni Browne and Dave King.

Stein on Writing. Sol Stein.

The Elements of Style. William Strunk, Jr.; E.B. White.

The Fire in Fiction. Donald Maass.

Writing the Breakout Novel. Donald Maass.

Index

www.ingramcontent.com/pod-product-compliance
Lightning Source LLC
Chambersburg PA
CBHW051945090426
42741CB00008B/1277